ARAB HISTORY AND THE NATION-STATE

The study of Arab historiography and of the emergence of the Arab nation-state as an object of historical treatment is a matter of considerable current interest. Despite its importance, no academic work has so far dealt with this subject as a major preoccupation of Arab historians and intellectuals.

This book discusses the development of modern Arab historiography and its study of the nation–state in the nineteenth century, and analyses the work of three contemporary Arab historians from Egypt, the Lebanon and Morocco. An important and highly readable account, it reaffirms the importance of historiography and proposes a revision of the manner in which modern Arab thought has hitherto been classified and interpreted.

The author: Youssef M. Choueiri is a lecturer in Arabic and Islamic Studies at the University of Exeter.

EXETER ARABIC AND ISLAMIC SERIES
General Editor: Aziz Al-Azmeh

1. *Arabic Thought and Islamic Societies*
   Aziz Al-Azmeh

2. *The Islamic Law on Land Tax and Rent: The Peasants' Loss of Property Rights under the Hanafite Doctrine*
   Baber Johansen

3. *The Muslim Conquest and Settlement of North Africa and Spain*
   'Abdulwāhid Dhanun Tāha

4. *Arab History and the Nation-State*
   Youssef M. Choueiri

5. *Allāh Transcendent: Studies in the Structure and Semiotics of Islamic Philosophy, Theology and Cosmology*
   Ian Richard Netton

ARAB HISTORY AND THE NATION-STATE

A Study in Modern Arab Historiography 1820–1980

YOUSSEF M. CHOUEIRI

Routledge
London and New York

First published 1989
by Routledge
11 New Fetter Lane, London EC4P 4EE
29 West 35th Street, New York, NY 10001

Printed and bound in Great Britain by
Biddles Ltd, Guildford and King's Lynn

British Library Cataloguing in Publication Data

Choueiri, Youssef M.
Arab history and the nation-state: a study
in modern Arab historiography 1820-1980.—
(Exeter Arabic and Islamic studies).
1. Arab historiography, history
I. Title II. Series
907'.20174927

Library of Congress Cataloging-in-Publication Data

Choueiri, Youssef M., 1948–
Arab history and the nation–state: a study in modern Arab historiography, 1820–1980/by Youssef M. Choueiri.
p. cm. — (Exeter Arabic and Islamic series)
Rev. version of thesis (Ph.D.)—University of Cambridge, 1986.
Bibliography: p.
Includes index.
ISBN 0-415-03113-3
1. Arab countries—Historiography. 2. Nationalism—Arab countries. I. Title. II. Series.
DS37.4.C46 1989
909'.04924'0072—dc19 88-25852
CIP

ISBN 0-415-03113-3

For Amal and Tarek

Contents

Preface

This study deals with Arab historians and intellectuals who had direct or indirect access to western education, knew a foreign language, and attempted to use academic techniques in their history-writings. It is, moreover, confined to a particular tendency of modern Arab historiography. Its main focus is that current of historical discourse which takes for its unit of study one specific Arab 'nation-state', and endeavours to endow its past with a distinctive national character. Thus other historical works are either excluded, or alluded to only briefly in order to illustrate a point or highlight a comparison. Furthermore, this is not a study of the history of the modern nation-state in the Arab World; rather, it is the history of its historiography represented by a selected sample of narratives.

The study consists of two parts, divided into six chapters with an introduction and a conclusion. Part I discusses the development of modern Arab historiography during the nineteenth and early twentieth centuries, with particular emphasis on Egypt, geographical Syria, and North Africa. Part II is a critical analysis and a somewhat extensive assessment of the writings of three modern Arab historians: Shafīq Ghurbāl (Egypt), Kamal Salibi (Lebanon), and Abdallah Laroui (Morocco). These historians were selected for a number of interrelated reasons: their crucial role in founding an indigenous school of history, the use of their works as authoritative sources, and their representative character of a cross-section of Arab intellectuals. Other historians whose output and influence met the same criteria were left out either for lack of space or in order to avoid repetition. One such whose name stands out is the Iraqi sociologist and historian 'Alī al-Wardī. Another is the Egyptian historian Muḥammad Ṣabrī. Hence, a process of elimination imposed itself as a necessary step so as to avoid compiling an encyclopedic list of subjects and historians, and for the sake of concentrating on one single theme. However, the selection of the national identity as a theme in modern Arab historiography does not imply its positivity or beneficiency. Nor does it signify a depreciation of other themes, be they Islamic, socialist, pan-Arab, or purely local histories of urban and rural communities.

The present work is a revised version of a doctoral dissertation submitted in 1986 at the University of Cambridge. In preparing both the original and revised versions, I am indebted to many persons and institutions.

I should like to express my gratitude to Dr Martin Hinds and the late Professor Marwan Buheiry.

I wish to thank Professor Ahmed Abdel-Rahim of Kuwait University, Dr Basim Musallam, Mr Albert Hourani, Professor Aziz al-Azmeh, Dr Murad Ghorbal, Dr Derek Hopwood, and Professor Malcolm Lyons.

I am particularly grateful to the staff of the Library of Cambridge University, The British Library, the Library of the Faculty of Oriental Studies, University of Cambridge, the Bibliothèque Nationale of Paris, and the Library of the University of Exeter.

My thanks go to Ms Jane Woo and Mrs Sheila Westcott for typing the manuscripts.

Portions of the introduction, chapter 2 and the conclusion appeared in *Middle Eastern Studies* and *Arab Affairs.* I am grateful to the publishers of those journals for their permission to reprint.

I am grateful to Mr Paul Auchterlonie for compiling the index, and Miss Helen Wythers of the editorial staff of Routledge for her probing queries and helpful suggestions.

Introduction

Despite claims and counter-claims, modern Arabic thought has not yet found its historian. A fashionable industry until less than a decade ago, it has now either stagnated, or has been silently bypassed.

The study of Arabic thought as an academic subject in the Anglo-Saxon world dates back to the pioneering works of Charles Adams, J. Heyworth-Dunne and Hamilton Gibb. These works, published between 1932 and 1947, dealt with the thought of Arab intellectuals in a relatively sympathetic manner, and endeavoured to enumerate the positive aspects of their contributions. Another trend, which developed after the Second World War, sought to redress the balance and reach less positive conclusions. Its main representatives included G.E. Von Grunebaum, Bernard Lewis, Elie Kedourie, and a host of other historians or political scientists.

By and large, the first trend espoused the reformist movement set in motion by Jamāl al-Dīn al-Afghānī (1838–97) and Muḥammad 'Abduh (1849–1905), attempting at the same time to infuse it with a more solid structure or basis of analysis. This surge in interest can be said to have culminated in the works of Albert Hourani and Jacques Berque. These writers and historians did not perceive themselves as outsiders, observing the new developments in the Arab World from a calm and detached distance. They almost considered themselves as custodians of a school of thought that had to be encouraged and supported. Consequently, great hopes were placed on groups of Arab intellectuals to bring about a transformation of traditional modes of thought and methods — not unlike similar transformations in Europe.

The other trend looked at Arab intellectuals either with indignation or disgust. Arab intellectuals were, on the whole, regarded as deranged persons, individuals infatuated with European ideas and fascinated by every new craze or method, without realizing their untenable position. Thus, the analysis would either ridicule the whole enterprise by concentrating on the minute details of someone's personal life, or establish a direct link between his ideas and scandalous behaviour. Alternatively, a return to Islam was advocated as the only viable solution to such a futile enterprise.[1] Historical Islam was, in its turn, depicted as an all-encompassing system which was blunted, arrested, and unable to evolve. If some Muslim thinkers come into contact with Europe, they still fail to grasp the totality of a concept, the flow of events, or the inner logic and philosophy of western civilization. They thus remain at the low level of the immediate, bewitched by an atomistic theory.[2]

A general dissatisfaction began to be voiced against this type of study towards the end of the 1960s. It was then felt that no history of ideas could be written without taking into account economic structures and social conditions. Such a dissatisfaction is clearly manifested in Maxime Rodinson's approach and his numerous publications.[3] Protests circulated against purely cultural approaches which did not pay sufficient attention to material circumstances. These protests gathered momentum with the appearance of the *Review of Middle Eastern Studies* from 1975 onwards. This *Review* brought together a number of Marxist-oriented scholars who took upon themselves the task of weeding out the harmful effects of these two trends. Most of the output of orientalists, whose books were used as standard texts in oriental studies, were subjected to a critical evaluation. Moreover, this exercise aimed at presenting an alternative reading of the same subject under scrutiny. Edward Said's *Orientalism*[4] summed up and attempted to elaborate the conclusions of this last trend without, however, sacrificing his own humanism or broad liberal ideals. Said's book wiped the slate clean, leaving only a handful of names clinging to its margins. Although Said's study heralded the birth of a new methodology, demolishing the discipline of orientalism from outside its citadel, it did not succeed in breaching the inner walls of orientalist discourse. It may well be asked: what have Herodotus, Dante, Flaubert, and Gibb in common, apart from the fact that they all refer in their discussions to something called 'oriental'? The whole enterprise of Michel Foucault's *Archaeology of Knowledge*, on which Said presumably relied, would become meaningless if such extrapolations could be derived from its method. A timeless western world is postulated as an instinctive enemy of an orient which is under the threat of constant reduction or subjugation. It is no wonder that Said's *Orientalism* was hailed with enthusiasm by Islamic fundamentalists and accorded a privileged status in their essentialist repertoire. Hence, it is easy to lose sight of both the recent ascendancy of the west and the equally recent decline of the orient.

In deciding to study the discourse of Arab intellectuals, one is faced with a number of methodological and empirical dilemmas. It seems that no clean break can be accomplished without adopting a new method capable of illuminating a relatively systematic theme. Focusing on a dominant aspect of modern Arab historiography enables one to deal with a genre which has been largely unexplored or has received only partial treatment. Viewed as a conglomeration torn between 'Traditional Islam' and its primordial identities, the Arab World is faithfully reproduced in its 'Oriental repose' and fragmented character. The illusion of permanent structures, and distinct cultures subsists on an obsession with absolute ideological utterances or their manifest consequences. Hence, most studies by western scholars have concentrated on Arab political thinkers, journalists, religious leaders, or the memoirs of some prominent politicians.

Studying history-writings offers a number of advantages and helps to situate the formation of concepts and the methodology of intellectual movements in their proper environment.

Arab intellectuals are generally preoccupied with their own national history. Ever since al-Jabartī (1753–1825)[5] there has been an incessant struggle to come to terms with this history, either positively or negatively. It is the site of controversies, endeavours of restoration, embellishments, and demolition. The history of the Arabs, or Islam, forms the background against which theoretical discussions are launched. Every new idea or movement is justified by having recourse to its precedents. Even sexual liberation is embraced in terms of historical examples. The works of the Egyptian feminist writer, Nawāl al-Sa'dāwī, spring to mind in this respect.

Apart from this universal preoccupation with national histories, an established tradition of history-writings has developed in the Arab World, dating back to al-Ṭahṭāwī. However, this is not to imply a uniformity of conceptualization, nor a continuity of one single tradition. Nevertheless, it was al-Ṭahṭāwī who first promised his countrymen, upon his return from Paris in 1831, that he would translate all the relevant history books published in France.[6] Even the modern Arabic novel made its first appearance in the guise of historical narratives. Salīm al-Bustānī in the 1870s and, later, Jurjī Zaydān pioneered this new genre. In fact, the nineteenth century witnessed a ceaseless search for historical examples, origins, and precedents. Producing history became a widespread industry in which every Arab intellectual dabbled, one way or another. Before al-Bustānī began publishing his encyclopedia, two Beirutis, Salīm Shiḥādah (1848–1907) and Salīm al-Khūrī (1834–75) launched their own historical and geographical encyclopedia in 1875 under the title *Āthār al-Adhār.* The original reformists, al-Afghānī and 'Abduh, both taught and wrote historical expositions.

While Napoleon's historical career gained wide popularity among the first generation of reformers, such as Muḥammad 'Alī of Egypt and Aḥmad Bey of Tunisia, the North African historian Ibn Khaldūn (1332–1406) was rediscovered by reformist ministers and their followers. Consequently, Ibn Khaldūn acted as the dominant intellectual figure throughout the second half of the nineteenth century. His main work, *Kitāb al-'ibar,* was first published in Cairo in 1867. The Tunisian statesman Khayr al-Dīn and his associate the chronicler Ibn Abī al-Ḍiyāf reinterpreted certain Khaldunian themes to bolster their arguments against unbridled royal authority. 'Abduh taught and commented upon his *Muqaddima* in a series of lectures he delivered in Cairo at the School of Dār al-'Ulūm in 1878.[7] European political concepts were invested with Khaldunian intellectual categories, be it the function of group solidarity ('*aṣabiyya*), oppression, just sultans, or the rule of law. Whatever the relevance of Locke, Voltaire, or Montesquieu, their theoretical formulations were appropriated in the light of local conditions, with Ibn Khaldūn's work acting as a constant source. His *Prolegomenon* seemed to solve the twin problems of the century: the causes of the rise and decline of nations, and the proper organization of political societies.

History-writings are more coherent (irrespective of their objectivity) when their authors are compelled by the nature of their work to adhere to certain rules of precision and articulation. Abstract concepts are, as it were, seen in action. They become immanent and inhere in the events, thus denuding themselves of their artificial resemblance to European ideas or affinity with traditional ones. Hence, if one studies the period which extends roughly from 1850 to 1919 (with variations from one Arab country to another), it emerges in its own right as an independent episode, clearly differentiated from the eighteenth or the twentieth centuries. Instead of seeking the origins of Arab nationalism in nineteenth-century geographical Syria or elsewhere, one should study the twin phenomena of local patriotism and Ottomanism which meant loyalty to the Ottoman state as a political rather than a religious institution. Arab nationalism was alien to both al-Ṭahṭāwī and al-Bustānī, in addition to ʻAbduh, Adīb Isḥāq, Shiblī al-Shumayyil, Faraḥ Anṭūn, al-Kawākibī, and Muṣṭafā Kāmil. These thinkers were as far removed from Arab nationalism as ʻAflaq, the founder of the Baʻth party, is from Ottomanism.

The first glimmerings of a modern Arab historiography emerged at the dawn of the nineteenth century in conjunction with the rise of a relatively well-defined territorial unit, governed by a quasi-western state. The model of Muḥammad ʻAlī's Egypt, coupled with efforts of modernization by various Ottoman sultans and governors in the nineteenth century, formed the background against which the first stage of this modern intellectual movement was born. Then the direct impact of western culture, commerce, and military power modified and shaped the national identities of a newly constituted Arab intelligentsia.

Such a pattern of development repeated itself in various forms throughout most of the Arab countries. The tempo, pace and timing depended on the geographical location of a particular country, the internal autonomy it enjoyed, the scope of its contacts with Ottoman reform and western influence, its socio-economic structure, and the degree of state centralization.

North Africa had already settled into its present 'national' divisions by the time of the French conquest of Algeria in 1830. By 1912 all the Maghrib had fallen, directly or indirectly, under French, Spanish or Italian colonialism, while Egypt and the Sudan became *de facto* parts of the British dominions. After 1860 a new 'state' was created in Mount Lebanon in the wake of the Druze–Maronite civil war, and as a direct result of the intervention of the Great Powers. The new autonomous administration formed the nucleus of the French Grand Liban of the 1920s. Only the Arabian Peninsula, except in its peripheral fringes, escaped any large-scale western influence until the middle of the twentieth century.

Thus between 1830, the date of the French Algerian invasion, and 1919, at the end of the First World War, and with the subsequent introduction of mandatory systems in the Fertile

Crescent, the main geographical and urban centres of the Arab World had been exposed to the various pressures and influences of the western powers. France and Britain were the two main actors, followed by Italy, Germany, and other European nations. This western expansion into the heart of the Arab World was accompanied by an internal movement of reform. Local rulers, Ottoman governors, or European consuls and representatives served in their own way to define the geographical boundaries and territorial limits as we know them today.[8]

These reforms, undertaken by enlightened national leaders or directly imposed to satisfy European interests, involved a number of specific measures. They included the reorganization of the administration, the creation of a new army, the implementation of a more efficient tax system, a network of modern schools and colleges, and the introduction of the printing press. This whole system, often ill-conceived and superficially implemented, operated within an economic sector linked with the markets of the west, or controlled by western credit banks, financial houses, and companies. New groups of merchants, intermediaries, businessmen, government bureaucrats, army officers, school teachers, journalists, and lawyers were the salient products of such a long process. They were destined to play a major part in shaping the national image of the new states, especially in the post-independence period at the end of the Second World War.[9]

Most modern Arab historians have increasingly tended to devote their academic research to the past of their own national states. Furthermore, the past of the Arabs, or historical Islam, undergoes at their hands a process of redistribution and reallocation among the new political entities. In the Arabian Peninsula, for example, the rise of Islam and the careers of the rightly guided caliphs figure as dominant themes leading, by a leap of imagination, to developments in the contemporary landscape. The Syrian historians, particularly the Sunnis and Greek Orthodox, are more inclined to feel at home with the Umayyad dynasty (661–750) and its crucial role in shaping the destiny of both Islam and Arabism. Islamic Spain, as an extension of this Damascus-based dynasty, is equally of special significance. However, for reasons of history, geography, and economic factors, most Syrian historians exhibited until quite recently an apologetic attitude whenever their historical treatises were confined to their own state. Even then, Syria, which historically included the present republics of Syria, Jordan, Lebanon and Palestine, would still be dealt with in its original geographical boundaries, extending from the Taurus Mountains to Sinai, and from the Mediterranean to the Euphrates and Iraq. While the Iraqis are generally preoccupied with the 'Abbasids (750–1258), as their country happened to be the seat of such an illustrious dynasty,[10] the Egyptian academic historians display, for obvious reasons, a keen interest in the Faṭimids (969–1171), the Ayyūbids (1171–1250), and the Mamlūks (1254–1517). In North Africa, the successive dynasties of the Almoravids (1053–1149), the Almohads (1147–1269), the Marinids (1269–1465), the Ḥafṣids (1236–1574), and the other local state-building dynasties claim the attention of Maghribi historians.

Moreover, the pre-Islamic, or ancient, past of almost all the Arab countries has been reclaimed and integrated into the national history by various native scholars and state educational institutions. Consequently, this modern trend is not a mere continuation of older traditions. Nor does it resume or hark back to early origins in a faithful manner of duplicate acts. The entire system of thought which defined the discourse of historical Islam, with its basis, conditions, rules, objects of study, concepts, statements, and sites, was disrupted beyond recognition under the impact of Ottoman reform and European capitalism. Thus, the political fortunes of Islam and its dynasties figured in the multi-volume works of Muslim annalists and chroniclers, such as al-Ṭabarī (838–923), Ibn al-Athīr (1160–1233), or al-Maqrīzī (1364–1442), as the main themes that unfolded and recurred in certain territories, irrespective of geographical boundaries or national allegiances. In the modern period, these territories are chopped up, delimited and rearranged into national entities. The new territory, designated as a fatherland or a nation-state, ceases to be an accidental theatre of a cyclical recurrence of events echoing the laws of the universe. It becomes in its own right the subject of historical treatment, lending its name to whichever dynasties are deemed worthy of the characteristics of its national identity.

The story of various Arab states with European commercial penetration, military domination, and financial control has become a familiar one. The national identity makes its gradual appearance as European supremacy manifests itself against the background of a reluctant recognition of stagnation or decline. (For further explanation of this symbiotic process see below pp. 197–200). The Tanzimat period,[11] which opened with the reforms of the Ottoman Sultan Selim III (1789–1807), heralded the birth of new conditions that made possible the emergence of the concept of the 'fatherland' as an object of historical treatment.

Hence, this study aspires to being a preliminary rehabilitation of historical analysis as a description of abrupt change and transformations. It focuses on the emergence of structures, new systems of thought and analysis, as well as their reorganization and dissolution. Its division into two separate parts corresponds to two radically different periods in modern Arab historiography and intellectual discursive formations. Individual authors, rather than being the subject of their discourse, are simply considered as representative examples. A synthesis at this stage, encompassing the general history of Arab thought in the nineteenth and twentieth centuries, can be only provisional and tentative.

The works of Arab historians singled out in this book are taken as serious academic products which point up, reflect, and condense the transitional nature of Arab societies. Although the function they serve and the methodological approach underpinning certain arguments are not lost sight of, it is their interpretative relevance to actual facts and intellectual rigour that receives thematic exploration. Had this study confined itself to a functional analysis, it would have resulted in either an anthropological treatment or an investigation of apologetics.

The style of the book and the thrust of its description may appear highly critical, even laced with overtones of cynicism, or perhaps as an ironic commentary on the state of modern Arab historiography. As a Lebanese and an Arab who has grappled with similar problems and experiences, the author cannot fail to share the anxieties and aspirations of his compatriots. In this perspective, the study may turn out to be an exercise in self-criticism.

NOTES

1. See, for example, Bernard Lewis, *The Middle East and the West*, London, 1968, p. 114.

2. For a partial list of works by authors mentioned in the preceding paragraphs see the bibliography.

3. See in particular his *Islam et capitalisme*, Paris, 1966 and *Marxisme et monde musulman*, Paris, 1974.

4. E. Said, *Orientalism* (London, 1978).

5. For further details on al-Jabartī's career and historical approach see chapters 2 and 4.

6. *Takhlīṣ al-ibrīz ilā talkhīṣ Bārīz* (Būlāq, 1834), pp. 207–8.

7. Rashīd Riḍā, *Tārīkh al-ustādh al-Imām*, vol. 1 (Cairo, 1931), pp. 135–6 and 777.

8. See M.S. Anderson, *The Eastern Question, 1774–1923* (London, 1966); A. Williams, *Britain and France in the Middle East and North Africa* (London, 1968); Jamil M. Abun-Nasr, *A History of the Maghrib*, 2nd edn (Cambridge, 1975, 1980).

9. For the economic impact of the west on the Middle East and North Africa, see Z.Y. Hershlag, *Introduction to the Modern Economic History of the Middle East*, 2nd revised edn (Leiden: E.J. Brill, 1980); Samir Amin, *The Maghrib in the Modern World*, (Harmondsworth, Penguin, 1970); Roger Owen, *The Middle East in the World Economy 1800–1914*, (London, 1981).

10. It is conventionally assumed that the reign of the 'Abbasids marked the apogee of Arab/Islamic civilization, be it in agriculture, commerce, craftsmanship, administration, philosophy or literature.

11. The Tanzimat period is traditionally restricted to the decrees and regulations formulated by Ottoman sultans and officials between 1839 and 1878. However, the Tanzimat, or reforms, extended over a longer period beginning with the military and fiscal innovations of Sultan Selim III in 1792, and culminating in the wide-ranging modernizing policies of Sultan 'Abd al-Ḥamēd (1876–1909).

Part I

Pioneers and amateurs 1820–1920

1

Patriotic intellectuals and enlightened Patrons: al-Ṭahṭāwī and the Egyptian identity

Modern Arab historiography had its origins in the 1830s under the rule of Muḥammad ʻAlī, who came to power in 1805 and eliminated the old order of the Mamlūks in Egypt. It began as a translation movement within the general framework of the policies of the new regime.

Those who were engaged in translating historical works from European languages considered their task as having a practical end. Such an end fitted into the ambitious plans of the new ruler, who aimed at modernizing his society and strove to emulate Europe in its industrial development. Although the army constituted the focal point of these plans and received the lion's share of the government expenditure, it was soon realized that a modern army required the rudiments of an industrial base and an efficient agricultural sector, in addition to an educational system which could provide the bureaucracy and the armed forces with new recruits. Since such a model was European-inspired, and no native group had the resources or the ability to launch it, foreign advisers, technicians, and specialists were imported to run and supervise the new system. They co-ordinated its functions and trained a certain proportion of Egyptians to master its secrets. Soon student missions were sent to Europe to study its sciences and technologies and return to their native land to serve in its newly created institutions.

A nucleus of translators and western-educated writers came into being with the establishment of the School of Languages as a separate institution in 1835. Rifāʻa Rāfiʻ al-Ṭahṭāwī (1801–1873) was appointed its director and became the inspiring spirit of a new style of writing. The school was formed to translate into Arabic or Turkish military and technical manuals from various European languages, especially French and Italian. However, Ṭahṭāwī did not confine his school to such a limited purpose. He had already published in 1834 a literary work upon his return from France.[1] In it he described his five-year sojourn in Paris, and dwelt on the manners and customs of the French in contrast with those of the Muslims in general, and the Egyptians in particular.

Muḥammad ʻAlī regarded history, especially historical biographies of eminent personalities and leaders, as a mine of information and a wealth of experience, from which he could extract the right ingredients and learn either to avoid mistakes or copy success.[2] Hence Ṭahṭāwī's inclinations for historical and geographical subjects struck a responsive chord with his master. The list of books bearing on the present subject and translated under the supervision of Ṭahṭāwī highlights his concern to act as a loyal interpreter of his patron's wishes and tastes. Thus Voltaire's *Histoire de Charles XII* and his *Histoire de l'empire de Russie sous Pierre le Grand*, in addition to Robertson's *History of the Reign of the Emperor Charles V*, and three other books on the kings of France and other European countries, were the main works translated to serve as textbooks and reading material for the would-be state officials. In fact, the total list of history books translated from French into Arabic down to the end of Muḥammad ʻAlī's reign (1849) amounts to less than ten items.[3]

Books printed at the Egyptian press of Būlāq in the 1830s and 1840s were widely circulated in the Arab World. The Egyptian administration in Syria under Muḥammad ʻAlī's son, Ibrāhīm Pasha, established a number of military schools in various Syrian cities and towns. The sons of some Syrian notables were even sent to Cairo to study in the state sector of education. Books covering a wide range of subjects, including history, geography, and sciences, were made available to teachers, pupils, and educated people in Aleppo, Damascus, Latakia, Tripoli, Jaffa, and Gaza.[4] In Morocco we find the traditional historian al-Shaykh Aḥmad Ibn Khālid al-Nāṣirī (1835–97) writing in 1869 a commentary on a historical work printed at Būlāq press and dealing with ancient history, especially Greek and Roman.[5] The reformist Tunisian politician Khayr al-Dīn (1823–89), in his introduction to his political treatise *Kitāb aqwam al-masālik fī maʻrifat aḥwāl al-mamālik* (1867), refers to a number of books published by the Egyptian press, singling out a work translated from the French on the Middle Ages.[6] He also advises his fellow Muslims to read al-Ṭahṭāwī's *Takhlīṣ al-ibrīz*, especially the chapter dealing with the arts and sciences in France.[7] Most books printed at Būlāq were circulating in Tunis from 1840 onwards, thanks to the efforts of Khayr al-Dīn and his colleagues, and the sponsorship of the modernizing Prince Aḥmad Bey (1837–55). One of the books especially singled out as having a wide influence on the Tunisian educated élite[8] was Ṭahṭāwī's translation of Georges-Bernard Depping's *Aperçu historique sur les moeurs et coutumes des nations.*[9]

Born into a family with a long tradition of religious piety and learning, educated at al-Azhar, influenced by his reformist teacher Shaykh Ḥasan al-'Aṭṭār (1766–1835), al-Ṭahṭāwī went to Paris in his capacity as the imam and guide of a student mission in 1826. It was on his own initiative that he studied the French language, culture, and literature, and started to compare the new ideas with the notions and precepts of Islam. He acquired his knowledge of the west, ancient Egypt, and pre-Islamic Arabia under the supervision of French scholars and orientalists, such as Edmé François Jomard (1777–1862), Silvestre de Sacy (1755–1838) and Caussin de Perceval (1759–1835). We catch a glimpse of the eclectic and one-sided nature of such a knowledge in the introduction to one of the first books translated by Ṭahṭāwī into Arabic. He informs us that Jomard, the tutor and director of the student mission to which Ṭahṭāwī was attached, advised him to translate Depping's *Aperçu historique* into Arabic, stressing at the same time that 'I should leave out all the statements that are derogatory and defamatory of Islamic customs or what is useless and of no benefit whatsoever'.[10]

Such an attitude was typical of Ṭahṭāwī's approach and set a trend in modern Arabic intellectual discourse that has persisted to the present day. For him, the criticism of Islam in the political and historical thinking of a western writer is a mere aberration and does not affect the essentially converging contents of the two philosophies: the European and the Muslim. Hence the suppression of the aberration ensures the general flow and correctness of the argument, and restores it to its proper place.

Muḥammad 'Alī himself encouraged Ṭahṭāwī to publish his books, awarding him large sums of money or plots of land,[11] or even bestowing on him military titles. Thus, on presenting his master with a translation of a work on geography in 1834,[12] he was promoted to the rank of major (*ṣāgh*) in the Egyptian army. *Takhlīṣ al-ibrīz* was translated into Turkish, on the recommendation of the Pasha, and made compulsory reading for army officers and state employees.

THE CONCEPT AND USE OF HISTORY

In 1838 three translators of the Egyptian School of Languages published a book on ancient history, culled from various French sources.[13] Al-Ṭahṭāwī justified its publication in a short introduction which summarized his concept of history and its utility in general.

He starts by stressing the natural sociability of man and his disposition towards association and civilization. Man, moreover, is impelled to live in a political state and under the rule of a government, whereby he endeavours to create the means by which his perfection can be accomplished. These almost instinctive drives can be harnessed only by those who have experienced the events of history and fathomed the biographies of great men. It is a well-known fact that 'history preserves for posterity what has fallen into oblivion. Were it not for the illuminating lantern of history, past events would become like straws scattered by the wind. The benefits of history are both for the élite and the common people. It is the counsel of every prince, and the prince of every counsel, the entertainer of every vizier, and the partisan of every conversation partner. If it is asked a question, it instantly comes up with the proper answer, manifesting the wonder of wonders, from which virtuous hearts derive repose, and perfect souls yearn for, be they those of sages, masters, kings or sultans.'[14]

But if such benefits are to be properly distilled from history, the direct patronage of an enlightened ruler becomes an essential requirement. For Ṭahṭāwī, his ideal ruler was the great Khedive,

> the prodigy of his age, the shining example of pride, the magnet of admiration, whose munificent hand is never withdrawn, nor are his abundant benefactions remotely emulated by anyone. . . . Muḥammad 'Alī Pasha whose name is on everyone's lips, and who has been called by

various honorific titles, especially by the monarchs of Europe. Is he not nicknamed at their courts the restorer of Islamic civilization, and the suppressor of traditional superstitious beliefs?[15]

The generosity of the Pasha, and his reputable credentials as a pious Muslim, admired and sanctioned by the advanced countries of Europe, do not exhaust the preconditions of bestowing a special privilege upon the singular task of translating a history of the ancient peoples. Added to those admirable qualities is the Pasha's great fondness of history and his equal curiosity about earlier monarchs. He is 'immensely well-versed in the biographies of the great leaders of ancient times'. Since the history of those periods, and Greek history in particular, is deficient in Arabic, and the humble subject ought to live up to the expectations of his master, 'I gave the books to a number of individuals in order to translate the relevant materials at the earliest possible time.'[16]

History, seen in this light, becomes an integral part of the revival of Egypt. It is the science of human association and statehood. It serves to mould the subject in the image of the ruler. It revives the forgotten glories of the past, and the great deeds of illustrious leaders. Such a revivification is identical to a re-enactment of remarkable experiences, whereby direct knowledge opens the way for unlimited benefits. History calls forth, for its renewal, a powerful leader who restores it from oblivion and breathes new life into its mummified body. Hence, reading or writing history is a call for action and active participation in society. It is nothing less than a political philosophy in the classical sense of its objectives. It is an activity that does not confine itself to narrating facts and events; it tells us what ought to be done.

Muḥammad 'Alī, in his ambitious policies and generous assistance to the advancement of the arts and sciences, embodied history in the making. As a governor of Egypt, he no longer derived his authority or legitimacy from the Ottoman Sultan, who was theoretically his master. His legitimacy, Ṭahṭāwī believed, finds its confirmation in the honorific titles Europe had bestowed upon him, be they real or fictitious. The frame of reference for such an ideal ruler is contained in the biographies of illustrious men of the ancient and modern world, especially Alexander the Great, Louis XIV, Peter the Great, and

Napoleon.[17] What the west had accomplished, the Pasha was anxious to emulate within a short period of time. His task, as we are given to understand, is made easier since he was the epitome of an accomplished example of how to learn from history and its makers. The translations were therefore meant for those who had joined him in his lofty and honourable endeavours, but who lacked his wider vision and knowledge of historical precedents.

The translation movement came to an almost complete halt under the reign of ‘Abbās (1849–54). Ṭahṭāwī was banished to the Sudan and put in charge of an elementary school. It was a fate that he bitterly resented and deplored in a long poem, turning his anger against the Sudanese people and climate.[18] However, he was restored to favour under Sa‘īd (1854–63), and a new phase in his career was inaugurated. It was during this period that he supervised the publication of Ibn Khaldūn's *Prolegomenon* (1857) and other classics of Arabic literature. But it was not until the reign of Ismā‘īl (1863–79) that the translation and literary movement witnessed a large-scale revival.

EGYPT RESURRECTED

Ṭahṭāwī was perhaps the first Egyptian to write and publish a history of ancient Egypt, this being in 1868–69.[19] Although the work itself is an intelligent compilation derived from European and some Arabic sources, its introduction provides us with a more complete idea of his theoretical assumptions and conceptions about history as a discipline, and helps us to assess his original contribution to modern Arabic historiography.

In accordance with the customs of those days, the introduction itself is preceded by a number of ‘eulogies’ expressing the appreciation and admiration of the author's companions or associates, who were either religious leaders or state officials. The first eulogy is by Muṣṭafā al-‘Arūsī (1799–1876) who, as a rector of al-Azhar mosque and university from 1860 to 1870, sought to introduce a number of reforms into the examination system of that old seat of Islamic learning, but to no avail. His eulogy is written in rhymed prose, and does not go beyond stating that he found Ṭahṭāwī's work ‘the most graceful book in the world of historical arts’.[20] Nevertheless, such a favourable opinion expressed by one of the highest religious authorities in

Egypt was presumably clear enough to allay the fears and opposition of the other '*ulamā*'. Another shaykh and Azharite teacher, Muḥammad al-Damanhūrī (d. 1869), is more forthcoming in exalting the benefits of a history book on ancient Egyptians. Man, we are told, yearns by nature to know the stories of ancient times, but is mainly motivated by his drive to 'keep abreast of the conditions pertaining to the fatherland in which he was brought up ... so as to be fully aware of the present state of its progress as well as the previous endeavours of his predecessors stretching back over a period of hundreds and thousands of years'. Furthermore, the narrated chain of events allows the modern Egyptian to ascertain 'who was virtuous and took the opportunity to promote the cause of the fatherland and further its development. . . . For history is the discerning eye of time, its mirror, the soul of its body and the source of its life.'[21]

The emergence and diffusion of true knowledge about the history of Egypt are naturally attributed to Khedive Ismā'īl. Hence the efforts of Ṭahṭāwī, the indefatigable scholar and historian, find their full expression under the enlightened reign of the new ruler and give birth to a new history 'the like of which we have never come across before, especially in its remarkable style, directness and easiness ... his history is a shining morning light or a bright lantern glowing and radiating throughout the fatherland'.[22]

Another contributor, Aḥmad Khayrī Bey, who was at the time the private secretary of Ismā'īl, draws our attention to the deficiency of Arabic historical sources on ancient Egyptian history. He points in particular to the fabulous tales of *Isrā'īliyyāt*, which were transmitted by later narrators without any proper criticism. The distorted transmission made it impossible to distinguish truth from falsehood. The time, however, was now ripe for new and stricter methods which enable the historian to arrive at a satisfactory result. The source of these methods is therefore self-evident and close at hand, for 'the European nations have devoted their attention to precise discoveries, studying ancient monuments and old scripts and were able in this way to arrive at reliable historical information. How often have we expected the students of foreign languages to translate into Arabic what those nations have accomplished?' He goes on to say that this task had now been fully realized by 'the erudite virtuous scholar Rifā'a Rāfi' al-Ṭahṭāwī' who wrote the history of the mother of the world [i.e. Egypt], compiling and translating from well-known European history books, or relying on Arabic sources for the part dealing with the Islamic era.[23]

'Alī Mubārak (1824–93), who was a state official and an intellectual, and considered by some to be the main rival of Ṭahṭāwī,[24] contributed a brief appraisal of the book. Mubārak seems to be more interested in emphasizing the crucial role of Khedive Ismā'īl in sponsoring such 'a new history' and acting as the patron of the sciences and arts in general. The merit of Ṭahṭāwī is perceived to be his 'elegant style' and ability to present a narrative free from 'invented stories and fabulous tales'. As a result, it is deemed beneficial to society and the inhabitants of the fatherland.[25]

As for Ṭahṭāwī's introduction, it is an amalgamation of traditional Islamic invocations and formulas, interspersed with some new ideas dealing with the method of history and its periodization. It thus opens with a Qur'ānic verse which presumably sanctions the writing and transmitting of history as a pious religious vocation.[26] His aim is to tell an instructive story based on fact, acting as a guidance for faithful people.

Ṭahṭāwī's narrative consists of a series of moral anecdotes linked together as a chain of events unfolding in one specific geographical area. It covers all the states which ruled Egypt throughout the ages, and all the races who inhabited its land, 'be they its indigenous people or the zealous foreigners who desired to settle in it . . . both before and after the coming of Islam'.[27]

We are told that he confined himself to a concise and comprehensive account, avoiding superstitious stories and fabulous inventions which contradicted common sense and reason. Such tales, he stresses, depreciate the exalted status of history and turn it into a useless activity. The sources and references on which he relied are briefly alluded to. They comprise 'Arabic and non-Arabic, old and modern works', without any further elaboration. In the text itself he does sometimes mention the names of his authorities, without indicating, however, any titles, page numbers, or dates of publication.[28]

Hence the new type of history Ṭahṭāwī aspired to create uses as its tools reason, comparison of sources, clarification of contradictory statements, and the arrival at a satisfactory synthesis designed to warn and instruct. Its meaning is closely linked with the available evidence[29] furnished by an indiscriminate use of European and Arabic references. In words reminiscent of Ibn Khaldūn's *Prolegomenon*, Ṭahṭāwī informs the reader that his history 'is in appearance the history of the mother of the world . . ., but in reality it comprises the history of all kingdoms and monarchs.'[30]

It is dedicated to his new patron Ismā'īl 'the guardian of the Egyptian land, the restorer of its former splendour and the renewer of the Islamic community', who sponsored and authorized the publication of its history. Since Ismā'īl's son, Tawfīq, was preparing himself to succeed his father in due course, the benefit and utility of history are dwelt upon at length. It is the royal science *par excellence*. Learning history is more worthy of the sons of princes and sultans, as its purpose is the knowledge of the actual conditions of past nations and states, former prophets, sages, and eminent leaders. Thus the reader gains the talent of learning from experience, shunning the bad and the false, and endeavouring to follow in the footsteps of the righteous. History, moreover, is a new life; the person who studies it increases his own age, and acquires the skill and ability for attaining the best outcome. History is a moral resurrection. It restores bygone times. It teaches later generations the genealogies. 'It was said that in the scriptures there is one book containing information about the conditions of past nations and the duration of their lifetime.'[31]

Thus, as far as the methodology and use of history are concerned, Ṭahṭāwī is still treading the beaten track of familiar Islamic notions. Even when he mentions the ability to distinguish between two contradictory statements and test the evidence with the aid of reason and comparison of sources, he does not depart from the methodology of *al-Ḥadīth* and other auxiliary religious sciences.

What is new in this history of ancient Egypt concerns the unit of study. Egypt is dealt with, perhaps for the first time, as a distinct geographical unit which has a permanent existence (but not development) over time. It is singled out as the only ancient nation that lost neither its territorial unity nor its leading moral and civilizing role over a period of seventy centuries. Under the Pharaohs, it was an awe-inspiring power, dominating its neighbours by its military strength. Then with the coming of Alexander the Great, his successors the Ptolemies, and under the Romans and the Byzantines, Egypt maintained its prominence both morally and intellectually. Its scientists and philosophers spread their learning and ideas far and wide. The Middle Ages witnessed the Muslim conquest of Egypt, which made it more prosperous and powerful than any other kingdom. It became the pivot of Islamic lands, the seat of the *Sharī'a* and the frontline of its defence. Its sultans defeated the Frankish monarchs and their large armies. They recovered Jerusalem and other places from the crusaders. The king of France, Louis IX, came to Egypt on a crusade to conquer and settle. As a condition of his release, he was compelled to pay his ransom and return to France. As a result of these encounters and contacts between Europe and the Muslim world, especially in the Near East and Arab Spain, civilization spread from the Orient to the west. 'Egypt deserves all the credit for disseminating this delightful and gratifying culture.'[32]

At the turn of the nineteenth century the French failed to establish a foothold in Egypt, and it fell to a new leader of exemplary perfection, Muḥammad 'Alī, whose 'resolution and firm will' were equal to those of Alexander the Great, one as 'energetic and vigorous' as Chosroes and Caesar. His grandson Imā'īl followed in his footsteps, and endowed Egypt with all the modern administrative and educational institutions. He built a new and strong army, reaffirming the powerful position of his country, and strove to turn it into a meeting place for the prominent men of east and west.[33]

The other new concept is the periodization of history, which is divided by Ṭahṭāwī into two domains, sacred and human. The first deals with religion and the stories mentioned in the holy books. The second has two main periods, ancient and modern. Its subject matter is human affairs down to the present. Then it is subdivided into either universal or particular. The former includes the history of all nations, and the latter is confined to the history of one single nation, such as the Egyptian, the Phoenician, the Babylonian, the Persian, the Indian and the Greek. 'Apart from the history of Egypt, the history of the Hellenic nation is the most beneficial of all the histories of Asian Kingdoms [*sic*], in view of the courage of its people, their freedom, glory, political competence and the perfection of their civilization.'[34]

As for Egypt itself, its history falls into three major cycles: the period of ignorance (*al-jāhiliyya*), the advent of Christianity, and the Islamic era, which forms the modern cycle extending into the present times.[35]

Al-Ṭahṭāwī was, first and foremost, acting as the ideologue

of Muḥammad 'Alī and his family. Writing a history of Egypt was for him an opportune occasion to highlight all the past events having a bearing on his positive view of his master's policies. As a consequence the present mirrors the past and prefigures its re-emergence. The age of Alexander the Great is thus depicted in the most glowing of terms. He is praised for his forbearance, justice, munificence, and his respect for the customs and beliefs of the Egyptians. Moreover, his founding of Alexandria opened the way for the settlement of all races from the east and the west. The city became a new world centre of commerce and trade, and has remained so ever since. When the fortunes of the city declined momentarily, another Macedonian conqueror appeared on the scene. He revived the splendour and youth of Alexandria, and made it once again, with its new European institutions, a thriving centre of the world. 'Muḥammad 'Alī has assured the perpetuation of what Alexander the Great had set out to achieve.'[36]

Bearing in mind the policies of Khedive Ismā'īl, which opened up Egypt to foreigners, especially to European creditors, speculators, and businessmen, al-Ṭahṭāwī does not fail to find parallels for these auspicious steps in the history of his country. The Ptolemies, the successors to Alexander, he informs his compatriots, granted 'full liberty to foreigners as well as the indigenous population', governing them with a code of standard just laws, following the example of their master in the wake of his conquest of Egypt. They refrained from interfering with the national customs of their subjects, 'be they religious or temporal'. Their love for learning and sciences made Egypt a great country, despite the decline of its military power and influence.[37]

The rise of Islam informs Ṭahṭāwī's image of the world, and moves him to consider the Arab conquest of his country a turning-point that endowed it with its present identity and crowned its specific character. Egypt under Islam became 'the pivot' of all the Muslim lands and 'the seat of a new religion' proclaimed by 'the best of all people'. The foundation of the Islamic state was preceded by 'miraculous portentous events'. The Arabs decided to assemble in one single national body, exhibiting a determination to stress their independence and constitute a civilized association capable of creating a powerful state. The other precursory signs consisted of the calamitous wars which had erupted between the Byzantines and the

Persians. Their conflict did not cease until the prophetic mission was fully revealed. These exhausting wars drained their energies, compelled the rulers to burden their respective subjects with unbearable taxes, and divided the Christians of the Byzantine empire into hostile factions. All these signs portended the emergence of Islam to implement the pressing need for sweeping reforms and spiritual guidance across the lands of the two corrupt empires. The holy wars launched by the Prophet's companions brought Egypt, amongst other countries, into the fold of Islam, and its history became an integral part of all that is connected with the Prophet, his mission and life, as well as the career and conquests of his companions.[38]

Al-Ṭahṭāwī devotes an entire volume of his fatherland's history to the life of the Prophet, his deeds and the various institutions of the new Islamic state in the Arabian Peninsula. Using for his sources the *Sīra* of Ibn Isḥāq (d. 767) in its recension by Ibn Hishām (d. 834), in addition to many other religious commentaries and biographies, he elaborately depicts the career of Muḥammad the Prophet, the members of his family, his wives, his companions, his servants, and all those who came into contact with him. He equally describes in detail the political, religious, military, social, and economic institutions which the Prophet built for the welfare of the Muslim community. His meticulous and sometimes original historical reconstruction of the early period of Islam invests his subject with a timeless significance functioning as an exemplary model for all ages.[39]

Proud of his Arab noble ancestry, earnest in urging his Azharite colleagues to revive the sciences which were their own, welcoming the Muslim conquest of Egypt as a divine happening,[40] he felt compelled to refute the defamatory tale hanging over the Arab capture of Alexandria. The refutation comes up as an interruption of his chronological narrative; in 48 BC Julius Caesar set fire to his fleet to prevent its falling into the hands of the Egyptian rebels and to protect Cleopatra from their assault,

> the fire spread to the Royal palace and destroyed the Ptolemaic library.... Hence the ascription of its destruction to 'Amrū b. al-'Āṣ by the order of the Commander of the Faithful 'Umar b. al-Khaṭṭāb, may God be pleased with them both, was a rumour spread by historians who were ignorant of the aforementioned fire.... It is therefore absurd to level

at the Commander of the Faithful the blame for burning the science books of the ancients.[41]

RELIGION AND SCIENCE

History, then, is neither mute nor silent. It speaks through its tangible signs, and if properly interrogated, it communicates its laws and reveals the inner secrets of human life. At this point a question poses itself: if history is a moral tale and a treasury of experiences and instructive lessons, is any sense of the past likely to emerge? To depict ancient times in relative terms, having regard to place and time, is tantamount to an act of depriving the narrative of its moral and exemplary value. It turns the present into unexplored territory, requiring new tools of study, different methods and an original approach. Translating outdated texts, or compiling a continuous story from various references, leaves the field essentially as it was. The past remains virtually untouched or ahistorically grasped. History as a process developing over time is frozen and atomized.

Ṭahṭāwī's lack of historical consciousness is further illustrated by his treatment of new sciences and technological advances. They are initially perceived as mere 'external things' or, in other words, superficial developments, that may be easily imported.[42] His rigid idea of science as an almost changeless technical skill allows him to speak of ancient and medieval Egypt as the permanent possessor and inventor, and Europe as a late borrower.[43] Brushing aside centuries of backwardness and changes, all that Egyptians had to do now, since a centralized political authority had been re-established, was to resume their former inventive activities unhindered. Science in this way has no philosophy or history. Progress, even in its rudimentary meaning, remains an alien concept in Ṭahṭāwī's repeated appeals and endeavours aimed at resurrecting the body and soul of his ancient fatherland. Scientific discoveries do not follow any logical sequence, nor do they arise as a result of new experimental methods and verifiable data and facts.

His traditional background and upbringing dominate his historical approach. The recurring themes of his writings land him in awkward intellectual positions, spelling disastrous consequences. We are able to observe the inner tensions and contradictions of his mind, when he tries, for example, to explain the astronomical theories of Ptolemy concerning the rotation of the sun and other stars around a fixed earth. Ṭahṭāwī informs his readers that the Ptolemaic system was universally adopted by the astronomers until Copernicus demonstrated the fixed position of the sun and the rotation of the earth. 'Although', he continues, 'Copernicus nullified Ptolemy's doctrine … and this theory has been adopted and sanctioned by the Europeans, let no one despair of the progress of the human mind, whereby the Europeans will end up by readopting Ptolemy's doctrine, following the lapse of a certain extended period equivalent to the interval that elapsed between the time of Ptolemy and that of Copernicus.'[44]

One is at a loss to comprehend such an astonishingly naïve opinion, until Ṭahṭāwī justifies his theory of 'regressive development' by referring to a verse in the Qur'ān which, to his mind, contradicts Copernicus and renders his arguments futile. He thus warns his readers:

> The rotation of the earth should not be mentioned except in the context of reporting the statements of either Copernicus or Pythagoras … and not in the context of discussing religious beliefs which are sanctioned by the unequivocal text of the Qur'ānic verses, such as the saying of God 'and the sun hasteneth to her place of rest. This, the ordinance of the Mighty, the Knowing'.[45] We, the community of the Sunnis, should, therefore, believe in the rotation of the sun, following in the footsteps of our venerable ancestors.[46]

The concept of science as a process of qualitative change is consequently excluded. History as development over time does not figure in the world of Ṭahṭāwī's mechanistic paradigm.[47]

Hence Egypt itself, the well-defined territorial unit, is pictured, in Ṭahṭāwī's writings, as a giant machine which existed as a nation since the dawn of history in the most perfect shape. If the machine happened to be rusty and malfunctioning, a simple operation should restore it to its former perfection. Once the machine is lubricated with the technical skills of Europe, all its parts will be set in motion, regulated and supervised by the new just prince and his family.

The historical and political doctrine of Ṭahṭāwī structures his image of the world and of the past, and situates him in a traditional semi-medieval world as regards polity and the role of government. Despite the persistent efforts of contemporary Egyptian and Arab writers to cast Ṭahṭāwī in a modernist liberal mould,[48] his ideas remain firmly rooted in his religious background and Azharite education. What he borrowed from western political notions fitted into his own prior approach to society, the state and the role of the prince. He was mainly interested in justifying and legitimizing the policies and practices of his patrons. He managed, with relative success, to present the autocratic rule and authoritarian character of Muḥammad ʻAlī and some of his successors as being in accordance with the ordinances of the holy *Sharīʻa.* Any western innovation that might clash with the established order was reduced at his hands to a mere superficial contradiction, leaving the main body of his argument intact. Thus the concept of 'liberty' in the west, and in France in particular, is nothing more than 'what we ourselves call justice and equity'.[49]

In his major theoretical work, *Manāhij al-albāb*, the inhabitants of Egypt are divided into four classes: the holders of power, the '*ulamā*', the military, and the rest of the people — peasants, workers, craftsmen, merchants.[50] How does al-Ṭahṭāwī see the relationship between these four classes? The task of the holders of power is considered in the first place as one of 'the most sublime religious duties', for without them the whole society would fall into a state of complete chaos and confusion. Moreover, the king is to his subjects like a soul to the body. There is no life in the community except through his power to rule, restrain, and deal out justice.[51]

The kings have 'rights called prerogatives, as well as duties towards their subjects'. One of the king's prerogatives is that he is the deputy (or caliph) of God on earth, and only God can hold him responsible for his actions, and he is thus not answerable to any of his subjects. The '*ulamā*' and other leaders of the community may only point out to him, in a gentle and courteous manner, what he may have overlooked, without casting doubt on his intentions.[52] The king is, therefore, above all his subjects. No one should engage in active resistance to his authority, no matter how harsh his rule may turn out to be. Patience and prayers are the best course open to the community of believers, until God answers their pleas by guiding the monarch to the right path again. The state being one and indivisible, there cannot be any intermediate power or institution between it and the society it governs. The king, as the central authority, unites by virtue of his position the three powers of the state: the legislative, judiciary, and executive. The role of parliament is confined to deliberations and the submission of their decisions to the monarch for approval. A system of constitutional representation whereby the monarch was elected by the majority of the people led in the past to 'corruption, seditions, wars and controversies'. A king is called to account by inner restraints and moral inhibitions. First, there is his conscience which acts 'as a judge who does not yield to bribery'. Then the moral power of public opinion, whether in one's own kingdom or in neighbouring countries, serves to make a monarch aware of his bad deeds, and overwhelmed by a feeling of disgrace and ignominy. Finally, history itself propels monarchs to be just and magnanimous. The narration of their deeds to future generations impels them to be virtuous for fear of infamy.[53]

ANOTHER AZHARITE

It is perhaps appropriate at this juncture to compare al-Ṭahṭāwī's historical and political ideas with those of another Azharite '*alim* and historian. Al-Jabartī (1753–1825) witnessed the invasion of Egypt by the French, the end of Mamluk power and the rise of Muḥammad 'Alī. His chronicle '*Ajā'ib al-āthār fī al-tarājim wa al-akhbār*[54] represents a bridge between traditional Islamic historiography and the birth of a modern Arabic school of historians.[55] He nevertheless clung to his old beliefs and considered Muḥammad 'Alī a heretic who violated the norms of religion. The chronicle dwells at length on the way the new ruler imposed illegal taxes on the people, destroyed the power of the Mamlūks, and deprived the '*ulamā*' of their property and status. He thus highlights facts which al-Ṭahṭāwī chose either to ignore or to interpret in a more positive and favourable manner.

Al-Jabartī's political theory is bound up with a cosmology in which the various elements are classified in a defined and hierarchical order. While al-Ṭahṭāwī places the holders of power at the top of his list, al-Jabartī relegates them to the third rank, coming after the prophets and the '*ulamā*'.[56] If the prophets are the guides of the nation and the pillars of religion, the '*ulamā*' act as their heirs, the élite of the élite, and the followers of the true divine laws. As for kings and holders of power, they are those who strive to apply justice and equity amongst their subjects and to enforce law and order. They protect the weak against the strong, and the noble against the mean. Justice lies at the basis of a government and ensures the stability of the nation, 'whether the state is Muslim or non-Muslim'.[57]

The decline of the *'ulamā*'s social and economic position, brought about by the deliberate measures of Muḥammad 'Alī, permeates the pages of al-Jabartī's chronicle and constitutes its recurring theme. He does not hide his opposition to such a development or his abhorrence of its various manifestations. He even condemns some of his colleagues who were currying favour with the Pasha, and had fallen victim to the love of earthly glory, money, and high office. Nevertheless, he resignedly realized his limited ability to resist the trend of events, and satisfied himself with writing down its chronological sequences, both as a witness and a helpless opponent, charged with a preordained mission.

Reflecting and expressing the ideas of his socioreligious group, al-Jabartī speaks as an outsider, registering his protests, and enumerating the 'pernicious innovations' of an ungodly usurper, withdrawing, at the same time, into his corner of seclusion and obscurity.[58] Hence history assumes a far-reaching purpose. It indicates the participation of its author in the re-creation of a cosmological order that has been disrupted and overturned. The impious policies of the Pasha, the multiplication of taxes, the receding of the Golden Age beyond redemption,[59] the corruption of state officials, and the complicity of some notorious *'ulamā'* and religious leaders, are mirrored by the parallel negligence and dearth of history-writing which

> our contemporaries have ignored, forsaken and abandoned, and come to consider as the work of the idle. . . . But they are excused, for they have more important tasks to perform. The conditions of time have been overturned; its shadows have faded; the rules of its calculation have been riddled and disorganized, rendering it impossible to record its events and facts in a register or a book.[60]

Al-Jabartī's feelings of indignation, desperation, and fury are matched by a serene sense of satisfaction and achievement on the part of al-Ṭahṭāwī. Time has come full circle, and the golden age is dawning again. What was blasphemous and heretical has become commendable and the revealed truth itself.

Nevertheless, al-Jabartī was no less enthusiastic than the ideologue of Muḥammad 'Alī for justice, science, and beneficial public works. Neither was al-Jabartī lacking in his praise for the Europeans, particularly their competence in battles, elaborate organization, and intellectual curiosity. He contrasts the exemplary manner in which the French conducted the trial of General Kléber's assassin (even though they only believed in reason as the sole arbiter in affairs, and had no religion) with the beastly atrocities of the soldiers who replaced them, and professed to be Muslims and holy fighters.[61]

The idea that the Europeans borrowed scientific discoveries from the Egyptians rears its head in al-Jabartī's chronicle, albeit on a smaller scale than the one postulated by al-Ṭahṭāwī. Speaking warmly and enthusiastically of his father's numerous talents as an accomplished scientist, scholar, and successful merchant, al-Jabartī tells us that one day

> he was visited by a number of Frankish scholars (*ṭullāb*) who started to study under him the science of geometry. This was in the year 1159 (1746). They offered him as gifts some precious instruments of theirs. Then they returned to their countries of origin and began to spread there the science they had learnt, putting the theory into practice, and inventing wonderful machinery such as windmills, devices for dragging heavy weights, watermills etc. . . .[62]

When a team of English amateur archaeologists unearthed some Pharaonic mummies and statues, al-Jabartī went to see them, in the company of Ibrāhīm Mahdī al-Inglīzī, at the house of the British Consul.[63] He does not comment directly on these relics of ancient Egypt. Nevertheless, he singles out the same European qualities that al-Ṭahṭāwī was later to celebrate in his writings. He informs his readers that 'the English Franks' wanted to examine the Pyramids 'because they are inclined by nature to study exotic things and investigate the particular aspects of knowledge, especially the ancient monuments, the wonders of the lands, and the paintings and the statues which are in the caves and temple ruins' of Egypt.[64]

Finally, al-Jabartī is no less proud of Egypt and its role in serving Islam and advancing the cause of its civilization. But, unlike al-Ṭahṭāwī, he yearns for a lost world, a golden age which Egypt enjoyed under the Mamluk Sultans as a military and religious power.[65] He was lamenting the end of an era and the disappearance of the values and norms which he thought the new ruler had precipitated. Being a shaykh and a gentleman of independent means, he was able to concentrate on his scholarly work and persist in his defiance of the Pasha to the end of his life. Al-Ṭahṭāwī, deprived in his early youth of a reliable income as a result of the new ruler's confiscations of his family tax-farms, entered al-Azhar at the age of 16, and then the service of the master of Egypt.

Al-Ṭahṭāwī embraced wholeheartedly 'the innovations' of Muḥammad 'Alī and never lost his enthusiasm for the new order, even under the most adverse conditions. The position he occupied as the main ideologue of the political system turned him into a submissive admirer and unquestioning adherent of its activities.

His historical writing is designed, like his political theory, to justify, warn, and instruct. It forms a series of anecdotes which succeed one another chronologically, and each ends with a moral rule, whether in verse or prose. He had ceased to be medieval without becoming modern. What he offered was not a new interpretation of his country's past, but rather a wider selection of examples reiterating the same edifying principles of righteous behaviour.

NOTES

1. *Takhlīṣ al-ibrīz ilā talkhīṣ Bārīz* (Būlāq 1250/1834). On al-Ṭahṭāwī's life and career see Ḥusayn Fawzī al-Najjār, *Rifā'a al-Ṭahṭāwī* (Cairo, 1962).
2. Al-Ṭahṭāwī, *Manāhij al-albāb* (Cairo, 1912), p. 207; Jamāl al-Dīn al-Shayyāl, *al-Tārīkh wa al-mū'arrikhūn fī Miṣr fī al-qarn al-tāsi' 'ashar* (Cairo, 1953), p. 41.
3. See T.X. Bianchi, 'Catalogue Général', *JA* T.11, 1843, pp. 25–58.
4. A. Tibawi, *American Interests in Syria* (Clarendon Press, Oxford, 1966), pp. 68–70.
5. Aḥmad al-Nāṣirī, *Kitāb al-istiqṣā' li-akhbār dūwal al-Maghrib al-aqṣā* (Casablanca, 1954), p. 26. The historical work concerned is entitled *Bidāyat al-qudamā' wa hidāyat al-ḥukamā'* (Būlāq, 1838). The above-mentioned source was the first modern history written on

Morocco by a native of that country. It was first published in Cairo in 1894.

6. i.e. *Qurrat al-nufūs* (Būlāq, 1844), 2 vols.

7. Khayr al-Dīn, *Aqwam al-masālik fī ma'rifat aḥwāl al-mamālik* (Beirut, 1978) pp. 133 and 200–1. A reprint of the 1867 original edition.

8. Aḥmad Ibn Abī al-Ḍīyāf, *Itḥāf ahl al-zamān bi-akhbār mulūk Tūnis wa 'ahd al-amān*, vol. V (Tunis 1964), pp. 31–32; Aḥmed Abdesselem, *Les historiens tunisiens* (Paris, 1973), pp. 133–4.

9. (Paris, 1826).

10. *Qalā'id al-mafākhir fī gharīb 'awā'id al-awā'il wa al-awākhir* (Būlāq, 1249/1833), p. 3. The book was first translated by Ṭahṭāwī in 1829, while he was still in Paris. *Ibid.*, pp. 111–12.

11. 'Alī Mubārak in his *Khiṭaṭ*, vol XIII (Būlāq, 1305/1887), p. 56, calculates that Ṭahṭāwī received 250 feddans as a gift from Muḥammad 'Alī, 200 feddans from Sa'īd, and 250 from Ismā'īl.

12. *Al-Ta'rīfāt al-shāfiya li-murīd al-jughrāfiya* (Būlāq, 1834).

13. *Bidāyat al-qudamā' wa hidāyat al-ḥukamā'* (Būlāq, 1254/1838). Translated by M. al-Zarābī, A. Abū al-Su'ūd, and M. 'Abd al-Rāziq. Al-Ṭahṭāwī revised the edition and wrote the preface. I. Abu-Lughod in his book, *Arab Rediscovery of Europe* (Princeton, 1963), p. 60, mistakenly attributes the preface to the translators.

14. *Ibid.*, pp. 3–4.

15. *Ibid.*, p. 4.

16. *Ibid.*, pp. 5–6.

17. R.R. al-Ṭahṭāwī, *Manāhij al-albāb al-miṣriyya fī mabāhij al-ādāb al-'aṣriyya* (Cairo, 1912; 1st ed., 1869), pp. 207 and 214.

18. *Ibid.*, pp. 265–9.

19. *Anwār Tawfīq al-jalīl fī akhbār Miṣr wa tawthīq Banī Ismā'īl* (Būlāq, Cairo, 1285H.) This was intended as the first part of a multi-volume work covering the history of Egypt down to the author's time. However, this task was not accomplished. The first part takes us to the eve of the Arab conquest. The second part, published posthumously in 1874, *Nihāyat al-ījāz fī sīrat sākin al-Ḥijāz* [A Biography of the Prophet Muhammad], treats of the life of the Prophet, the early Muslim state and its institutions as exemplary for all ages.

20. *Anwār Tawfīq al-jalīl*, pp. ii–iii.

21. *Ibid.*, pp. iii–iv.

22. *Ibid.*, pp. vii–ix.

23. *Ibid.*, p. ix.

24. See, for example, J. Heyworth-Dunne, *Introduction to the History of Education in Modern Egypt* (London, 1938), pp. 296–7. He believes that 'Abbās disliked Ṭahṭāwī and banished him into exile partly at the instigation of Mubārak who took over 'the same work that Rifā'ah used to undertake in the School of Languages and in the Translation Bureau'.

25. Ṭahṭāwī, *Anwār Tawfīq al-jalīl*, pp. x–xi.

26. 'We shall tell you the most beautiful story … in it you shall find instruction.' Qur'ān, xii, 3, and xii, 111.

27. Ṭahṭāwī, *Anwār Tawfīq al-jalīl*, pp. 2–3.

28. Herodotus is quoted, for example, on pp. 53–78, 121 and 249–50; the Egyptian priest Manetho pp. 54 and 96; Strabo, p. 87; Aristotle, p. 121, Mariette, p. 107; and the Muslim historians Ibn 'Abd al-Ḥakam (d. 871), and al-Maqrīzī (1364–1442), on pp. 88–9.

29. *Ibid.*, p. 3.

30. *Ibid.*, p. 3.

31. *Ibid.*, pp. 4–9. Cf., the opinion of the fifteenth-century Muslim biographer and religious scholar al-Sakhāwī on the use of history in his treatise, *al-I'lān bi-al-tawbīkh li-man dhamma ahl al-tārīkh*, translated by F. Rosenthal in *A History of Muslim Historiography* (Leiden: E.J. Brill, 1952), pp. 201–62. Al-Sakhāwī's statements are reproduced by Ṭahṭāwī word for word.

32. Ṭahṭāwī, *Anwār Tawfīq al-jalīl*, pp. 9–10.

33. *Ibid.*, pp. 10–11.

34. *Ibid.*, pp. 7–8. Dividing history into divine and human, universal and particular was a practice and concept familiar to the French historians of the sixteenth and seventeenth centuries. See, for example, Jean Bodin, *Method for the Easy Comprehension of History*, translated by Beatrice Reynolds (Columbia University Press, New York, 1945), pp. 17–18; L'Abbé Lenglet du Fresnoy, *Méthode pour étudier l'histoire* (Paris, 1713), Part 1, pp. 6–7.

35. Ṭahṭāwī, *Anwār Tawfīq al-jalīl*, pp. 11–12.

36. *Ibid.*, pp. 155–7.

37. *Ibid.*, pp. 225–8.

38. Ṭahṭāwī, *Anwār Tawfīq al-jalīl*, pp. 10 and 548–52.

39. *Nihāyat al-ījāz fī sīrat sākin al-Ḥijāz* (Cairo, 1874). This biography, which covers 332 pages, was published posthumously by al-Ṭahṭāwī's son, 'Alī Fahmī Rifā'a, undersecretary of the Ministry of Public Instruction.

40. Cf. al-Ṭahṭāwī, *Manāhij al-albāb*, p. 373.

41. Ṭahṭāwī, *Anwār Tawfīq al-jalīl*, p. 212. It is now believed that the library did not perish until AD 272, when the greater part of the Brucheion was destroyed during the reign of Aurelian. See chapter 2, p. 33, n. 33.

42. Ṭahṭāwī, *Takhlīṣ al-ibrīz*, p. 4.

43. See, for example, *Manāhij al-albāb*, p. 391, where the everlasting prominence of Egypt is attributed to 'a divine mystery'.

44. Ṭahṭāwī, *Anwār Tawfīq al-jalīl*, pp. 230–1.

45. Qur'ān, xxii, 37.

46. Ṭahṭāwī, *Anwār Tawfīq al-jalīl*, p. 231.

47. Most historians of science stress the close connection between the rise of a modern historical consciousness and the new scientific approach. Herbert Butterfield, in *The Origins of Modern Science* (London, 1949, p. 203), maintains that 'the introduction in modern times of a view which envisaged the whole universe in terms of historical process was a new thing ... and represents an important stage in the development of the modern mind ... science and history had come together to present the idea of the whole of nature advancing slowly but relentlessly to some higher goal.'; R.G. Collingwpood, in *The Idea of Nature* (Oxford University Press, 1976, p. 9), reaches a similar

conclusion. 'The modern view of nature, which first begins to find expression towards the end of the eighteenth century and ever since then has been gathering weight and establishing itself more securely down to the present day, is based on the analogy between the processes of the natural world as studied by natural scientists and the vicissitudes of human affairs as studied by historians'; Benjamin Farrington, in *Greek Science* (Harmondsworth, Penguin, 1963, p. 312), sums it up aptly: 'the greatest achievement of modern science has been the rebirth of the historical sense.'

48. See, for example, Khaldun S. al-Husry, *Three Reformers* (Beirut, 1966), chapter II; Louis 'Awaḍ, *Tārīkh al-fikr al-miṣrī al-ḥadīth* (Cairo, 1969), vol. II, pp. 104–7.

49. Ṭahṭāwī, *Takhlīs al-ibrīz*, p. 306.

50. Ṭahṭāwī, *Manāhij al-albāb*, p. 348.

51. *Ibid.*, p. 348.

52. *Ibid.*, p. 354.

53. *Ibid.*, pp. 349–69.

54. Three vols (Dār al-Fāris: Beirut, n.d.).

55. David Ayalon in his article 'The historian al-Jabartī and his background', *BSOAS*, vol. XXIII (London, 1960), p. 218, believes that 'al-Jabartī should be considered one of the greatest historians of the Muslim World of all times, and by far the greatest historian of the Arab World in modern times'!

56. Al-Jabartī, *'Ajā'ib al-āthār*, vol. 1, pp. 14–15.

57. *Ibid.*, pp. 15–16.

58. *Ibid.*, p. 9.

59. *Ibid.*, vol. III, p. 494, where al-Jabartī explicitly expresses his yearning for the old days of the Mamlūks under whose reign 'Egypt Felix was unrivalled'.

60. *Ibid.*, p. 9.

61. *Ibid.*, vol. II, 359–60.

62. *Ibid.*, vol. I, pp. 440–66.

63. Professor C. E. Bosworth in his article 'al-Jabartī and the Frankish archaeologists', *IJMES*, vol. 8 (1977), pp. 229–36, identifies Ibrāhīm Mahdī al-Inglīzī as the famous Swiss traveller and orientalist John Lewis Burckhardt and the British Consul as Henry Salt.

64. Al-Jabartī, *'Ajā'ib al-āthār*, vol. III, pp. 571–2.

65. See note 59.

2

Two Histories of Syria

It is generally agreed that the Egyptian occupation of Syria in the 1830s unified the country politically and economically, and opened its main cities to western influence.[1] The new administration encouraged a sustained growth in commercial and financial involvement of European powers in the country, and led to the proliferation of European and American missionary schools and colleges. Soon after the withdrawal of the Egyptian forces from Syria, as a result of internal factors and the intervention of the European powers, the Ottoman authorities embarked on a variety of modernizing schemes, and announced their intention to implement relatively secular laws throughout the Empire.

These laws, despite their ambiguities and shortcomings, paved the way for a new type of history-writing based on a semi-modern notion of national consciousness. Thus Syrian patriotism was born under the authoritarian rule of the Ottoman Sultans towards the middle of the nineteenth century, and in response to the modernizing policies of their local representatives.

One of the first Syrians to embrace and propagate the idea of a Syrian fatherland was Buṭrus al-Bustānī (1819–83).[2] He conveyed in his writings its existence as a separate, well-defined historical unit, with a distinctly Arab culture in the process of adopting certain western characteristics deemed essential for its survival.

A Maronite of a well-known Lebanese family, al-Bustānī was educated at the comparatively modern seminary of ‘Ayn Waraqah. He adopted Protestantism as a young man, and worked with the American missionaries in Beirut, who sought his assistance in translating the Bible into Arabic. He entered the services of the American Consulate in Beirut as a dragoman in the late 1840s and kept his post there until 1862, when he resigned and nominated his son Salīm (1848–84) to replace him.

The eruption of the Druze–Maronite civil war in 1860, and the massacre of the Christians of Damascus by some Muslims of the city, provided al-Bustānī with a tragic opportunity to articulate and communicate his national and secular views. Towards the end of 1860 he started publishing a broadsheet called *Nafīr Sūriyya* (the *Trumpet of Syria*). In one article after another he appealed to his compatriots to put the welfare and interests of their Syrian fatherland above those of sectarianism and factionalism. The birth of a clear notion of Syrian patriotism can thus be traced to that date. Al-Bustānī served to impress upon his readers the picture of an ideal national community, working within the Ottoman Empire for the benefit of all its members, irrespective of religion, race, or any other divisive factor. He was joined in his endeavours by a number of colleagues and students, who were largely confined at that stage to either Protestant converts or Greek Orthodox and Uniate Catholics. One of the first literary and cultural societies was established in 1847, this being the Syrian Society. It was modelled on European academic organizations bearing the modern name of the country. It appears that its founders were the three American missionaries William Thomson, Cornelius Van Dyck, and Eli Smith. The first served as its president, then the third was elected in the same capacity in 1852. Al-Bustānī acted as the secretary and editor of the Society's journal.[3]

Syria was generally referred to by its inhabitants and other Arabs as '*Barr*' or '*Bilād al-Shām*' ever since its conquest by the Muslim armies in the first half of the seventh century. Nevertheless, the Ottoman authorities revived the old name of the Roman period, and started calling the country *Sūriyya* in their official decrees and proclamations.[4] In 1865 Rāshid Pasha, the Governor of Syria, and one of the leading Ottoman supporters of the reform movement in the Empire, founded a Turkish–Arabic official gazette in the city of Damascus, bearing the same name.[5] Thus the European influence and the reforms initiated by Ottoman officials helped to concentrate the minds of some Syrians on a distinct geographical unit. When a native inhabitant adopted the 'new' name, such a step denoted, in more than one instance, a change in his cultural outlook. The country ceased to be a mere territory and became a *Waṭan* (fatherland), the focus of national feeling and loyalty, expressing itself in literature, poetry, historical writings, and the espousal of western political notions.[6]

Soon some sections of the Muslim communities, especially in the urban centres of Syria, began using the 'new' name of their country. Thus in a chronicle written *circa* 1868, a Damascene notable and later Naqīb al-Ashrāf (the head of the descendants of the Prophet Muḥammad) of his city, al-Sayyid Muḥammad al-Ḥasībī, 'uses the term Sūriyya (which was just coming into general use) instead of the older Bilād al-Shām, to mean the geographic region of Syria (including Lebanon, Palestine and Trans-Jordan)'.[7]

In 1863 al-Bustānī founded in Beirut a new 'National School' for boys. Its secular curriculum included the teaching of modern languages, such as French and English, as well as mathematics, history, geography, Latin, and Greek, in addition to Turkish. For the teaching of Arabic, al-Bustānī engaged three leading authorities in the subject: Nāṣīf al-Yāzijī (1800–71), Yūsuf al-Asīr (1815–89), and Salīm Taqlā (1849–92). This school forged close links with the Syrian Protestant College (renamed the American University of Beirut after 1920) when it opened in 1866. The SPC represented the consummation of American educational activities in Syria.[8]

When al-Bustānī started publishing *al-Jinān* as a fortnightly magazine in 1870, he assigned the editorship to his son, Salīm. He also engaged a number of his associates and students to contribute various literary and historical articles to it. One of those contributors, whose history-writing will be discussed later, was Jūrjī Yannī.

Salīm al-Bustānī, in a series of editorials in *al-Jinān*, sought to elaborate and give wider applications to his father's theories, particularly the role of history and the past in shaping one's image of the present and the future. Besides his editorship, Salīm taught history and natural sciences at the National School. By 1871 he left the American Consulate and dedicated his time to his new work. He also pioneered a new genre in Arabic literature, the historical novel. Most of his novels were serialized in *al-Jinān*, or the other two newspapers which he also edited, *al-Janna* and *al-Junayna.*[9] In his writings he was trying to anchor the general principles, announced by Sultan 'Abd al-Majīd (who ruled 1839–61) in 1856, concerning, *inter alia*, the equality of all Ottoman subjects before the law, to a broader western concept. Thus a recurring theme permeates his numerous articles: the separation of religion from the state, and the necessity of establishing a national bond transcending religious sects and communal groups. The Bustānīs by that time had ended their direct involvement with the American missionaries,[10] and started to work in close co-operation with the new generation of Ottoman governors and officials who were intent on reforming the institutions of the Empire along broad western lines. Later on, their interests were widened as they resorted to Khedive Ismā'īl, seeking his financial assistance in order to launch the first modern encyclopedia in the Arabic language (*Dā'irat al-Ma'ārif*).[11]

THE BURDEN OF THE PAST

Salīm considered the nineteenth century a turning-point in the history of the world, heralding a fresh historical stage in the destiny of the Ottoman Empire and his own country, Syria. For him, it was the century that brought forward new principles according to which the civilized nations conducted their internal and external policies. These principles constituted 'the spirit of the age'. Any nation whose members deviated from these common principles was judged incompatible with that spirit. It violated the conditions and terms set by the strong nations and was doomed to be conquered by their superior military and industrial power. History is the means by which one is bound to reach such a conclusion.[12] Nevertheless, to al-Bustānī, the nineteenth century was still a mere extension and continuation of the Enlightenment and the French Revolution.

Hence, he undertakes to tabulate for his readers the elements of the spirit of the age.[13] Three principles define it: equality, absolute freedom which does not injure the rights of others, and the achievement of progress. Two impediments obstruct the emergence of the new spirit — religion and arbitrary politics. Religion constitutes an obstacle when it interferes in matters not related to its fundamental concepts and proper realm. Religious beliefs should be left to the individual and his conscience, and not used as a tool in the hands of the state to manipulate and suppress the minorities. 'The English state', for example, felt obliged, by the force of the new spirit, to admit into its institutions those of its subjects who were debarred from holding 'official positions' because of their religion or sect, and relieved the Catholics and the Irish of 'their burden to cover the expenses of the Protestant churches'. So much so that many of the Jews, 'who are the smallest of its communities, have reached the highest positions' in the state.[14]

The policies of a modern government should be in agreement with the new spirit. Otherwise, it would be constrained to comply, and become the victim of stronger, more advanced states. The new nations had replaced the religious bond with the national and had thus met the requirements of the new civilization. The Ottoman state was on the way to meeting the spirit of the age, although 'it still adheres to the religion of Islam'.[15]

The geographical unit which ought to claim the national allegiance of Salīm's compatriots remains a moot point. Syria is not mentioned by name. However, it is not difficult to identify what he held to be his proper fatherland, if we scrutinize his other articles. In an article entitled 'Who are we?'[16] Salīm, or his father,[17] lists in a proud tone the various races that ruled Syria, which developed a flourishing material and intellectual culture, and whose intermixture constituted its present population. He declares

> Some of us belong to the Arabs who spread East and West, seized and dominated the Arabian Peninsula, Persia, Africa, Morocco and India. Their conquests reached as far as Spain and most European countries. They unfolded the banner of justice, knowledge, industries and agriculture in all the regions they ruled over … some are descended from the Syriac Aramaeans and Chaldaeans, the peoples of conquests, courage and power … and who were renowned for their love of sciences and learning. … Others trace their ancestry to the Greeks, celebrated for their philosophy, industry, trade, audacity and initiative … some of us are a mixture descended from the commingling of those great peoples. Finally, we are the progeny of those who gave the world its religions, taught it the art of craftsmanship, invented for it the fundamentals of all its beneficial facilities … and opened to it the trade routes by land and sea.[18]

It is clear that al-Bustānī excludes the Turks from his list and confines himself to extolling the virtues and merits of his putative Syrian ancestors. The fact that the Arabs precede the others in his scheme of classification is not accidental or based on a random selection. He believed that a nation derived its distinctive personality partly from a common language. He thought that Arab customs and the Arabic language should prevail and be adopted by all the people of Syria, so as 'to become one nation with an Arab national identity'.[19] Were it not for their language, 'the Ottoman Turks would also have joined us in our nationality', Salīm continues, whilst hastening to proclaim his allegiance to 'the authority of a state which has embraced the religion of our majority, whose laws are our laws and whose country is near ours'.[20]

Salīm had no doubt that his country was the best in its climate, water resources, soil, and wealth. Its language was the most eloquent and the most widespread. But all these glories have disappeared along with many others — schools, sciences, books, libraries, commerce, agriculture, great leaders, statesmen, scientists, and the prosperity Syria once enjoyed.[21] It is true that some schools have opened their doors to a few native pupils, and commerce has been revived by a handful of merchants, but to what end? This practice is at the expense of agriculture and industry, which are the most important sources of wealth, particularly in a country like Syria. Europe has flooded the local market with its goods and products, and created a false consumer boom. 'How can we hope to compete with them if our transportation is still the backs of camels and donkeys while they use the wind and steam.... How can we succeed in advancing our industry and the relegation of theirs if every Arab praises their industry and denigrates his country's?[22]

While al-Ṭahṭāwī was trying to patch up a political philosophy tailored to suit the needs and tastes of his patrons, Salīm al-Bustānī was bent on inculcating 'a philosophy of history' in the minds of his countrymen. He thought of human development as the constant operation of fixed laws, the discovery of which depended on a proper understanding of the historical process. The Arabs, or Syrians, had fallen behind because they failed to diagnose their maladies and grasp the deep-seated sources of their backwardness.

> One has to discover the illness and its causes before prescribing the remedy. This is the secret of medical treatment.

> Knowing the proper cure is an easy task in comparison with knowing the disease. . . . It is this task which has defied the outstanding doctors of politics and master scholars of history who exert all their efforts in examining the maladies of nations and their aetiology.[23]

However, not all nations suffer from the same ailments. These vary with the variations of time, space, religion, tastes, innate temperament, and the political organization of each nation. It is, therefore, almost impossible for a foreigner to comprehend the causes of a nation's internal afflictions. It is equally implausible for a patient to treat himself properly on his own. The answer to the problem lies in conducting 'meticulous research, free from prejudice and fanaticism, into the mirror of the world, which is history itself. Because in comparing the past of a nation with its present, and discovering the reasons of its rise and fall, the thick veil obscuring the reality of the present is thereby removed'.[24]

History has a just and perceptive eye. It reads the past faultlessly, diagnoses the present accurately, and predicts the future precisely. Clio's tears, streaming down her face, convey to the Syrians their sordid and lamentable recent history. She is earnestly exhorting the rulers of the land to govern justly and fairly, 'for the governed person follows the path of his governor in all matters, be they good or bad'.[25]

The diffusion of science and the cultivation of learning provide the remedy. They cure the fatherland of sectarianism and of the corruption of religion. Proper scientific knowledge paves the way to national unity and constructs the foundation of a healthy future.[26] Ever since the Arab caliphate split into warring factions, Syria has been experiencing 'constant turmoil and gloomy darkness'. The Syrians, witnessing the dawn of a new age, ought to put the 'dark ages' behind them and take stock of their present conditions. History shows their past devoid of a national bond which unites the various communities within one single distinct territory, and inspires them to achieve success and ward off all foreign intrusions. A nation's knowledge of its future is *ipso facto* dependent on the knowledge of its past. It must calculate the distance it has traversed in all its ups and downs, so as to foretell the concealed future and chart its course.[27]

One studies the past not simply to revive it, or freeze its

arrested development, but to transcend it and incorporate it into the philosophy and sciences of the nineteenth century. The past is not a prison. Nor is it an object of worship. Rather it is to be judged in the light of the present industrial, technological, and political systems of the west. Consequently, the dark historical episodes of some nations are better glanced at, if only to be consigned to the dustheap of oblivion. Salīm al-Bustānī identified his newly acquired education with that of European societies, and imagined himself standing on the threshold of a new era. For him, Syria was also capable of joining his generation in their futuristic adventure, if only it showed the inclination and possessed the will. It no longer had to endure the perpetual spells of sectarian strife, social fragmentation, and economic backwardness. Furthermore, the spirit of the age, in all its manifestations, was encircling its borders and infiltrating its vulnerable fortifications. It had to make one of two choices: it either adopted the new spirit voluntarily, or it would be forced to do so and suffer the humiliation of foreign subjugation. The past had become a burden to be discarded and dismantled. History conclusively proved the sheer uselessness of a foredoomed resistance. It is, however, a prospect that invites hope and great expectations, rather than discouragement and despair. 'We are perhaps justified in rejoicing at the disappearance of a past like ours, and in awaiting the advent of a morrow which augurs happiness and prosperity for our nation.'[28]

As early as 1859 Buṭrus al-Bustānī had castigated his contemporaries for priding themselves on the role of their Arab ancestors in bestowing the sciences and arts upon the world. Granting that they were correct, he went on, 'our ancestors' scientific attainment of the highest level neither makes us scientists, nor does it entitle us to indulge in boastfulness, unless we ourselves are so'.[29] Hence he deemed it appropriate to relate and recall some relevant 'historical facts and issues', which might throw light on the efforts and merits of the medieval Arabs.[30]

As we read al-Bustānī's concise lecture, it slowly emerges that he is undertaking the task of secularizing the Arab past, so much so that its religious dimension pales into insignificance. Initially he sketches in broad strokes the pre-Islamic past of Arabia. So illiterate, we are informed, were the Arabs and so primitive that they could boast of no meaningful knowledge, except that of their tongue, the composition of poetry, and the art of oratory. Their community was divided into two main social groups: the dwellers of towns and villages, engaged in agriculture and trade, and the wandering Bedouins. With the rise of Islam at the beginning of the seventh century, some of them adopted the new faith, while others did not. 'Then numerous wars and quarrels broke out among the believers and unbelievers, for which there is no room here. Moreover, history does not help us a great deal in bringing to light the true state of their affairs, owing to their remote ancientness and their neglect of this refined art [i.e. history-writing].'[31]

Al-Bustānī was thus delimiting the character of his national identity by glossing over what was to become for Arab nationalists the most noteworthy twin events of their history: the life of the Prophet and the rise of Islam. He uses as a convenient expedient the antiquity of a forgotten past and the silence of his available sources. The fact that he describes, in the same breath, the more ancient and mistier pre-Islamic era in relatively ample detail demonstrates the thrust of his argument. As his text indicates his reliance on Arabic and European sources for his data and somewhat extensive quotations, his other pretext can be easily dismissed. It is apparent that he chose to skip such a central historical epoch as a result of a comparative approach, aimed at establishing a new linear sequence of events. The illustrations he furnishes to buttress such a purpose serve to deprive the Prophet's religious message of its role in awakening the Arab intellectual potentialities, the same qualities which al-Bustānī depicts in more than glowing terms.[32] He readily and wilfully accepts the fictitious story that 'Amr b. al-'Āṣ, the conqueror of Egypt, destroyed the great Alexandrian Library, acting under the orders of the caliph 'Umar b. al-Khaṭṭāb. He dwells at length on this fabrication, quotes his source in full,[33] deplores the irreplaceable loss of the library, and attributes such regrettable behaviour to 'the ignorance and heedlessness' of the Arabs and, by implication, the Commander of the Faithful 'Umar.[34]

The landmarks of Arab history and its worthy achievements did not take place until the adoption of Greek science and the translation into Arabic of books fetched from Constantinople, especially under the reign of al-Ma'mūn in Baghdad. But it was in Spain that the Arab sciences and arts bloomed and blossomed. Al-Bustānī lists the Spanish cities blessed with this culture and in doing so transliterates their Latin letters into

Arabic. This suggests he was copying from purely western sources, and was totally oblivious of their Arabic equivalents.[35] Finally, throughout his historical description and analysis, not once does he mention the Muslims either as a religious community or as a political entity.

Such a reading of Arab history would seem to a devout Muslim such as al-Ṭahṭāwī thoroughly suspicious and ludicrous, verging on blasphemy.

However, neither al-Ṭahṭāwī's ardent defence of one of the four rightly guided caliphs, nor his ability to demonstrate Islam's encouragement of learning and the acquisition of knowledge, mean he was a more objective historian than al-Bustānī. Had the evidence, or his sources, pointed to a contrary conclusion, he would almost certainly have suppressed it.

Unlike al-Ṭahṭāwī, al-Bustānī did not produce a proper history of his country. He devoted the rest of his life to his school, magazine, and, above all, the editing and publication of his encyclopedia. The task was undertaken by two young members of his immediate circle: Ilyās Maṭar (1857–1910) and Jūrjī Yannī (1856–1941).

MAṬAR'S SYRIA

Ilyās Maṭar[36] was one of the first western-educated Syrians to attempt writing his country's history according to the rudiments of European scholarship. He was born into a prominent middle-class Greek Orthodox family in the southeastern Lebanese town of Ḥāṣbayya. In the 1860 civil war the town was sacked by the Druze forces. The Maṭars found refuge further north in the palace of the Druze notable Sa'īd Junbulāṭ, and eventually settled in Beirut. There the father resumed his trading activities, and educated his four sons at various missionary schools. Ilyās Maṭar studied first at his sect's school (Les trois docteurs), then moved to the Catholic Patriarchal School, where he learned modern languages, among other subjects. Two of his teachers were the Arabic scholars Salīm Taqlā and Nāṣīf al-Yāzijī who were also attached to al-Bustānī's National School. In 1874 he graduated from the Syrian Protestant College (SPC) with a degree in pharmacy. However before receiving his degree, he had to sit for his final examination in Istanbul, in conformity with Ottoman regulations. He also carried with him his 'History of Syria' which he submitted to the Ottoman Ministry of Education for the authorization of its publication. Having satisfied both his examiners and the official censors, he was introduced to the Ottoman Minister of Education and historian Aḥmad Cevdet Pasha (1822–95),[37] with whom he formed a lifelong intellectual and professional association. He served as a tutor to the minister's son for ten years, and studied medicine and law. He was exceptionally active and successful in Istanbul as a lawyer, editor, medical doctor, teacher, and civil servant, so that 'he continued receiving simultaneously the salaries of four posts for twenty years until he was retired in 1909 owing to his affliction with a disease'.[38]

It was during his study at the SPC that Maṭar decided to write a history of Syria.[39] At that time his spiritual patron and one of his chemistry teachers was his fellow townsman Fāris Nimr (1856–1952). Nimr was a freemason, a member of various cultural and scientific societies, first in Beirut and later in Egypt, and a close associate of the American physician Cornelius Van Dyck who taught medicine at the SPC. Nimr ascribed to himself a leading role in a 'secret society' founded in Beirut about 1875, and was responsible for distributing political pamphlets in Beirut, calling on 'the Syrians' and 'the sons of the fatherland' to resist Turkish domination, and achieve some sort of independence.[40] It is not unreasonable to assume that he encouraged Maṭar to compose his history before the latter's career witnessed a change of direction.

Prior to its publication, al-Bustānī's magazine *al-Jinān* ran advertisements for Maṭar's history on its back cover, signed by the author himself. After the laborious task he had faced, and the painstaking research he had undertaken in composing 'a history of our Syrian country', he alludes to the journey which took him to the Ottoman capital. 'I submitted it', he informs his readers, 'to the Board of Education, whereupon they scrutinized it thoroughly. Since no fault or flaw was found in it, I was authorized to print it on the strength of a sublime decree, in addition to the normal benefaction of receiving a prize in conformity with the laws of our sublime state'.[41]

Maṭar's book came out when the Ottoman reform movement was in full swing. Its publication indicates both a growing Syrian consciousness of a distinct national history, and an Ottoman proclivity to encourage a limited cultural, non-political, autonomy. Given the circumstances of its subjection to a strict censorship, and possibly the convictions of the author, *Tārīkh al-mamlaka al-Sūriyya* does not carry a clear political message. Nevertheless, what it lacks in patriotic overtones, it makes up in its concentration on a well-defined territorial unit, endowed with all the essential characteristics of a nation.

Living up to the literary traditions of his day, Maṭar opens his work by invoking the inevitable benefits of history. It is thus a treasury of wisdom and knowledge, and a mirror in which one may observe the conditions of kingdoms and nations.[42]

He justifies the writing of his book as a matter of patriotic duty and moral obligation. Having acquired, he maintains, a deep knowledge through reading and pondering history books dealing with various nations, he was impelled by 'an inner feeling' to delve further into the past. But the more he studied his historians, the sadder he felt:

> I saw with my own eyes that each country had a written history recollecting its regions and communities, in addition to its conquerors and sovereigns, with the exception of our Syrian country. For I have not come across any history of it whatsoever, save some scattered fragments here and there.[43]

His disappointment and amazement led him to read more history. As he contemplated the relevant material, it suddenly dawned on him how extensively the fame of Syria had spread. His quest was not in vain. The Syrian past deserves to be commemorated and celebrated. Syria is the land of prosperity, beautiful scenery, and rich fertile soil. It boasts of outstanding virtuous men who excelled in science, literature, and learning. Syria was one of the most renowned kingdoms, and is still one of the most eminent. It is believed to be the cradle of civilization, and the place of origin of the most important and significant inventions. All the nations are envious of its possession by the Ottoman state. In it are located the holy places and the lands promised by God to the descendants of Abraham.[44]

The reign of Sultan 'Abd al-'Azīz (1861–76) is highlighted as a vindication of Syria's inherent capabilities and resourceful talents. Under his rule it became wealthy and powerful. How, indeed, could it fail to reach such heights, since the Sultan 'made a tour of the European nations and was received with exceeding hospitality and seemly respect. It all goes to prove the perfection of his characteristics and the excellence of his attributes'?[45] The honorary titles the European monarchs had bestowed on al-Ṭahṭāwī's patron, as a recognition of his enlightened rule, take on at the hands of Maṭar a more tangible authenticity. Muḥammad 'Alī did not lose his identity. Rather, he re-established his popular acclaim as the rejuvenator of Islam. 'Abd al-'Azīz went to Europe in person, entered its courts, subjected himself to the careful scrutiny of the civilized circles, and was pronounced to be their mirror image. The Ottoman Empire, embodied in the personage of the Sultan, had become another Europe.

If the Sultan is reduced to a western monarch, stripped of his Islamic shadows, Maṭar does not lose sight of his own identity. He flaunts his 'Arab zeal' which kindled his imagination, and inspired him to relate the glorious past of his 'beloved fatherland'. The fruit of his efforts is nothing less than 'a book containing the most pleasant of events and the most abundant of historical questions'.[46] It is obvious that Maṭar was walking a tightrope, trying to perform a balancing act between his loyalty to the Ottoman state and his burgeoning Syrian consciousness. His fatherland has a long history of glorious accomplishments, but these find their culmination under the benign authority of its sultan residing in Istanbul. He is motivated by a deep Arab commitment to the culture of his country, and proud of his inherited racial ability, which confirms the intrinsic civilized nature of a new national community. He dedicates his book to the 'peerless' historian and 'my master' Aḥmad Cevdet Pasha, the Ottoman Minister of Education, and sings his praises in a long, sycophantic poem. Furthermore, in reciting the bygone splendours of Syria, he stumbles on the Palmyrene queen Zenobia. Her grandeur triggers in his mind the illusion of a renewed role of Syria under another Zenobia, the queen 'who carved for herself an immortal name in the annals of the nations'. Then this unexpected burst of pregnant recollection is dampened by his incantation: 'let us reiterate the praise of our most magnificent Sultan'.[47] Bearing in mind his background, education, and his intellectual environment, it would be quite legitimate to read an implicit message into his allusion to the days of Zenobia. It manifests a latent desire for an autonomous Syrian entity or perhaps an independent nation. Palmyra met all the requirements of a prosperous 'secular' power worthy of imitation. From a caravan and market city it developed into a military power. It defied the legions of the Roman Emperors and defeated the armies of the Parthians. Its energetic Arab queen brought various parts of Syria under her authority and extended her frontiers far beyond, reaching into Egypt and the heart of Asia Minor. When she was finally overthrown by Aurelian in AD 272, and taken to Rome in golden chains, she astonished her captors by her dignity and pride.[48]

Nevertheless, in Maṭar's work, Syria is looked at more as a geographical unit inhabited by a distinct people, than a political national entity. It is defined as a clearly bordered territory, stretching from the Euphrates and the Syrian desert in the east to the Mediterranean in the west, and from Asia Minor in the north and the Sinai Peninsula in the south. When it fell under Roman domination, it was designated by the name Syria, the origin of which is still disputed.[49] As its people are an intermixture of many races, it is impossible to trace their ancestry. According to the historical evidence, the Syrian people are a racial synthesis composed of the remnants of the Arabs, the Tatars, the Turks, the Greeks, and all the other nations which brought Syria under their rule.[50]

In a brief historical sketch Maṭar covers the various races and dynasties which settled in Syria or conquered its territory. The scope of his narrative encompasses the Canaanites, the ancient Israelites, the Assyrians, the Babylonians, the Persians, the Macedonians of Alexander the Great, and the Romans. When he reaches the date of the Arab conquest he totally ignores the Prophet Muḥammad or the birth of Islam, and shifts his story in rapid succession to 'Umar b. al-Khaṭṭāb, and other Arab caliphs down to the Mamluks and the Ottomans.[51]

The remainder of the work's contents represents more of a topography than a continuous narration of events. It concentrates on the physical features and natural life of the country, roaming over its mountains, climate, fauna and flora, its minerals, and agricultural products. Maṭar pays particular attention to the growth and progress of the city of Beirut,[52] especially in the educational fields. Its missionary and native schools are dwelt on at length as concrete evidence of a new age. The author provides his readers with a rare glimpse into the total population of Syria, classified into their respective sectarian and religious categories. Whereas the Syrians were deemed to have lost any distinct racial affiliation or origin and considered in their entirety as a *sui generis* amalgamation, their sects obstinately refuse to decompose and merge into a solid compound.

Instead they are visibly paraded in a systematic arrangement, proudly unfolding the banners on which are inscribed their exact numbers. The Sunni majority figure at the top of the list, designated simply as 'Islam', the colloquial Arabic name for Muslims. After the Sunnis, there follow in a descending order the Greek Orthodox, the Maronites, the Greek Catholics, the Druzes, the Nuṣayris and Ismā'īlis lumped together, down to the Shi'ites, the Armenians, and others. The Ottoman Millet system is thus reproduced in its full imposing majesty, and substantiated as an accurate device of mathematical genius and tax-collecting efficiency. The grand total amounts to 1,660,000 sectarian individuals, although the Armenians keep both their racial and Syrian identities. Maṭar expresses his regret at failing to grace his table with the number of Syrian Jews. Nor was he able to include a few pages on the fundamental tenets of each sect: the Ottoman Ministry of Education censored such an ambitious plan.[53] It seems the Ottoman authorities were already aware of various European schemes calling for the creation of a 'Jewish Kingdom' in Palestine, and did not wish to publicize their number, no matter how insignificant it was.[54]

The topography and history of the Syrian main towns and the autonomous Sanjaks of Mount Lebanon and Jerusalem monopolize two-thirds of Maṭar's panoramic sketches. Consequently, his history degenerates into a disjointed series of events. The separate entities sprawled over a specific geographical unit emerge as a mosaic with no identifiable character. Relying on the observations and accounts of two main French sources,[55] he ends up by seeing his own country through the pages of relatively outdated descriptions. Only Beirut escapes this fate, it being his home town. The whole text has no punctuation or footnotes. Occasionally the page number of a quoted reference is provided, but either the author, the title, or the date of publication is missing.[56]

Maṭar wrote his 'history' when a new generation of western-educated Syrians was groping for a new definition of its role within the structure of the Ottoman Empire. The tension revealed in his convoluted narrative was apparently resolved upon his admission into the administrative hierarchy of Istanbul. His promise to write another volume on ancient and modern Syrian history, dealing exclusively with political events, was never fulfilled.[57]

Another compatriot of his took up the challenge, and

decided in his own way to grapple with the same problem. He undertook to write the most comprehensive history of Syria in Arabic, based on European models.

YANNĪ'S HISTORY

Jūrjī Yannī's history of Syria[58] was published after the accession of Sultan 'Abd al-Ḥamīd (1876–1909) to the throne, and the brief spell of an unprecedented constitutional and parliamentary life in the Empire which lasted for almost two years. However the Russo–Turkish war of 1877–78 brought in its wake a suspension of the constitution. Midḥat Pasha, the Grand Vezir and the inspiring spirit of the constitutionalists, was dismissed from his post and appointed to the governorship of Syria. Banished from the centre of power, Midḥat sought to apply his reformist ideas in his new province. As a governor, he endeavoured to obtain from the Sultan wider authority and freedom of action in order to implement his policies speedily and effectively. The Sultan, bent on amassing more power in his hands, did not respond favourably to another challenge to his autocratic rule. Nevertheless, Midḥat proceeded with his programme of reforming the antiquated and corrupt Ottoman administrative structure in Syria. His policy of decentralization involved wider participation by the local people, the appointment of more Syrians, Muslim and Christian, in the institutions he created or overhauled. He encouraged various literary and cultural societies, and patronized the foundation of new ones, especially amongst the Muslims of Beirut, Damascus, and Sidon. His open-mindedness expressed itself in the promotion of Arab culture and the use of the Arabic language in his administrative machinery. The emergence of a nascent Syrian consciousness was allowed to flourish, even in its political dimensions. The fact that he was capitalizing on Syrian grievances against the Porte is a redundant conclusion.[59] Midḥat was engaged in a power struggle with an autocratic sultan, and considered Syria as a convenient *point d'appui* from which to launch his political comeback. To the Syrians his reforms were interpreted differently. Some took the opportunity to further their own cause, while others saw in them a direct threat to their entrenched interests.[60] The latter group represented on the whole a wide variety of Muslim notables whose authority and economic survival depended on preserving the status quo. Nevertheless, a rising stratum of Muslim merchants, entrepreneurs, and reformist *'ulamā'* of the middle rank rallied to Midḥat's cause and welcomed some of the changes he intended to introduce. One such was the Damascene *'ālim* Shaykh Salīm al-'Aṭṭār. He responded to the formation of a Comité de la Patrie, sponsored by Midḥat, in these words: 'Désormais, il ne devait plus être question de distinction entre chrétiens et musulmans, et qu'il fallait songer uniquement à l'intérêt général, c'est-à-dire à l'intérêt des Syriens.'[61] Furthermore, whereas the Syrian Society of 1847 had Christian members exclusively, its successor, the Syrian Scientific Society, founded in 1857 and still in existence during Midḥat's governorship, had no less than fifty Muslim members of prominent families, whether in Beirut, Damascus, or other Syrian cities.[62] Ilyās Maṭar's *History of Syria* has at its end 'eulogies'[63] penned by Muslim Syrians who all had a sound religious background (Yūsuf al-Asīr, Ḥusayn Bayhum, Shaykh Muḥammad Rashīd, Muṣṭafā al-Ḥalabī). One noteworthy eulogy is written by the son of the legendary Algerian leader 'Abd al-Qādir al-Jazā'irī, who had been exiled by the French to Damascus. According to the memoirs of a contemporary Muslim notable, Munaḥ al-Ṣulḥ,[64] a delegation of prominent Muslims contacted 'Abd al-Qādir in 1877 during the Russo–Turkish war with the aim of achieving 'Syrian independence', without disowning the Ottoman Sultan as the caliph of all Muslims. However no concrete result came out of these developments. On 1 August 1880, Midḥat was transferred to Izmir after twenty months of his Syrian governorship. Yannī's history reflects both the expectations and disappointments of those years. With its publication the momentum generated by Ottoman reforms came almost to a standstill, especially in the political sphere. Finally the Syrian Protestant College (SPC), which in its turn planted the seeds of scientific ideas and liberal debates, saw the same weapons being used to undermine its missionary purpose. Its Syrian students and instructors who embraced Darwinism and the theory of evolution were expelled. The American culprits had their contracts terminated or were forced to resign. Jurjī Zaydān (1861–1914), who was then a first-year medical student, emigrated to Egypt, and later embarked on a variety of literary and other, wide-ranging activities. Fāris Nimr, Ya'qūb Ṣarrūf and Shāhīn Makarius followed in 1884, and relaunched in Cairo their celebrated scientific magazine *al-Muqtaṭaf*.[65]

Yannī, an Orthodox Christian of Greek origin, was born in Tripoli in 1856. Some members of his family were traders who enjoyed close connections with the local American Consulate. He was educated privately and in the local schools of his town, and acquired a knowledge of such foreign languages as Italian, French, and English. In 1868 he enrolled at the newly founded National School of al-Bustānī.[66] Four years later he started writing a series of articles in the magazine *al-Jinān* on the Franco-Prussian war. He initiated or joined a number of literary and cultural societies both in his home town and in Beirut. Shortly after publishing his history he became an active member of the Oriental Scientific Society which replaced the now defunct Syrian Scientific Society.[67] In dropping its Syrian identity card, and adopting the colourless oriental designation, the new society was yielding to the hardening attitude of the Porte. It was a calculated step which betrayed its political function as an umbrella for various discontented Syrians.

Yannī was not known for any active involvement in politics. Nevertheless, his house in Tripoli became a literary salon, and a meeting place for political and social debates. Two members of his generation who frequented his house were Rashīd Riḍā (1865–1935) and Faraḥ Anṭūn (1874–1922). Both emigrated in the same ship to Egypt in 1897 and established a reputation in journalism and political thought, the former rallying to the defence of Muḥammad ʻAbduh as one of his disciples, and the latter attacking both as enemies of science and secularism.[68] Following the declaration of the Ottoman constitution in 1908, Yannī founded with his younger brother Ṣamū'īl (1865–1919) a printing press and an Arabic periodical *al-Mabāḥith*, which continued to be published until 1936 when he was aged 80. In 1919 Muḥammad Kurd ʻAlī and his Syrian compatriots founded the Arab Academy in Damascus and invited Yannī to join them as a founding member.[69] Thus, unlike the other disciples of al-Bustānī and some Syrian Protestant College graduates, he did not consider leaving Syria and settling in Egypt or elsewhere.[70] An amateur historian, he was a quiet and subdued scholar not known for outbursts of rhetoric or sycophancy to the powers that be. He preferred the world of his well-stocked private library to the hustle and bustle of political intrigues. Consequently his history is not dedicated to a prince or a sultan. The title of his book does not follow the customary style of encapsulating its contents in rhymed prose, as was the case with both al-Ṭahṭāwī[71] and Maṭar. Nor does he include a long poem to sing the praises of a patron and win favours. This spirit of independence exhibits itself in the use of his sources, and the way he compares one historian's judgement with another. Although he relies on *Syrie, ancienne et moderne* by the two French historians David and Yanosky as one of his main sources, he does not follow their narrative uncritically. Whereas Yanosky decides arbitrarily not to include in his narrative of ancient Syria either Judaea or Phoenicia, Yannī opts for Strabo's geographical definition of the country, which Yanosky himself casts doubt on. As a result, Yanosky's Phoenicia, for example, is considered to have had a history quite separate from the rest of his central Syria.[72] Yannī, on the other hand, devotes eleven chapters to the Phoenicians, gleaned from other ancient and modern sources. He describes and discusses their origin and colonies (whether in the Mediterranean, the Atlantic, or North Africa), their commercial activities, navigation, and industry; their language, religion, and government.[73] In this wide-ranging narrative there is no undue national pride or exaggerated trumpeting of Phoenicia's role in inventing the alphabet and teaching the world the art of seafaring, as other nationalist-minded Lebanese tend towards in the twentieth century. For Yannī, the Phoenicians were not so keen on achieving national independence, nor did they possess a heightened sense of patriotism. The submission of Phoenicia to other nations was a familiar feature of its long history. It often opened its doors to conquerors without much resistance, and was happy to obey the great empires. It only wanted to pursue its trading activities unhindered, preserve its autonomy, and practise its indigenous customs and traditions.[74]

The various races, empires, and conquerors are then dealt with in a dry and dispassionate narration of events. But the rise of Palmyra as a Syrian kingdom, with an empire of its own, brings the rule of foreign powers to an end. The narrative suddenly sparkles with flashes of patriotism and offers a momentary pause for wider reflection. Here Yannī brings some of Yanosky's judgements to his aid, but without attributing them; then he makes his own conclusions about that fateful encounter between the mighty Roman army and the brave Syrian queen of Palmyra. He first translates into Arabic Yanosky's following sentences: 'Zenobie, veuve d'Odenath, prit le gouvernement de la Syrie. Les habitants reconnurent avec joie l'autorité d'une reine de leur nation.'[75] But in order to convey the pregnant meaning of such a statement, Yannī finds a better substitute for the colourless term 'les habitants', and replaces it with one of his own — 'the Syrians'. Having ascertained her credentials as a loyal and wise 'daughter of the fatherland', he makes Zenobia's battles and conquests in Asia Minor and Egypt an index of an inherent Syrian desire for independence, obliterating the long and endless subjugation to outside powers. The memory of Palmyra's brief glory is tinged with a yearning for a lost world superimposed on a melancholy resignation:

> It is apparent that Aurelian did not wish to see another state rival his mighty empire in greatness and influence. He therefore set about the destruction of its authority by means of war, and succeeded in achieving his aim. He thus deprived Syria of its desire to enjoy, if only for a short period, the bliss of independence from foreigners. With the capture of its queen, the country returned to its former servitude, as if it [Syria] is fated not to control its own affairs.[76]

The Arab conquest of Syria which began in 634 opened a new chapter in its history, and Yannī is anxious to trace the causes of such a momentous event. After narrating the moral and political corruption of the Byzantine Empire and the gradual decline of the Persians, he turns his attention to Arabia and the rise of Islam. Keeping to a Christian tradition that does not consider Muḥammad a prophet, he simply designates him as 'the founder of the Islamic mission'. Nevertheless, he paints a sympathetic portrait of the new prophet and his religious ideals. The successive Arab victories are seen as a direct result of the religious bond that forged the tribes into an awesome army of believers. The defeat of the Byzantines and the departure of their notables, princes, and administrators from the country meant the end of the Roman civilization. Some Syrians embraced Islam, and joined the front ranks of the Muslims, acting as guides and local informants. Others refused to pay the poll-tax or to be converted and took the third option of emigrating with their former masters. The social structure of the country witnessed a complete change in the wake of these new developments. Mu'āwiya's reign in Syria (660–680) turned it into the centre of a great empire. The history of the Umayyad dynasty is no longer a story of alien rulers. The struggle between Mu'āwiya and the Caliph 'Alī is viewed as a political conflict between two 'national' entities, rather than a religious civil war. The Syrians were attached to their new ruler, showing him all the loyalty he deserved for his justice, intelligence, forbearance, and prudence. When Syria finally succumbed to the rising power of the 'Abbasids and the capital of the empire was transferred from Damascus to Baghdad, misery and grief became the order of the day. It was reduced to a mere province ruled by oppressive governors who eventually led it to ruin.[77]

Yannī condemns the Crusades and the Frankish kings who instigated them. Despite the dreadful condition of Syria, he asserts, the Arab provinces were still 'rich and prosperous'. The Frankish hordes descended on the Holy Land as a wave of barbarian invaders. Their leaders were oblivious of the power of the Arabs and decided to launch their campaigns for their own selfish purposes, capitalizing on the lack of knowledge of the European masses. Europe at the time was enduring the adversities of 'poverty, drought, civil wars, social divisions and confusion'. Her inhabitants were enslaved to the notables and princes, paying blind obedience to the fanatical clergy. The entry of the Crusaders into Syria brought in its wake 'calamities and tribulations'. For it was their intention 'to ruin it, and afflict it with all misfortunes, as well as to plunder its wealth and divert it from pursuing its quest of civilization and the flourishing Arab culture. However, they benefited a great deal from their coming, namely in emulating the example of the Muslims in their material and moral way of life'. Having copied various sciences, and systems of organization and administration, the Crusaders transplanted this advanced culture to their own countries. 'In this way they planted the seeds of what we witness today in the flowering civilization of their descendants.'[78]

The Mamlūk period is disposed of in less than a page, while the Ottoman period, extending from 1516 to the author's own time, fares little better.[79] Perhaps Yannī was following the model set by the French historian Jules David, who in his turn condensed the history of the Turkish Empire into a few pages.[80] Although Yannī relies extensively on David's narrative of the Arab conquests and the Crusades, he chooses not to agree with him on every point. Where the two narratives converge is in their approach to the history of Mount Lebanon, seen as the refuge of a proud and free-spirited minority. The inhabitants of the hills and mountains never submitted to the Muslim invaders, and were jealous of their freedom to the extent of launching one revolt after another, earning for themselves 'the nickname of rebels or *Marada*'.

Here Yannī departs from his relatively neutral narrative and reveals his preferences. He even passes over in silence the Maronites' defiance of the Byzantine authorities, restricting their resistance to the constant Arab–Muslim attempts to conquer their fortified strongholds,[81] whereas David, being a passionate French Catholic, highlights the enmity of the Maronites towards both the Muslims and the Byzantines:

> Lorsque les Arabes eurent conquis la Syrie, leur rapide victoire jeta d'abord l'épouvante dans la montagne: les Maronites se fortifièrent et laissèrent passer l'ouragan. Mais plus tard, quand les forces Musulmanes se dispersèrent sur le monde, quand les ennemis des Chrétiens diminuèrent en nombre et en hardie, les Maronites se montrèrent de nouveau au delà de leurs frontières, et commencèrent avec les Mahometans une guerre qui ne cesse plus. Les Maronites ne connaissaient ni paix ni trêve; et lorsque les grandes cités de la Syrie suspendaient les hostilités avec les Arabes, les Maronites n'en combattaient pas moins. Ils allèrent même jusqu'à mépriser l'autorité de l'empereur de Constantinople; et malgré ses ordres, ils ne déposèrent jamais les armes. Ce fut, d'après les traditions du pays, cette persistance à agir indépendamment des princes byzantins qui les fit appeler par les Arabes les *rebelles*. La cour de Constantinople les traitait comme des sujets révoltés, et le gouvernement des khalifes comme des ennemis mortels.[82]

This image of Mount Lebanon by a French orientalist, preaching the gospel of the Maronites and calling upon his government to turn Lebanon into 'une Suisse orientale',[83] must have made an enduring impression on many a Christian of Yannī's generation, who were avid readers of such historical sources. During the nineteenth century it remained a vague idea, particularly for non-Maronite Christians living outside the confines of Mount Lebanon. The Greek Orthodox and Catholic communities were mainly concentrated in the urban areas of Ottoman Syria. Hence they sought to generalize the idea of a new Switzerland and to apply it to the whole of geographical Syria, hoping to extract further concessions from the Porte under the pressure of European powers. In this manner Yannī considers the reign of Sultan 'Abd al-Majīd (1839–61) as heralding a qualitative change in the fortunes of his country. The Sultan initiated reforms designed to curb the harsh and arbitrary rule of his governors, and make them conform to the rules of the *Sharī'a* and the law. From then on all subjects were equal before their government, in spite of the persistent corruption and indiscriminate attitude of the tax-collectors. Sciences and knowledge, on the other hand, were non-existent in Syria during its 'dark ages', which did not terminate until the arrival of the Europeans and the Americans. The westerners spread across Syria with the sole aim of 'diffusing knowledge and refining morals'. They built schools, introduced printing presses and established benevolent societies. Thus the media and means of learning multiplied and became available to wide sections of the population. Soon the Syrians started to imitate the example of these westerners and to emulate them in the process of self-enlightenment. New schools were opened, particularly in Beirut and its environs. Within a few years Syria experienced an awakening (*yaqẓa*) which, if kept to its past momentum, must lead to everlasting success. As for trade and industry, Syria was still lagging behind Europe. Foreign goods dominated its market. Its agriculture was primitive and neglected by the new sons of wealthy families, who gave up cultivating the land and began seeking other employment after graduating from the new schools. All the ports of Syria were run or used by foreign ships. Moreover, there was only one proper road in Syria, running between Beirut and Damascus, which was administered by a French company. Some of 'the honourable valis' had given orders for the improvement of the Jaffa–Jerusalem road and Midḥat Pasha had started repairing two other roads.[84]

Thus ends the history of Syria on a note at the same time gloomy and relatively optimistic.

Yannī's historical narrative is yoked to a political theory, expounded in the introduction to his work and interspersed throughout the text. Man is by nature inclined to follow 'his selfish interests' and deviate from the right path. He seldom learns from the lessons of his past. The first families and tribes, following the Deluge, were led by greedy individuals who appropriated all authority to themselves and prevented their communities from falling into disorder. Laws soon emerged to preserve the rights of man, and bind his rulers by them. Absolute freedom was subordinated to justice. Following Montesquieu's classification of political systems, Yannī divides states into three categories: republics, monarchies, and despotisms. With the hindsight of experience one can detect five causes underlying the rise of nations, and three others which account for their downfall. The set of five causes include:

1. religious solidarity as illustrated by the rise of Islam
2. the ability to achieve victory in war and create an efficient system of administration, such as the case of the Assyrian Empire
3. the capacity to establish political authority by the sword coupled with a love of learning and philosophy – Egypt, the Greeks, and the Romans being the ideal models
4. the foundation of sovereignty on justice and liberty; both of these virtues were manifest under the reign of Caliph 'Umar b. al-Khaṭṭab, while the United States of America is another perfect example
5. a talent for practising trade and commerce; the Phoenicians and the Palmyrenes serve as twin models.

The downfall of those nations or kingdoms sets in when, first, maladministration, negligence, and moral decadence become prevalent (such was the fate of the Romans in Syria), and second, as a consequence of oppression, dissensions, and internal divisions (witness the ruin of the Greeks, the Byzantines, and the Arabs). Finally, nations decline with the constant eruptions of wars and the successive changes of dynasties. It suffices to mention Syria and Egypt as an indisputable proof.[85]

Yannī inserts into his narrative, and at the relevant junctures of events, his commonplace homilies. The voice of history, to which man, as an inherently evil being, refuses to listen, echoes in a concatenation of clear messages, against the background of one fallen empire after another. It is true that 'the subject and scope of history are the exploration and elucidation of the actual events which lie at the source of the rise and fall of nations'. Nevertheless, 'one of history's basic principles is to act as a receiving mirror in which one can observe the unfolding future of the nation'.[86]

Yannī's history is relatively neglected nowadays. It seems to have suffered at the hands of some scholars who refer to it as a mere local history of the author's home town.[87] Such references serve to shroud it in further obscurity and are an indication of a total ignorance of its contents. More importantly, it shared the same fate that befell the national entity whose fortunes it aspired to narrate.

Before its final demise, the concept of a Syrian national identity gained wider currency in the wake of the Young Turkish revolution in 1908. Its momentum reached its peak at the end of the First World War, when, in 1920, a Syrian kingdom was proclaimed under the leadership of King Fayṣal. However the French hastened to dismantle the new political entity, and proceeded to create Greater Lebanon and four other mini-states out of geographical Syria. Palestine became a British mandate which did not terminate until the creation of Israel in 1948. Another son of Sharīf Ḥusayn, ʻAbdallāh, who joined the cause of the Allies in 1916, carved out for himself an Emirate in Transjordan. The British authorities were more than willing to lend him their support and limit his ambitions to a smaller kingdom, instead of his original demand for a larger independent Arab kingdom. Fayṣal was compensated for his lost kingdom by his appointment as the king of a new Iraqi state under British mandatory powers.

Syrian nationalism as a political and intellectual movement lingered on in the 1920s, typified historiographically by a multi-volume history and topography which was the result of a team effort on the part of leading Syrian personalities and scholars headed by Muḥammad Kurd ʻAlī.[88] With the quelling of the Syrian Revolt of 1925 by the French, the movement petered out, except for a few isolated pockets among the minorities, especially the Greek Orthodox of Lebanon and the ʻAlawīs of Northern Syria. In the 1930s Arab nationalism gradually replaced Syrian localism. The Syrian identity was submerged and came to be looked at as a reactionary response aided and abetted by such British agents as King ʻAbdallāh of Jordan, or anti-Arab parties represented by the Syrian Nationalist Party founded in 1932 by a Greek Orthodox Lebanese, and the son of Dr Khalīl Saʻādah, who graduated from the Syrian Protestant College in 1883, left Lebanon and eventually settled in Brazil. At the same time in Greater Lebanon, Maronite and Catholic intellectuals and politicians endeavoured to foster a new Lebanese identity based on a new reading of its history. Phoenicia emerged into full daylight as a resurrected western nation under the protection of the mistress of liberty, the Republic of France.

NOTES

1. Georges Douin, *La mission du Baron de Boislecomte* (Cairo, 1927), pp. 228–34; John Bowring, *Report on Syria, Parliamentary Papers* (London, 1840), vol. 21, pp. 104–8 and Appendix D; William Polk, *The Opening of South Lebanon, 1788–1840* (Cambridge, Mass., 1963), pp. xviii–xx.

2. On Buṭrus al-Bustānī see *Dā'irat al-Ma'ārif*, edited by Salīm al-Bustānī, vol. VII (Beirut, 1883), pp. 589–93; *al-Muqtaṭaf*, vol. VIII (Beirut, 1884), pp. 1–7; A.L. Tibawi, 'The American missionaries in Beirut and Buṭrus al-Bustānī', *St. Antony's Papers No. 16*, MEA, No. 3, ed. Albert Hourani (London, 1963).

3. For further details see, *A'māl al-Jam'īyya al-Sūriyya* (the *Proceedings of the Syrian Society*), Beirut, 1852, pp. i–iii, where a list of the members and their respective posts is provided by Buṭrus al-Bustānī. Out of 48 resident and non-resident members, 15 were foreigners, mainly American, English, and Armenian. The rest were all native Christians (Greek Orthodox, Uniate Catholic, and Protestant). The majority were resident in Beirut, one in Damascus, three in Tripoli, two in Palestine (Ḥaifa and Ṣafad), and one in Sidon. It is worth noting that, in the introduction to the proceedings (p. iii), al-Bustānī expresses the Society's gratitude to the English member, Charles Henry Spencer Churchill (1828–77), for his unswerving support as well as to 'the Austrian Oriental Society' for donating some books.

4. Philip K. Hitti, *History of the Arabs*, 10th edn (London, 1977), p. 726.

5. Philippe de Ṭarāzī, *Tārīkh al-ṣaḥāfa al-'arabiyya*, vol. I (Beirut, 1913–33), p. 67.

6. Thus in the fourth issue of *Nafīr Sūriyya* al-Bustānī felt the need to spell out the connotations of the new name: 'Syria, otherwise known as Barr al-Shām … is our fatherland … and the inhabitants of Syria, whatever their creed, sect or race are the sons of our fatherland', *Nafīr Sūriyya*, 25 Oct. 1860.

7. K. Salibi, 'The 1860 upheaval in Damascus as seen by al-Sayyid Muhammad Abu'l-Su'ud al-Hasibi', in William R. Polk and Richard L. Chambers (eds), *Beginnings of Modernization in the Middle East* (University of Chicago Press, 1968), p. 189.

8. *Al-Jinān*, vol. IV (1873), pp. 626–9; A.L. Tibawi, 'History of the Syrian Protestant College', *MEJ*, vol. XVI (1967), pp. 1–15 and 199–212.

9. *Dā'irat al-Ma'ārif*, vol. VII (Beirut, 1883), p. 580; Philippe de Ṭarāzī, *Tārīkh al-ṣaḥāfa al-'arabiyya*, vol. II (Beirut, 1914), pp. 68–9; Yusuf Sarkīs, *Mu'jam al-maṭbū'āt al-'arabiyya* (Cairo, 1928), pp. 559–60. He also translated a 'history of modern France' (Beirut, 1884).

10. A. Tibawi, 'The American missionaries in Beirut', pp. 166–68. It was probably the financial difficulties which the American mission was experiencing at the time that made al-Bustānī look for alternative sources of financial support. Cf. A. Tibawi, *The American Interests in Syria* (Oxford, 1966), pp. 145 and 159. See also, Butrus Abu-Manneh, 'The Christians between Ottomanism and Syrian nationalism', *IJMES*, 11 (1980), p. 289, where the same view is reiterated.

11. *Dā'irat al-Ma'ārif*, vol. I (Beirut, 1876), pp. 3–4. Ismā'īl subscribed to one thousand copies of the encyclopedia and donated to al-Bustānī a large library, after his failure to secure financial assistance from the Ottoman authorities.

12. *Al-Jinān*, vol. 1 (1870), p. 385.

13. See also Buṭrus al-Bustānī, *Khuṭba fī ādāb al-'Arab* (Beirut, 1859), pp. 27 and 39, where the nineteenth century is similarly hailed to have ushered in knowledge, inventions, discoveries, industry, and arts.

14. *Ibid.*, pp. 386–7.

15. *Ibid.*, p. 388.

16. *Al-Jinān*, vol. I (1870), pp. 160–1.

17. The editorial is not signed. Another article follows immediately signed by Salīm which we shall also discuss.

18. *Ibid.*, p. 160.

19. *Al-Jinān*, vol. I (1870), p. 647.

20. *Ibid.*, p. 647.

21. *Al-Jinān*, vol. I (1870), p. 160. Salīm is here rehearsing a passage in his father's lecture (*Khuṭba fī ādāb al-'Arab*), pp. 26–7.

22. *Al-Jinān*, p. 162.

23. *Ibid.*, p. 163.

24. *Ibid.*, p. 163.

25. *Ibid.*, p. 163.

26. *Ibid.*, p. 164.

27. *Al-Jinān*, vol. I (1870), pp. 641–8.

28. *Ibid.*, p. 648.

29. *Khuṭba fī ādāb al-'Arab*, p. 4. Al-Bustānī uses the Arabic plural of al-ādāb (literature) to convey the meaning of the French terms 'les lettres et les sciences'. Cf. L.A. Sédillot, *Histoire générale des Arabes*, 2nd edn, vol. II (Paris, 1877), p. 2 (1st edn, 1854).

30. *Ibid.*, p. 4.

31. *Ibid.*, pp. 4–6.

32. *Ibid.*, pp. 16–17.

33. Al-Bustānī was probably drawing on the chronicle of Bar Hebraeus (d. 1286). Cf. E. Gibbon, *Decline and Fall of the Roman Empire*, ed. J.B. Bury, vol. V (London, 1898), pp. 452–5. Gibbon was the first western historian 'to deny both the fact and the consequences' of the alleged event.

34. Al-Bustānī, *Khuṭba*, pp. 6–7.

35. *Ibid.*, pp. 8–13. Thus the transliteration gives us Cordova, Seville, and Granada, instead of Qurṭuba, Ishbīliyya, and Gharnāṭa respectively, as the Arabs rendered these names in their language. Cf. Khayr al-Dīn al-Tūnisī, *Aqwam al-masālik*, p. 134, where he translates a

passage from Victor Duruy's *Histoire du moyen age* concerning the great centres of Arab knowledge, and renders the Spanish city names in their original Arabic version.

36. On Maṭar see Ṭarāzī, *Tārīkh al-ṣaḥāfa al-'arabiyya,* vol. II, pp. 227–9.

37. On Cevdet, see, H. Bowen, 'Ahmad Djewdet Pasha', *The Encyclopaedia of Islam,* 2nd edn, E.J. Brill, Leiden, 1979, pp. 284–6.

38. Ṭarāzī, *Tārīkh al-ṣaḥāfa,* p. 229.

39. Ilyās Dīb Maṭar, *al-'Uqūd al-durriyya fī tārīkh al-mamlaka al-Sūriyya* (Beirut, 1874).

40. George Antonius, *The Arab Awakening* (London, 1938), pp. 179–86; Zeine N. Zeine, *Arab–Turkish Relations and the Emergence of Arab Nationalism* (Beirut, 1958), pp. 56–7 and 68, n. 15. Both reproduce personal interviews with Fāris Nimr. The first traces the birth of Arab nationalism to the foundation of the 'Beiruti Secret Society', while the other sees in its emergence a latent Lebanese nationalism promoted by a handful of Christians. Nimr managed to produce two conflicting accounts of the same event when he was 'at the ripe age of 80', according to Antonius, *ibid.*, p. 81, and almost 90 by the time Zeine tried to elicit more information from him. Being his son-in-law, Antonius tends to exaggerate his role, calling Nimr 'one of the most outstanding figures in the Arab World'. *Op cit.*, p. 81, n. 1.

41. *Al-Jinān,* vol. V (15 June, 1 July, and 15 July, 1874).

42. Maṭar, *Tārīkh al-mamlaka,* p. 2.

43. *Ibid.* Maṭar uses '*mamlaka*' to mean a country, a dominion, or a kingdom. The various Ottoman territories were designated *al-Mamālik al-'Uthmāniyya.*

44. *Ibid.*, pp. 2 and 21.

45. *Ibid.*, pp. 2 and 14. 'Abd al-'Azīz made his journey to Europe in 1867. It was 'the first made by an Ottoman Sultan for any purpose but war. He was received at the courts of Paris, London, and Vienna, and also met the King of Prussia.' See Bernard Lewis, *The Emergence of Modern Turkey* (London, 1968), p. 121.

46. Maṭar, *Tārīkh al-mamlaka,* p. 3.

47. *Ibid.*, pp. 3 and 22.

48. Maṭar gleaned his portrait of Zenobia from the French traveller Baptistin Poujoulat's *Voyage à Constantinople, dans l'Asie Mineure, en Mésopotamie, à Palmyre, en Palestine et en Égypte,* vol. II (Paris, 1841), 110–54. Maṭar used this work as a main source in his topographical and historical description of Syrian towns and regions. Dealing with Palmyra under a separate heading (*Tārīkh al-mamlaka,* pp. 59–60), he translates the following passage, toning down its political implications:

> sı Palmyre n'avait jamais été qu'une cité commerciale, le voyageur n'irait pas la troubler aujourd'hui dans le silence de son désert; mais la postérité s'est occupée d'elle parcequ'elle est devenue le siège d'un empire, parceque de grands intérêts politiques se sont agités sous ses murs, et surtout, enfin, parceque la gloire des arts y a laissé d'impérissables traces.

Poujoulat, *Voyage*, p. 114. By 1874 Zenobia had become a cult figure for some western-educated Syrians. In 1871 Salīm al-Bustānī, for example, published in Beirut his historical novel: *Zenobia malikat Tadmur.*

49. Maṭar, *Tārīkh al-mamlaka*, p. 8.

50. *Ibid.*, p. 19.

51. *Ibid.*, pp. 6–14.

52. *Ibid.*, pp. 106–20. On 'the spectacular growth of Beirut' in the last century see Leila Tarazi Fawaz, *Merchants and Migrants in Nineteenth-century Beirut* (Harvard University Press, 1983).

53. Maṭar, *Tārīkh al-mamlaka*, pp. 19–20.

54. In Poujoulat's *Voyage* (vol. II, pp. 597–610), one such plan is discussed and rejected as a British bid to extend commercial and missionary interests in Syria at the expense of long-standing French influence.

55. Poujoulat's *Voyage*; Jules David and Jean Yanosky's *Syrie, ancienne et moderne* (Paris, 1848).

56. Maṭar, *Tārīkh al-mamlaka*, pp. 45, 63, 91, and *passim*. The whole text covers 184 pages.

57. *Ibid.*, p. 58.

58. Yannī, *Tārīkh Sūriyya* (Beirut 1881).

59. See, for example, Najib E. Saliba, 'Midḥat Pasha in Syria', *IJMES*, vol. 9 (1978), pp. 307–23; Shimon Shamir, 'Midḥat Pasha and the anti-Turkish agitation in Syria', *MES*, vol X (1974), pp. 115–16. Both highlight Midḥat's reforms while questioning at the same time his sincerity as a committed Arab nationalist!

60. Albert Hourani, 'Ottoman reform and the politics of Notables', in W. Polk and R. Chambers (eds), *Beginnings of Modernization in the Middle East* (Chicago, 1968), p. 63.

61. Archives des affaires étrangères, Schmid to Freycinet, Damascus, 21 April 1880, quoted in Najib E. Saliba, *op. cit.*, p. 321.

62. See 'Abd al-Karīm Gharāyiba, *Sūriyya fī al-qarn al-tāsi' 'ashar* (Cairo, 1961–62), pp. 242–4, where a list of the 1868–69 members is reproduced.

63. Maṭar, *Tārīkh al-mamlaka*, pp. 185–9.

64. 'Ādil al-Ṣulḥ (ed.), *Suṭūr min al-risāla* (Beirut, 1966), pp. 91–101.

65. Nadia Farag, 'The Lewis affair and the fortunes of al-Muqtaṭaf', *MES*, vol. VIII (1972), pp. 72–83.

66. Jūrjī Yannī, 'al-Nahḍa al-adabiyya fī Ṭarābulus', *al-Machriq*, vol. XXV (1927), pp. 371–2; *al-Muqtaṭaf*, vol. VIII (1883), p. 122.

67. Philippe de Ṭarāzī, *Tārīkh al-ṣaḥāfa al-'arabiyya*, vol. I, p. 134.

68. Rashīd Riḍā, *Tārīkh al-ustādh al-Imām Muḥammad 'Abduh*, vol. I (Cairo, 1931), p. 805; A. Hourani, *Arabic Thought in the Liberal Age* (London, 1970), pp. 253–9.

69. Jūrjī Yannī, 'al-Nahḍa al-adabiyya fī Ṭarābulus', p. 375; Y. Dāghir, *Maṣādir al-dirāsāt al-adabiyya*, vol. III (Beirut, 1972), pp. 1428–9.

70. *Majallat al-Majma' al-'Ilmī al-'Arabī*, vol. II (1921), p. 364 and vol. IX (1929), p. 8.

71. Rifā'a Rāfi' al-Ṭahṭāwī published in 1868–69 the first part of a multi-volume history of Egypt under the title, *Anwār Tawfīq al-jalīl fī akhbār Miṣr wa tawthīq Banī Ismā'īl* (Cairo, 1285 H).

72. Yannī, *Tārīkh Sūriyya*, pp. 7–10; David and Yanosky, *Syrie ancienne*, pp. 1–5.

73. Yannī, *Tārīkh Sūriyya*, pp. 13–63.

74. *Ibid.*, pp. 25 and 65.

75. Yanosky, *Syrie ancienne*, p. 81.

76. Yannī, *Tārīkh Sūriyya*, pp. 186–7.

77. *Ibid.*, pp. 209–55.

78. *Ibid.*, pp. 273–82.

79. *Ibid.*, pp. 283–301.

80. David and Yanosky, *Syrie moderne*, p. 354–9.

81. Yannī, *Tārīkh Sūriyya*, p. 218.

82. David, *Syrie moderne*, p. 115.

83. *Ibid.*, p. 365.

84. Yannī, *Tārīkh Sūriyya*, pp. 302–4.

85. *Ibid.*, pp. 4–6.

86. *Ibid.*, p. 209.

87. See, for example, Aḥmad Ṭarabīn, *al-Tārīkh wa al-mū'arrikhūn al-'Arab fī al-'aṣr al-ḥadīth* (Damascus, 1970), p. 102, where he affirms that Yannī dealt exclusively with 'the history of Tripoli'. It seems Ṭarabīn misinterpreted a brief allusion to the same work by Albert Hourani, 'Historians of Lebanon', in Bernard Lewis and P.M. Holt (eds) *Historians of the Middle East* (Oxford University Press, 1962), p. 238, where it is stated: 'Among the histories of Syria … we may mention that of Jirjī Yannī … which is important for the history of Tripoli'. In a personal communication, 23 Sept. 1985, Hourani stressed that he did not refer to Yannī's history as 'a mere local history'. He also indicated: 'I knew it was a general history of Syria, but most of its information seemed to me to be drawn from French works (although I did not investigate them as thoroughly as you), and it was his information about Tripoli which seemed to me to be the most original and important'.

88. *Khiṭaṭ al-Shām*, six vols (Damascus, 1925–28).

3

New Identities and Imperial Vistas

The Syrians who emigrated in the second half of the nineteenth century to Egypt, and other parts of the Arab World, contributed in their various ways to the propagation of new scientific ideas and western methods of research. They were, on the whole, graduates of the Syrian Protestant College who advocated the theories or common principles of Ottoman reforms and modern scientific knowledge. After settling in Cairo, the Greek Orthodox Jurjī Zaydān, who imbibed similar ideas during his short study at the SPC, was the first Arab to write a history of modern Egypt in a semi-academic style.[1] In 1911 he expanded and rearranged his text, adding new chapters dealing with social, cultural, and economic developments. This step constituted quite an innovation in the world of Arabic scholarship. No Arab scholar had previously taken the risk of updating his published text in the light of newly available facts, or considered the possibility of integrating new material that might alter his own version of explaining certain events. Zaydān is regarded by some Egyptian academic thinkers as the founder of their modern school of historiography and the pioneer in introducing the orientalists' research methods into the contemporary Arab World.[2]

Another SPC science graduate, of an Orthodox Christian family, was Na'ūm Shuqayr (1864–1922) who published in 1903 a history of ancient and modern Sudan.[3] The sources upon which he drew for his pioneering work included unpublished documents, personal interviews, and his intimate knowledge of the country, both as an officer in the Egyptian military service under Wingate, and as a director of the historical section, which was set up within the Sudan Government after 'the Reconquest' in 1898.[4]

As one Arab country after another succumbed to direct European military occupation or experienced the effects of wide-ranging policies, initiated by the indigenous or local masters, rewriting the new nation's history became a common feature and part of reforming the old education systems. This was the case, for example, in Iraq following its occupation by the British army towards the end of the First World War. The exEtonian director of education, Humphrey Bowman, formed an advisory council of local Iraqi nationals to assist him in reforming and unifying the school system in the three defunct vilayets of Musil, Baghdad, and Basra. One of the council's members was Père Anastase al-Karmalī (1866–1947), an accomplished Arabist whose family came originally from Syria. As 'a loyal friend, an engaging and convivial companion, and a scholar unsurpassed in erudition and in knowledge of Arabic literature',[5] al-Karmali, at the suggestion of Bowman,[6] composed in 1919 a history book devoted exclusively to Iraq as a territorial unit.[7] This was perhaps the first Arabic text that dealt on an equal footing with the history of ancient and Islamic Iraq, treating both as integral parts of a single political entity. Needless to say, it concludes with a section extolling the benefits and civilizing features of the British occupation.

In the 1920s the Palestinian Ilyās al-Ayyūbī (1874–1927), who was the head of the translation section in the Egyptian Senate House, and a protégé of King Fū'ād, produced various historical works extolling the accomplishments of Muḥammad 'Alī and his successors.[8] He based his narrative on western sources and some private papers of the palace. His works included a history of Muḥammad 'Alī (1923), two volumes on the reign of Ismā'īl (1923), and a general history of Islamic Egypt covering the periods from the Arab conquest down to the Ottoman occupation in 1517.[9]

CARTHAGE, ROME, AND ARABIA

In North Africa, some Tunisian intellectuals took the lead in reviving their ancient history and that of the Maghrib as a whole. They belonged to a new generation educated in modern schools and colleges, or in the Zaytūna University in Tunis, founded in the eighth century, and reorganized during the premiership of Khayr al-Dīn in the 1870s. The ruler of Tunisia, Aḥmad Bey (1837–55), inaugurated a new era in the history of his country. His reforms, which included the building of a new army, a navy, industries to serve military needs, and the abolition of slavery, were later widened by his successors to encompass the administrative and institutional innovations envisaged by the Ottoman Tanzimat.[10] These reforms, as in the case of both Egypt and the central Ottoman establishment, led to the bankruptcy of the state, which fell prey to European creditors. In 1869 a joint Anglo–French–Italian debt commission was installed to supervise the affairs of the government. In 1881 the French invaded Tunisia, and established a Protectorate two years later.[11]

However, following this experience, Tunisians began to develop a distinctive national identity, with a westernized indigenous élite bent on adopting Ottoman and European notions of nationality and loyalty to a geographical unit. Khayr al-Dīn al-Tūnisī (1823–89), whose political career spanned almost the whole period of Tunisian reforms, culminating in the premiership of the country between 1873 and 1877, represented the Tanzimat era and Ottomanism in their most articulate and refined form. His book *Aqwam al-masālik*, published in 1867, aspired to make available to state officials, religious leaders, and intellectuals a comprehensive description of the visible structures and political institutions of the major European states.[12] Loaded with Khaldunian concepts, drawing on the life and sayings of the Prophet Muḥammad, backed up by quotations from Muslim jurists and European historians, his introduction[13] comes out as the best documented defence of Ottoman reforms. Thus, by using civilization as a designation of the new spirit of the age, he fuses both Europe and Islam as two compatible cultural units. Europe, shorn of its Christianity, and Islam, purified of its petrified accretions, emerge as twin representatives of reason, science and progress. His system of classification and method of observation are employed to reveal the desired reforms in their most accomplished European embodiment, as well as to disclose the potential realization of similar institutions, once the essential elements of rejuvenation are enumerated.

In contrast to al-Ṭahṭāwī, who exalted royal power at the expense of other state institutions, Khayr al-Dīn sought to advance the interests and views of the bureaucratic and ministerial levels of authority. His line of argument downgraded the power of a king as God's caliph on earth, called on the '*ulamā'* to play an active role in the administration of the new state, and attacked those rulers and intellectuals who chose Napoleon or other dictators as their heroes and models.[14]

A close associate of Khayr al-Dīn, the historian Ibn Abī al-Ḍīyāf (1802–74) was another state official who became, in the wake of his visit to Istanbul in 1842, an enthusiastic supporter of the Ottoman Tanzimat.[15] He is considered one of the first Tunisians to advance a semi-modern concept of the nation-state, especially in the introduction of his otherwise traditional chronicle, *Itḥāf ahl al-zamān.*[16] It was not until the twentieth century that a modern concept of Tunisia as a nation came into being.[17]

Tunisia, which became an Ottoman province in 1574, reflected in its internal organization and historical vicissitudes the general pattern which characterized the Ottoman Empire at large. Even under direct French occupation, its political, professional, and religious élites continued to mirror in their ideological and national aspirations the various developments and conflicts which swept the central Ottoman establishment. Thus, whereas its secular, and broadly westernized élite (the young Tunisians) favoured the Young Turks, the '*ulamā*' adhered to the cause of the Ottoman Sultan and caliph.[18]

French archaeologists, historians, and orientalists had devoted painstaking efforts to the recovery and interpretation of the pre-Islamic Maghribi past ever since the occupation of Algeria in 1830. Their scholarly journals, academic societies, and learned treatises conveyed a gloomy, unflattering image of North Africa's 'dark ages'. The natives were depicted as helpless victims of powerful civilizations with no culture or national history of their own. The French intended to legitimize an essentially colonialist policy by a historical analogy with the Carthaginian and Roman colonization. The Berbers, the indigenous population, emerged devoid of a past worthy of recording. The French thus became the natural successors of a long chain of conquerors encompassing Phoenicians, Romans, Vandals, Byzantines, Arabs, and Turks.[19]

The intensity of the French assault on the Maghribi cultural and social heritage was met with an equally intense response. Tunisian, Algerian, and, later on, Moroccan historians began to articulate an image of their long forgotten past in national terms. They used the structure of French scholarship and turned its prototypes upside down.

The Berbers were accepted as the native inhabitants endowed with a national character and a potentially elaborate civilization. The Carthaginians ceased to be foreign invaders exploiting and plundering the wealth of their conquered territories. They were instead the kith and kin of the Berbers, with whom they formed one closely knit community. Only the Romans and the Byzantines were held as the most deadly and hated enemies of the local people. With the Arab conquest, North Africa regained its true identity, and both Arab and Berber joined in the glorious struggles of Islam. They worked and fought together for the welfare of one people and one nation. Then the Ottoman Turks appeared on the stage as the upholders of religion and the defenders of their brethren believers against European encroachments and imperialist policies.

One of the first North African intellectuals to offer a historical synopsis of these various periods of the North African past was the Tunisian historian Ḥasan H. ʻAbd al-Wahhāb (1884–1968). In 1913 he published a textbook of his own country's history.[20] He divided Tunisia's past into four cycles: the Carthaginian, the Roman, the Byzantine, and finally the Islamic. The latter was in its turn subdivided into three periods, coinciding with the initial Arab conquest, the Arab–Berber alliance, and Turkish rule and the dynasty of the Husaynids who came to power in 1706.[21] Both Hannibal, the Carthaginian military genius, and ʻUqba b. Nāfiʻ, the Muslim conqueror, figure in the text as Tunisian heroes struggling against the tyranny of the Romans and the Byzantines respectively. The French occupation is seen in exactly the same perspective as the Roman, for, as the author puts it, 'history repeats itself'.[22]

Aḥmad al-Madanī (1899–1977), another Tunisian historian who was to play a prominent role in Algerian politics, published in 1927 a history of ancient North Africa entitled *Carthage over Four Centuries.*[23] Relying on French sources, he devoted his history almost entirely to the pre-Islamic past of the Maghrib. His story revolves in its broad themes around two main characters, and the relentless wars one wages against the other. First, there is Carthage, the peaceful commercial state seeking to enter into non-colonialist relations with the Berbers and win their trust for the benefit of both communities. In the second act,

Rome intervenes as a colonial power bent on destroying the national entity of the Phoenicians and the Berbers, their willing allies. The struggles and battles which this foreign intervention entailed expressed a deeply felt nationalist rejection of all imperialist invaders. Thus Berber nationalism was to be tested and reasserted over four centuries down to the eve of the Arab conquest. Thereafter, the Maghrib regained its true identity and built a new civilization in which the genius of the Berbers and the Arabs manifested itself as that of one nation.

In 1929–32 an Algerian *'ālim*, Mubārak al-Mīlī (1880–1945), and a colleague of al-Madanī, produced a two-volume history of his own country.[24] Al-Mīlī was a member of the Association of Algerian *'Ulamā'*, founded in 1931. Its motto was: 'Islam is my religion, Arabic is my language, Algeria is my fatherland.' He was the first of his countrymen to devote an entire volume (280 pages) to the pre-Islamic past of his well-defined national unit. He deals in separate chapters with Algeria's prehistory, the Berbers, Carthage, Rome, the Vandals, and the Byzantines. His theme is virtually the same as that of al-Madanī. The one, but highly significant, difference is the focus of his study. Al-Mīlī is primarily concerned with proving the existence of an Algerian national identity throughout the ages. The Roman invasion of his country is seen as the most disastrous event which robbed the Algerians of their independence during the Phoenician ascendancy. Algeria did not resume its true role as a prosperous territory until eight centuries later, when the Arabs, the brethren of the Phoenicians, brought to the Algerians 'a natural religion, just laws and a virtuous civilization'.[25]

None of these history-writings, however, heralded a new departure from either the style or the approach of Yannī's and Zaydān's histories of the 1880s. They were composed by amateur historians, using secondary western sources, in order to promote the image of their respective countries as viable national entities. Others met the immediate needs of an occupying and colonial power, or simply responded to the demands of a new élite. A qualitative change in modern Arabic historiography was brought about by a new generation of professional historians. They first emerged in the wake of the First World War. Trained in European or American universities to master western academic methods of research, their contributions were made in their capacity as professors of history committed to the articulation of a new interpretation of the 'nation-state' and its genesis.

Once again, it was Egypt that led the other Arab countries in the historiographical field. We now turn to an examination of the Egyptian scholarly methods of rewriting national history.

NOTES

1. *Tārīkh Miṣr al-ḥadīth* (Cairo, 1889).
2. See, for example, Shafīq Ghurbāl, 'Maṣādir al-ilhām 'ind ba'ḍ al-mū'arrikhīn, *al-Hilāl*, vol. LXII (1 Nov. 1954), pp. 43–4; Jurjī Zaydān, *al-'Arab qabl al-Islām*, edited by Ḥusayn Mū'nis (Cairo n.d.), p. 7.
3. *Tārīkh al-Sudān al-qadīm wa al-ḥadīth* (Cairo, 1903).
4. On Shuqayr's career in the service of the Egyptian and Sudan occupation governments see Richard Hill, *A Biographical Dictionary of the Sudan* (London, 1967), p. 293.
5. Humphrey Bowman, *Middle East Window* (London, 1942), pp. 196–7.
6. Rufā'īl Buṭṭī, 'Anastase Marie al-Karmali 1866–1947', *Majallat al-Kitāb*, vol. III (1947), p. 756.
7. *Khulāṣat tārīkh al-'Irāq mundhu nushū'ihi ilā yawminā hādhā* (Basra, 1919).
8. See also p. 111, n. 62 for further details on al-Ayyūbī's history writings.
9. For a 'list of contributions by Syrians to Egyptian historiography' see Jack A. Crabbs, *The Writing of History in Nineteenth Century Egypt: A Study in National Transformation* (Cairo and Detroit, 1984), chapter 10.
10. For a sympathetic evaluation of these reforms see L.C. Brown, *The Tunisia of Ahmad Bey, 1837–1855* (Princeton University Press, 1974), Part 2.
11. Jean Ganiage, *Les origines du Protectorat français au Tunisie 1861–1881* (Paris, 1959).
12. *Aqwam al-masālik* is divided into three parts: an Introduction, Book I, and Book II. Book I is in its turn divided into separate chapters dealing with the histories, laws, political institutions, and the internal organization of various European countries and principalities. These are: the Ottoman Empire, France, England, Austria, Russia, Prussia, Germany, Italy, Spain, Sweden and Norway, Holland, Denmark, Bavaria, Belgium, Portugal, Switzerland, the Papal States, Württemberg, the Principality of Baden, and Greece. See pp. 90–432.
13. The Introduction was published in French by the author in 1868. Almost a century later it was translated into English by L.E. Brown under the title *The Surest Path* (Cambridge, Mass., 1967).
14. *Aqwam al-masālik*, pp. 128–31 and 226–7. Apart from Muḥammad 'Alī, the Tunisian Regent, Aḥmad Bey, professed a great

admiration for Napoleon Bonaparte. The director of his Bardo Military School, Luigi Calligaris, composed for him a biography of Napoleon which was translated into Arabic by General Ḥusayn and revised by Shaykh Muḥammad Qabādū. Ibn Abī al-Ḍīyāf, *Itḥāf ahl al-Zamān*, vol. IV (Tunis, 1963), pp. 36 and 104.

15. Ahmed Abdesselem, *Les historiens tunisiens*, pp. 346–7.

16. Cf. B. Tlili, 'Note sur la notion d'état dans la pensée de Ah'mad Ibn Abî Ad'-d' Iyâf', *Revue de l'Occident musulman et de la Méditerranée*, vol. VIII (1970), pp. 141–70.

17. Jamil Abun-Nasr, *A History of the Maghrib* (Cambridge University Press, 1975), pp. 347–54.

18. Arnold H. Green, *The Tunisian ulama, 1873–1915* (Leiden: E.J. Brill, 1978), p. 208.

19. These arguments are discussed in chapter 6, dealing mainly with the works of the Moroccan historian Abdallah Laroui.

20. *Khulāṣat tārīkh Tūnis* (Tunis, 1st edn, A.H. 1332; 3rd revised edn, 1953).

21. The dynasty of the Husaynids, founded by Husayn Ibn 'Alī, an Ottoman agha of Greek origin, ruled Tunisia until 1957 when, after independence, it was abolished and a republic was announced.

22. *Khulāṣat*, p. 22.

23. *Qarṭajanna fī arba'at'uṣūr* (Tunis, 1927).

24. *Tārīkh al-Jazā'ir fī al-qadīm wa al-ḥadīth* (Constantine, 1929–32, reprinted 1963). References are to the 1963 version.

25. *Ibid.*, p. 115.

Part II

The professional historians: managers of legitimation 1920–80

4

Muḥammad 'Alī and the Sphinx: Shafīq Ghurbāl's Histories of Egypt

When Shafīq Ghurbāl published in 1928 his first historical work, *The Beginnings of the Egyptian Question and the Rise of Mehemet Ali*, Egyptian historiography can be said to have entered a new stage in its development. It was subtitled by the author as 'a study in the diplomacy of the Napoleonic era based on researches in the British and French Archives'. Thus an Arab historian had decided to reconstruct a certain period of his country's modern history from original and unpublished sources.

Whatever his interpretations, or the use he made of the unpublished documents, the mere fact of his taking this essential step is a landmark in itself. It heralded a new development, ushering in a break with traditions, which was followed by other Arab historians.

Such a revolutionary achievement is better appreciated when contrasted with the dearth of similar studies in the Arab World during the same decade. It meant not only a change in the technicalities and procedures of research, but a fresh intellectual approach as well. It is true that others before Ghurbāl had contributed in their own way to the birth of a more balanced study of history. Their methods did not, however, constitute a clear-cut departure from the methods of the past, nor a major advance in distinguishing between primary and secondary sources. Seen in this light, it is not feasible to consider Muḥammad Ṣabrī's *La révolution égyptienne 1919–1921*[1] as marking 'the advent of professional Egyptian historiography'.[2] Sabrī's book is based on journalistic reports of western correspondents and reads like a propaganda pamphlet intended to convince the European public of Egypt's right to full independence.

Moreover, it continues the tradition of a familiar genre of polemic literature which uses historical arguments to demolish the claims of one colonial power or another. The writings of the Egyptian nationalist leader, Muṣṭafā Kāmil (1874–1908),[3] were perhaps the model for a plethora of political tracts which appeared during the first two decades of the twentieth century.[4] Ṣabrī, who studied history at the Sorbonne under the French historians Albert Aulard and Emile Bourgeois, launched his scholarly career as a secretary to the Egyptian delegation at the 1919 Paris Peace Conference. His hero at the time was Sa'd Zaghlūl, who led the 1919 Egyptian revolt against British occupation.[5] All his early works were either composed in a polemical spirit or in an endeavour to re-enact the French Revolution on the Egyptian stage. By the time Ṣabrī began to adhere to the basic principles of academic research, Ghurbāl had already established himself as the leading national historian at the Egyptian University. As we shall see, Ghurbāl did not entirely manage to divest himself of his generation's biases and ideological allegiances. Nevertheless, his was a serious attempt to understand the dynamics of his society.

Shafīq Ghurbāl was born in Alexandria in 1894, the son of 'Abd al-Ḥamīd Ghurbāl and Waṣīfa Badr al-Dīn. Both his father and grandfather were merchants. 'It is interesting to note that his grandfather was a Tunisian from Sfax where, incidentally, there are still large numbers of the original family [Ghurbāl is exclusively a Tunisian name]'.[6] Educated initially at the local schools of his hometown, Ghurbāl entered the Teachers' Higher Training College in Cairo, from which he graduated in 1915 with a diploma in history and the humanities. His parents wanted him to study law, engineering, or medicine, but he did not heed their advice. He had already made up his mind to become a true Egyptian citizen, charged with a more serious task in life. Reading, studying, writing, and teaching his country's history was, for Ghurbāl, the only worthy career to be pursued and accomplished.[7] In 1915, when he was twenty-one, the Ministry of Education awarded him a scholarship to study his favourite subject at the University of Liverpool, England. He graduated with an honours degree in 1919. It was during those years that he met his future English wife, Gertrude Humberstone, who was studying geography at the same university.

Upon his return to Egypt, he was rewarded with a position he had always coveted – teaching history at his former secondary school in Alexandria. Three years later, in 1922, he won another scholarship to study at the London Institute of Historical Studies, where he prepared his major work, *The Beginnings of the Egyptian Question*, under the supervision of the budding historian, Arnold Toynbee. Armed with his MA degree and a published dissertation, he was appointed in 1929 Assistant Professor of Modern History at the Faculty of Arts of the Egyptian University. Between 1930 and 1950 he became a leading authority on modern Egyptian and Arab history, and was recognized as the founder of the national school of Egyptian historiography.[8] He was several times appointed Under-Secretary of State for Education and headed both the History Department and the Faculty of Arts at his university. His other pioneering activities included the foundation of the Museum of Civilization in Cairo, the organization of the Egyptian Association for Historical Studies, and the publication of the *Egyptian Historical Review* in 1949. His appointment to either an academic or an administrative post depended on the whims of the government of the day. Never an active member of a particular political party, he none the less espoused the cause of a group of politicians who had broken away from the mainstream Wafd Party. This group, known as the Sa'dists, after the original leader of the Wafd, Sa'd Zaghlūl (d. 1927), was headed by Aḥmad Māhir, Maḥmūd Faḥmī al-Nuqrāshī, and Ibrāhīm 'Abd al-Hādī. They were all known for their close relationship with King Fārūq and for their enmity towards Muṣṭafā al-Naḥḥās. Thus, when the latter became Prime Minister, as he did in 1942 and 1950, Ghurbāl would lose his post at the Ministry of Education and return to academic life.[9] His retirement in 1954 coincided with the advent of a new military regime headed by Colonel Nasser. One year earlier his English wife died, and her loss was one of the most tragic events of his life.[10] However, he slowly emerged from his self-imposed isolation. Notwithstanding his lukewarm reception of the new regime's policies, he was appointed as director of the Arab League's Institute of Higher Arab Studies upon the retirement of the veteran Arab nationalist Sāṭi' al-Ḥuṣrī. He died in 1961 at the age of sixty-seven.

VIEWS OF HISTORY

To Ghurbāl, history-writing was almost a personal affair, mainly concerned with self-education and the development of the individual as a responsible citizen. Hence he maintained that the concepts and methods of history do not exert a direct influence on princes and political leaders. An active and ambitious statesman seldom derives proper lessons from the course of historical events. His actions and decisions are determined by more tangible and immediate exigencies. Revolutions are thus made not because the revolutionaries have academically studied the underlying currents of their country's past, nor as a result of deducing considered conclusions from the distant experiences of their forefathers and compatriots. A revolution is a work of art, executed according to a plan. Its outlines are modelled on foreign revolutions carried out under similar circumstances. 'History is therefore more influential in shaping the intellectual rather than the man of action.'[11]

Even if the revolutionaries link their action with a certain period of the nation's history, this should be taken metaphorically and not as a direct, uninterrupted connection between the two. After toppling the monarchist regime of King Fārūq in 1952, the Free Officers considered their movement as the continuation of the 1881 'Urābī Revolt. However, despite undeniable similarities, the preconditions which led to the emergence of each are not the same. Nor is the first a mere resumption and recommencement of the other. 'In history, there are no gaps of this nature.' The causes of the Free Officers' movement should be sought in the recent past of Egypt, particularly the failures of certain policies between 1919 and 1950.[12] It is, moreover, erroneous to view past events as an absolute struggle between right and wrong, or goodness and immorality. A conscientious historian should resist the temptation of setting himself up like a judge on the day of reckoning. It is more beneficial for him to avoid passing conclusive judgements and satisfy himself with a neutral presentation of the controversial views of two contending parties. Recourse to inflammatory language or disparaging remarks in depicting the conflict between the Sunnis and Shi'ites in Islam, for example, only serves to cloud the real issues and stir up old rivalries. It is not feasible for a twentieth-century historian to adopt the attitudes and principles of the protagonists of a revolution which took place in the seventeenth century. One should in this case follow in the footsteps of the English historians. They endeavour to see in the political struggles of their revolution the positive contributions of both King Charles I and Oliver Cromwell.[13] 'The purpose of historical research can never be the re-enactment of a conflict, for it is a useless exercise. Its validity resides in the attempt to give each person his due.'[14]

Ghurbāl aired these views after the revolution of July 1952. However, a few months before the fall of the monarchy, he allowed himself the pleasure of violating the same restraints so admirably advocated. He then contended that in order to bring out the proper significance of the internal developments which accompanied the Anglo–Egyptian negotiations (1882–1936), the historian would feel compelled to 'pass value-judgements' on the attitudes of the men engaged in these negotiations. He justified such an approach by invoking the imperative duty of citizenship which imposed on the native historian the necessity of contributing to 'the construction of public opinion', and the performance of 'political duties'. Writing such a study was for him an exercise in self-discipline, and a sincere attempt to organize his thoughts and make his 'judgements spring from correct understanding'. He goes on to say 'my writing is that of an Egyptian citizen who aspires to be a better one, capable of evaluation and discrimination'.[15]

Between 1952 and 1955 Ghurbāl's assesssment of the proper role of the historian underwent a noticeable transformation. Before the revolution he did not flinch from turning the study and writing of history into an exercise in civic education and ideological instruction. It was only when he witnessed the Free Officers' indiscriminate assault on the dynasty of Muḥammad 'Alī that his stance abruptly changed. Almost his whole academic career had been built on the elaboration and edification of Muḥammad 'Alī's achievements. It was not easy for him to stand back and watch his lifelong work being demolished at one stroke. As late as 1948 he wrote an article on the Palestinian question and the Arabs' struggle against Zionism, and did not fail to extol the noble pedigree of King Fārūq and his impeccable credentials as a holy warrior. After narrating the long unbroken relationship between Egypt and Palestine since the dawn of history down to his own times, he hails Fārūq as 'the successor (Khalīfat) of Saladin and the scion of Muḥammad 'Alī and his son Ibrāhim', and links his name with the second

Caliph 'Umar b. al-Khaṭṭāb.[16] In 1951 he wrote another article expressing his belief in gradual reform. He explicitly rejected the method of revolutionary change, which the Republic of Turkey had chosen, and considered the option taken by the monarch as an Egyptian innovation, constituting a compromise between modernization and preservation. Once again, the reign of Fārūq was highlighted as an intrinsic part of the new national identity. Its virtues were the beliefs it held that 'the nation is the origin of power and the government the servant of the people'.[17]

THE VILLAINS, THE IGNORANT, AND THE UNLUCKY

Ghurbāl's book, *The Beginnings of the Egyptian Question*[18] falls into fifteen chapters, and has as its theme the French invasion of Egypt in 1798 and the rise of Muḥammad 'Alī to power. 'The first seven chapters ... formed the substance of a dissertation approved in 1919 for the Degree of B.A. with honours in Modern History in the University of Liverpool. The rest of the study was approved in 1924 for the Degree of M.A. in the University of London and was awarded a mark of distinction.'[19] Arnold Toynbee, as the supervisor of the last part, wrote a prefatory note to the published version. In it he informs us that Ghurbāl

> is in personal touch with both East and West — with the East because it is his home, and with the West because he has lived and studied here — and at the same time he is so thoroughly detached from the passions and prejudices that enter his field of study — were it not his name printed on the title page — it would be difficult to guess from internal evidence whether the author were an Englishman, a Frenchman, an Egyptian, or none of these.

To Toynbee, Ghurbāl is so self-effacing and so objective that, although his work treats an emotional and still controversial subject, it earns the comment 'yet no reflection of contemporary politics can be discerned in Mr. Ghorbal's work'.[20] The controversies Toynbee alludes to had to do with the struggle of Egyptians for independence, and their direct confrontation with Britain as the colonial power of the day. However, the claim that Ghurbāl's national identity is totally obliterated throughout his narrative does not stand up to closer scrutiny. Toynbee's is one of those exaggerated statements which force one to beg to differ.

Ghurbāl was not writing a civil servant's report, nor was he anxious to please all the parties involved in deciding his country's fate. On the contrary, his prior commitment to the monarchist regime, his belief in the superiority of western civilization, and his adherence to a European concept of the nation-state, led him to conduct a thorough investigation of the process of 'westernization', of the eventual dissolution of the Ottoman Empire and the various 'events which led to the rise of Mehemet Ali'.[21] Ghurbāl went beyond his original task of extracting information from archives, and embarked on a tortuous journey in search of Egypt's birth as a nation-state. His purpose was to discover and register that 'wonderful episode' in which Egypt was reborn and reinvigorated as a new national entity. We are left in no doubt as to his opinion of all the actors who tried to solve the entangled task of delivering the new nation into the world. He showed in successive chapters how the Mamlūks, the Ottomans, the French, and the British had failed, one after the other, to grasp the inner dynamics of Egyptian society. Only one adventurer solved the riddle and was, as a result, awarded the title of the undisputed master of the land. Or, as he succinctly put it, 'Mehemet Ali made modern Egypt.'[22]

Ghurbāl has a story to tell. It is dominated by a single hero, Muḥammad ʿAlī. All the others are either villains, ignorant, or simply unlucky. Even the indigenous people and their leaders are dismissed as a negligible quantity with no spirit, or imagination. Such a story takes shape along familiar lines.

There are, first, the long, dark ages overshadowing Egypt ever since the establishment of the Mamlūk Sultanate in 1250. The whole history of the Mamlūks, whether as independent sultans or under Ottoman sovereignty, is lumped together and condemned with revulsion and disgust. Their sultans, who defeated the hordes of Mongols at the battle of ʿAyn Jālūt in 1260, and probably saved Islam and Europe from a barbarian invasion,[23] are made the butt of mockery and ridicule. Their subsequent resounding victories over the Crusading States in Syria do not even receive a passing reference. His depreciatory idea of the Mamlūks deserves to be quoted in full:

> A single fact sums up the history of Egypt before the landing of the French; the domination of the Mamelukes. Recruited from the slave-markets of Georgia[24] to serve as the Ayyubid Dynasty's bodyguard, they soon acquired such authority as to be able to destroy, in the year 1250, that dynasty and to elect as Sultan of Egypt one of their chiefs. The country became at once the theatre of civil wars and brigandage. The new Sultans were not more firmly established than their predecessors. Forty-seven of them followed one another in quick succession in the short period of two hundred and fifty years,[25] and when, in 1517, Selim the Grim turned his eyes from Europe to Oriental conquest, he was able to make short work of the sultans and to turn Egypt into a Turkish province.

Ghurbāl then relates the way the Mamlūk Beys gradually re-established their authority and reduced the Ottoman Viceroy to an impotent governor. The Porte, constantly engaged with defending its frontiers against the incursions of Austria and Russia, found itself unable to enforce its own rules in Egypt and compel the Beys to keep a regular payment of the Tribute. The repercussions inside Egypt were made worse by the baseless character of the Mamlūks.

> Strangers amongst themselves, they were not bound by the natural ties of family. Without relations, without children, the past was a blank. Ignorant and superstitious by training, the frequent murders rendered them ferocious, the tumults seditious, the cabals perfidious, the dissimulation cowardly and the unnatural vices corrupt.[26] A happy stroke of the sabre won the Mameluke pre-eminence. But the upstart did not change character; in a lordly station he had the soul of a slave. Power had no other end than procuring women, horses, jewels and retainers. Gold was to be had, whenever found. The poor peasant was as much pillaged as the 'Frank' or Levantine merchant.[27]

Thus the stage is set for a momentous act. The poetic language accentuates the tragedy of the land, haranguing the audience with a sad and deeply moving monologue. The reader is no longer aware of the slow and multifaceted aspects of a complex historical period. Short and pungent remarks introduce him to the main theme of the play. Baybars, Qalawūn, al-Nāṣir Muḥammad, Barsbay, and other sultans are dismissed as usurpers and brigands. Their living memories in countless Egyptian folkloric tales and popular literature are passed over in silence.

The 'slaves', with their tyranny, rapacity, prodigality, and intrigues, 'could not but attract the eyes of the outside world to the unhappy land'. The 'outside world' consisted at the time of various European powers competing for markets, colonies, and spheres of influence. It was only natural that the fair but unhappy land 'entered into the calculations of diplomacy in connection with the innumerable projects for the Partition of the Ottoman Empire'. And it was Napoleon, the son of the Enlightenment and the French Revolution, who appeared off the Egyptian coast in the summer of 1798.[28] The black curtain was lifted and the audience awaited the second act.

When the French disembarked, despite the menace of the English fleet under Admiral Nelson, the fate of the old order was sealed. 'The mob of the Mameluks, ferocious Bedouins and simple peasants armed with long flails gathered for the defence of Egypt's first port [Alexandria] was quickly dispersed by French advanced detachments, and before the evening of July 2nd, the French were masters of the place.' Bonaparte's Arabic Proclamation to the Egyptians is described by Ghurbāl in the following flattering terms:

> His profound study of the Koran, which together with the Bible, the Vedas, and Montesquieu's works, he grouped in his library catalogue under the heading of 'politics', had borne fruit in the remarkable proclamation in Arabic addressed to the Egyptians. It must be stated, however, that the French original composed by Bonaparte is truer to the style and spirit of the Koran than the Levantine interpreters' Arabic version.[29]

The reader is then informed in a footnote of al-Jabartī's criticism of the Arabic version, which constitutes one of a series of misleading statements about the true position of the Egyptian chronicler. In fact, al-Jabartī does not confine his criticism to the corrupt Arabic style. He was particularly offended by its pompous tone and general contents, and deemed it totally opposed to the true teachings of Islam.[30]

Forgetting, for a brief moment, his contempt for the Mamlūks as a disorganized mob, he affords us a description contradicting his earlier sweeping statements. The strangers and slaves suddenly spring into life as courageous soldiers ready to defend their land and acquit themselves with honour. Two engagements between the Mamlūks and the French are described thus:

> The Mamelukes, dazzling in gold and silver, armed with pistols and carabines of the best English make and with the finest sabres of the East and mounted on horses of the purest breed, dashed upon the [French] squares, caracoled round the flanks seeking a feeble point, but were stopped everywhere by a wall of raised bayonets, and some of the bravest expired within the French lines. The Mamelukes at last retired. In the meantime a lively engagement took place between the flotillas in which the Mamelukes acquitted themselves with honour and would have been victorious had it not been for the advance of the French troops towards the bank of the river and the sail of one of their ships catching fire accidentally.[31]

Following the narrative of the diplomatic reports and dispatches, Ghurbāl hesitates between letting the fate of Egypt hang on a single engagement, and accepting the concept of a confrontation between a dying inferior civilization and a young superior one. The first impression one gains, from the detailed narration of events, is that the Mamlūk chiefs committed tactical errors rather than strategic blunders, and lost the war and Egypt in an unfortunate encounter. Murād, the main Bey, besides his rival Ibrāhīm, 'committed the fatal mistake of not placing the river between himself and his enemies and thus imposing upon them the necessity of finding means for crossing it'. He then goes on to highlight the encounter as being between two equal armies and naval forces. We now learn that Murād's 'superior flotilla could have seriously hampered that operation and his cavalry could have fallen upon the French detachments as they effected their landing on the other side'. This ambivalent account is extracted from a dispatch sent by Damas to General Kléber. The argument unexpectedly shifts to a different level as the author uses another source; this time it is Napoleon's

Correspondence. The birth of a nation had begun. One superior civilization sealed the fate of another backward fossilized community. 'In the engagement which took place on July 18th and which marked the last effort of mediaeval warfare, the famous cavalry was shattered by the world's greatest soldier, and the most indispensable condition for the rise of a New Egypt was realised.'[32]

Bonaparte, having cleared the swampy grounds, proceeded to lay the foundations of a new national entity. He thought that the Egyptians lacked 'regular institutions', which would allow them to participate in the management of their internal affairs. He therefore recruited local notables and '*ulamā'* to join his *divans*, and communicate his decrees to the inhabitants. The '*ulamā'* were chosen on account of their submissive nature, the hatred they harboured for both the Ottomans and Mamlūks,[33] and their aspiration to a new order of things. The first assembly was convened on 4 September 1798, in order to discuss the formation of provincial assemblies, the introduction of a criminal and civil code, and the improvement of the laws governing property ownership and tax-collection. However, the whole project failed. The Egyptians refused to be made into new human beings. They pulled down the structure of the edifice, and demolished the elaborate schemes of the French generals and their ponderous savants. Formerly deprived of any semblance of institutions or regular laws, except of 'the tax-collecting type' and 'the occasional commands', the miserable natives stubbornly resisted reform or discipline. The spasms of an early smooth delivery changed into hysterical xenophobia:

> An orderly system of government and, especially, of taxation, so far from securing to them their property, seemed to the Egyptians, on the contrary, to close every loophole for escaping the payment of the tax, as they might occasionally have done under the old *régime.*[34]

Nelson's destruction of the French fleet at Abū Qīr (Abu-Kir), Napolean's recourse to forced contributions, the advancement of Levantines in the army and administration, and the drunkenness and frivolity of the French added insult to injury. Then the imposition of taxation on religious endowments, and another tax on residential property, led to the popular revolt of 21 October. This revolt is scantily alluded to by Ghurbāl, and only in such a manner as to make its brutal suppression by the French a laudable achievement: 'a judicious disposition of artillery enabled the men of the 13 vendémiaire to suppress the rising. Drastic measures were taken to prevent its recurrence.'[35]

With the failure of Napoleon's Syrian campaign, as a result of Sidney Smith's sea power and his capture of the French heavy artillery, the future Emperor left Egypt for France. His successor, General Kléber, had only one aim: the evacuation of the army under his command. The convention of al-'Arīsh was accordingly signed between Kléber and the Ottomans on 24 January 1800. However, the British, posing as the allies of the Porte, refused to let the French off the hook so easily. A war of nerves was imminent. The Cairenes sensed the dilemma of the French and launched another revolt in March 1800. It fell outside Ghurbāl's compass and he failed to register its existence. The historian's silence is deafening, and invites an explanation. The participants included the Ottoman military forces, the Mamlūks, the local inhabitants, artisans, shopkeepers, and various religious orders. Two leaders distinguished themselves in the uprising, 'Umar Makram and Muḥammad Bey al-Alfī. The first was the head of the descendants of the Prophet (*Naqīb al-Ashrāf*), and the second a prominent Mamlūk chief. Both were later to fall out with Ghurbāl's hero, Muḥammad 'Alī, and incur his wrath and enmity. Hence the historian's silence to cover up a momentous event which lasted for over thirty days, and opened the way for eventual French withdrawal from Egypt.[36] However, the revolt met with failure and the French were once again the masters of Cairo. An uneasy tension hung over the land. The stalemate was broken when 'a Syrian fanatic' assassinated Kléber. General Menou took over the command of the army and the country. Unlike his predecessor, he was set 'against the idea of evacuating Egypt'.[37]

The new commander-in-chief receives a sympathetic treatment from Ghurbāl. Even his conversion to Islam is considered a sincere and whole-hearted step.[38] He was a reformer and an honest man. He endeavoured to put an end to the various abuses which had cropped up under the administration of Napoleon and Kléber. He had a low opinion of the Copts, and their employment as tax-collectors was consequently terminated. 'It is difficult to explain how men like Bonaparte and Kléber could condone such abuses and continue to employ such vile agents', Ghurbāl comments, and goes on to probe the extent of Menou's correct approach.

> His ideas went beyond the removal of abuses. He conceived that the evil had its origin in the lack of stable institutions[39] and proceeded to endow the country with them .... [Menou] restored the ... assemblies of notables ... [and] elaborated codes of customs and regulations for the encouragement of agriculture, commerce and industry.[40]

Nevertheless, Menou's worthy cause had one vital flaw in it, namely his failure to grasp the peculiar local conditions. His 'grand design' included the establishment of a new system of taxation to replace the chaotic arrangements under the old regime. The French scholars jumped at the opportunity and systematized the prevailing conditions 'into a coherent theory of feudalism'. They equated Mamlūk and local *multazims* or tax-farmers with the feudal lords of Europe without the '*hommage*' or 'the oath of fealty'. However, Ghurbāl's alternative theory is no less confusing. He asserts that Islamic doctrine considers the land as 'absolute property'. The absolute ownership by individuals encompassed, in his opinion, 'the multezims' holdings' and 'house-property in towns', in addition to religious and charitable endowments.[41] If that was the case, why should the land held by Mamlūks as *iltizām* be considered 'pure usurpation', as Ghurbāl contends? It is true that the Mamlūks were not 'feudal knights'. But by what criteria can one differentiate between an Egyptian *multazim* and a Mamlūk one, given the fact that both adhered to the same Islamic doctrine as adumbrated by Ghurbāl? Would it not have been more useful and factual to study the development of the *iltizām* system within the historical context of the seventeenth and eighteenth centuries? Such a study would have shown the gradual appearance of a stratum of *multazims*, embracing Mamlūk officers, '*ulamā*', merchants, Arab shaykhs, and women who were in most cases either wives, daughters, or maids of Mamlūk *amīrs*.[42] The Islamic doctrine on its own is not a substitute for conducting a historical investigation of concrete cases.

Ghurbāl was obviously worried about the reappearance of the Mamlūks as a military and social force whose existence threatened the dawn of a new age. However, no sooner had Menou issued his orders for a cadastral survey, than the Battle of Canopus loomed on the horizon. On 21 March 1801, the British invasion of Egypt gathered momentum and 'killed the project' of Menou. Furthermore, the commander-in-chief was hampered in his efforts by a clique of senior officers, such as Damas and Reynier, who were openly hostile to his policies and dreams.[43]

The French army capitulated and evacuated Egypt. The British and the Ottomans took upon themselves the reorganization of the country's affairs. But before the historian proceeds to the third act, a general assessment of the French occupation and its long-term effects is called for.

> The short sojourn of the French in the Valley of the Nile had permanently affected its later history. The Mamelukes never recovered from the blows dealt them by the French. The Turks proved too weak to complete their destruction. An adventurer of genius turned the stalemate to his personal profit.[44]

With the expulsion of the French, the British sought to settle the internal affairs of Egypt, and encourage those local forces deemed friendly towards them. They thus entered into various pledges to restore the authority of the Mamlūks. The successor of Murād Bey, 'Uthmān Bey al-Jūkhdār, known as al-Tanburjī',[45] had joined the British Army on 15 May 1801, after receiving assurances from Sir John Hutchinson. The Mamlūk cavalry, numbering 1500, was described by Hutchinson as 'inferior certainly to none in the world'. He also calculated that the Mamlūks were received by the British 'at the most critical period of the campaign'.[46]

Hutchinson, who had replaced Abercromby as the Commander of the British expedition, did not have a high opinion of the Ottoman Empire. He thought it was in a deplorable state. The Turks were no longer capable of holding their dominions or reasserting their authority in Egypt, which had been 'nominal' in any case. Fearing that France would step in to fill the vacuum, he saw no alternative to handing Egypt back to the Beys. He therefore wrote them a letter on 5 May 1801, stating, among other things, that the aim of the British was to drive out the French 'and to establish all in those possessions and rights, which belonged to them'. The Mamlūks interpreted this promise to be no less than 'an ample indemnification for their losses and the full restitution of their property, power and influence in the country'. The Beys, having carried out their side of the bargain, pressed the British to fulfil theirs. They dreaded the hostile attitude of the Turks towards them, an attitude which amounted to a long-standing wish to liquidate them as a whole. The British Commander did his best to convince the Turks of the necessity to reinstate the Beys, and thus avert a confrontation between the two camps over the control of Egypt.[47]

Ghurbāl, once again, raises his doubts about the wisdom of the British General in giving pledges to the Mamlūks as to their future in Egypt. He finds it an opportune moment to reiterate his psychological theory about the base character of all the Mamlūks. His moralistic argument runs as follows:

> It was clear that the Turks were determined to carry out none of the terms they seemed to accept. The Beys had identical intentions. It is curious that Hutchinson did not realise this. It is possible to admire his sympathy with the under-dog, but it is difficult to understand the illusion not only of Hutchinson, but also of his colleagues as to the real character of the Mamelukes.[48]

The British Cabinet went on agonizing over this intractable problem. J.P. Morier, of the British Embassy in Constantinople, tried to tackle it by drafting a memorandum in July 1801. He suggested three alternatives. The first was outright British occupation under the guise of providing the Turks with 'an armed force for the protection of Egypt'. Such an arrangement with the Ottoman Empire should entail 'certain commercial privileges' for the British, and the entire destruction of the Mamlūks in order to 'secure the tranquillity of Egypt'. The second alternative was to take possession of the country along the lines which the French had contemplated. In this case the British would recognize the nominal sovereignty of the Sultan and reinstate some acceptable Beys in certain districts. But these Beys 'should at stated periods be removed from one government to another, that a long residence at any one place should not put it in their power to acquire such authority as to be troublesome, by exciting the natives to throw off our authority'. The third alternative to be adopted, 'in case we should find it impracticable to keep Egypt, would be an attempt to destroy it by inundation'. The last alternative does not stir the moralistic tone which Ghurbāl has voiced in other contexts. On the contrary, he even finds room in his wounded pride to forgive and forget. By so doing he had to falsify Morier's statement and quote him out of context. 'It is only fair to add', Ghurbāl equivocates, 'that Morier displayed a strong revulsion at the thought of inundating Egypt since he went on to say that his nation would "transmit to posterity a name as black as that of the incendiary of Ephesus".'[49] However, the truth was that Morier did not allow the memory of Ephesus to linger on in his conscience for more than a fleeting and aberrant moment. He immediately plucked up courage and stated, 'but we might defeat the ambitious projects of a rival power who, by the possession of Egypt, would gain such immense commercial advantages as not to feel the loss of her West India possessions'. Moreover, having convinced himself of the inevitability of his last 'resource', Morier raised the spectre of 'the political advantages' that France would derive from its possession of Egypt, and which 'would not be of less consequence than the commercial. For she would command Turkey, her influence would extend to Persia and from thence to India.'[50]

The British Cabinet, however, decided to satisfy itself with the role of a mediator between the Mamlūks and Ottomans. But the mediator was still acting under the fear of a new French invasion of Egypt. It was therefore essential for the British ministers to arrange the affairs of the occupied country before it was evacuated. Lord Elgin, the British Ambassador at Constantinople, was accordingly sent a plan to be negotiated with the Ottoman authorities, but without making them aware of its full contents. This plan receives Ghurbāl's full acclaim and total support. Although it amounted to a disguised occupation of Egypt, its long-term implications are hardly explored. Its sections, which clash with Ghurbāl's thesis about Britain's scrupulous abstention 'from exploiting the Turko–British Alliance for commercial privileges in the Levant', are simply ignored. He only voices his objection to the inclusion of the Mamlūks in the new arrangement. The first condition which the British Cabinet laid down for proceeding with the negotiations related to ascertaining 'the rights, privileges and territorial jurisdiction of the Mamlouks', the definition of 'the nature and extent of their military service', and the insistence 'that the performance of that service shall be made the condition of their tenures'. These demands were too much to swallow. 'This reveals', Ghurbāl retorts, 'the common mistake that Egyptian society was feudal.' The other conditions, which included the creation of 'a coercive military force under . . . the direction and control of British officers', and its chief command 'vested, if possible, in a British officer', are pronounced fair and beneficial. Ghurbāl's judgement is openly optimistic and flattering. The British plan anticipated what Muḥammad ʻAlī was later to succeed in implementing. Placing the revenues of the state 'under fixed regulations', forming an army 'under regular and strict discipline', inflicting 'severe penalties' on the tax-collectors 'if they exacted more than was due' – these were among the lasting bequests of the founder of modern Egypt. The fact that the same British plan looks forward to the 'infinite advantage to our Levant trade' and the opening 'to the commerce of Britain the markets of Egypt', is not alluded to. The teleological march of events does not permit such minor digressions.[51]

Ghurbāl obviously saw in the British proposals another opportunity for the Egyptian nation to enter the modern world. It did not matter to him who had to carry out the task nor for what ulterior motives. The prospect of seeing the implementation of a new order in his country excited his imagination, and moved him to compare the British and French endeavours so as to determine which deserved preference. Thus, the ideas of the British ministers offered in form 'the greatest possible contrast to the creations of Menou's fertile mind'. But the historian was not deceived, as he already knew the final outcome.

> The British scheme, as was proper, bore the cachet of the practical; it burnt no incense to liberty or to equality and omitted to theorise on 'feudal principle' or *impôt unique.* Had it been carried into effect, however, it would have proved just as revolutionary as any of Menou's projects.[52]

Ghurbāl allows himself at this point to over-ride his strict adherence to a chronological, almost daily, narration of events, and telescopes the trajectory of eighty years of historical developments. The plan under discussion is considered 'the first authoritative pronouncement on the problems of Egypt. The second was the famous Dufferin Report of 1883.'[53] What was the invisible bond which linked the two 'authoritative pronouncements'? The comparative method offers a clear answer:

> A slight comparison between the two documents reveals how fast events had moved between 1801 and 1883. During the interval, the viceroys had built up their power, expelled the Turks, welded the heterogeneous elements into a compact nation, accumulated a burdensome debt and attracted into the country a powerful *clientèle* from all lands. The plan of 1801 was intended to make the presence of the British unnecessary; in 1883 the British occupation was commencing its indefinite course.[54]

The viceroys, including Muḥammad 'Alī, spared no effort in forcing the Egyptians to become a regimented nation. Having contributed their well-meaning share, they sat back waiting for the British to administer the finishing touches.

> Mehemet Ali was able to play fast and loose with every kind of property because he found everything in chaos. But it was reserved for the British to make 'amende honorable', it was they who made effective Menou's promise, 'que ce serait par les lois seules que les habitants de l'Egypte seraient désormais jugés'.[55]

Why did Egypt have to wait so long to be formed into 'a compact nation' endowed with the best European laws? The British settlement of 1801, which could not have been 'fairer' or 'more beneficial' was an abortive attempt. Who is to blame? 'A large share of the responsibility for this unhappy state of affairs rests with the Ambassador at Constantinople', Lord Elgin. He ruined the chances of Ghurbāl's nation through his mediocrity, his preoccupation with various financial transactions, and his reluctance to communicate to the Porte the full instructions of his government. The British plan was consequently turned into an empty gesture.[56]

In the meantime the Ottomans were refurbishing their own plans. On 22 October 1801, they tried to carry out a swift and clinical operation, and the Capitan Pasha attempted to murder as many Mamlūks of Murād's party as possible. He only succeeded in ridding himself of five Mamlūks near Alexandria; whereas in Cairo the Grand Vizier arrested the Ibrāhimites. Hutchinson was enraged. He told the Turks to deliver their prisoners, or face the consequences. They duly gave in and released the Beys. Only one Mamlūk *amīr* escaped the fate of his brethren. 'He persuaded the Grand Vizier to let him proceed to Upper Egypt to collect the estates of several people who had died in the previous year's plague without leaving issue. There he fed the "imperial" cupidity for some time and waited in safety for events.'[57]

The British General, Sir John Stuart, was now given the chief command in Egypt. He was instructed by the Addington Cabinet to persuade the Porte to restore the status quo, or failing that, to convince the Ottoman authorities that they should grant the Beys the provinces of Upper Egypt above Gīzah. Once again, the Porte refused either to restore the Mamlūks to their former position or to grant them Upper Egypt, with only the promise of doubling their pensions. The issue at stake was the sovereignty of Egypt, and the Sultan was 'in no mood for concessions'. Meanwhile, Napoleon had made his peace with the Porte, and was urging the implementation of the terms of the Treaty of Amiens which stipulated the evacuation by the British of Malta and Egypt.

Stuart evacuated Egypt in March 1803. The Beys retired into Upper Egypt, while the Ottomans sought to regain their control through their Viceroy, Khosrev, and the Albanian contingent which had entered the country with the combined Turko–British expedition.

The British General, before evacuating the country, furnished the Beys 'with secret supplies of arms and ammunition'. Moreover, he took with him one of their chiefs, Muḥammad al-Alfī Bey, whose consideration, as Stuart thought, 'was high with both Mamelukes and Arabs'. He also left behind Major Misset to represent the interests of the British Government in Egypt, and Major Hayes to assist as an officer of the engineers in the repair of the fortifications and the defence of the country against any French invasion. 'Thus ended the first British occupation of Egypt, and with it the possibility of effective interference in her domestic concerns.'[58]

Having depicted the abysmal failure of the various parties to hasten the process of turning Egypt into a new nation, Ghurbāl turns his attention to the adventurer who knew how to exploit that 'wonderful moment'.

TWO RIVALS

As we reach this stage in the heart-rending struggle of Egypt, the story assumes at the hands of Ghurbāl a somewhat different complexion. We are no longer treated to a direct narration of events. The hero is about to appear on the stage. As the momentous hour approaches, the reader is showered with a wide assortment of celebratory remarks and ceremonial speeches. The historian's purpose is to detach Muḥammad 'Alī from the rest of the Albanians and the Turks, and to present him as an adventurer of genius. It was essential, therefore, to depict him as a towering pioneer who triumphed single-handedly, and seized all the opportunities with the masterly stroke of a veteran statesman. 'Power', we are told, 'was never to him, as it was to many a Turkish adventurer, the means of satisfying lust: he was rather impelled by it, by the desire to do great things and leave a great name.'[59]

In order to prove his case, and show why Muḥammad 'Alī's rivals are to be excluded from his strict code of greatness, Ghurbāl resorts to a variety of techniques, not least of which is the deliberate suppression of evidence.

The main rival of Muḥammad 'Alī between 1803 and 1807 was the Mamlūk chief, al-Alfī Bey. Ghurbāl tries to show this chief in the worst possible light. Since he believed that 'Alī, his hero and the future Viceroy of Egypt, was the only leader, local or foreign, who understood the realities of the situation, his rival is naturally subjected to what may be termed a campaign of character assassination. His moral, political, and social qualities are mercilessly ridiculed and pronounced to be dangerously defective in their various manifestations. However, before we enter into a full discussion of Ghurbāl's negative attitude towards al-Alfī, it is essential to see how he explains the exceptional success of Muḥammad 'Alī.

Ghurbāl takes great care to emphasize the complete independence of his hero's rise to power. His argument hinges on his repeated emphasis 'that events which took place in the years 1803 to 1806 and which culminated in the final confirmation of Mehemet Ali in 1806, were not directly or purposely affected by foreign influence'. Britain, France, Russia, and Austria were all absent from the scene. The laws of history were miraculously suspended. The outside world ceased to be attracted by the plight of the unhappy land; it observed from afar the exploits of a great man with a mission to accomplish. Ghurbāl then shows the sheer ineptitude and futility of all the local political, religious, and military forces. Khosrev, the Ottoman representative in Cairo and a former Georgian slave, was a useless arrogant viceroy. He had no knowledge of politics, administration, or war. The troops under his command, Turks and Albanians, were godless gangs, intent on the destruction and robbing of the Egyptians. As for the Mamlūks, they were roaming the countryside with the sole aim of plundering and perpetrating intolerable horrors, aided and abetted 'by their fellow-plunderers — the Bedouins'. Under these dire circumstances, the Egyptians suffered in silence. They endured untold misery and distress with the 'dull apathy' which is 'the trait of the Oriental'. Had the French occupation been of a longer duration, the Egyptian would have been impelled to question the validity of some of his religious beliefs, and begin to appreciate the importance of change in his customs and attitudes. But how was he to aspire to such a 'revolution' since 'his proper leaders', the '*ulamā*', were nothing but 'a narrow, covetous and subtle class, their learning amounted to no more than commenting upon earlier comments, and most of their efforts were directed to the accumulation of wealth and the cultivation of the powers that be'.[60]

In short, the outside world had ceased to exist, and the Egyptians were powerless, unable to evolve or constitute their society into a national entity. There was a deadlock that had to be broken. Various French and British generals and officials had correctly perceived the urgent need for change, but they were either unfortunate or hampered by the obscurantism and indolence of the orientals. A challenging task and a thrilling prospect offered themselves to the only pathfinder still hovering in the wings. The historian was no longer in doubt about the necessity of a surgical operation. Egypt, floundering and lurching aimlessly and pitiably, had lost its self-energizing capability.

> Conditions were then unfavourable to the evolution of national unity. There had to exist, before this could take place, a highly centralized authority, which should provide security and eliminate pretensions to exclusive privileges. It was indispensable also to create a healthier moral tone by the suppression of concubinage and unnatural vice, to propagate a connection – real or fictitious did not matter[61] – between

the Egypt of the Pharaohs and the Egypt of to-day,[62] so as to enable the country to cut itself loose from Pan-Islamic trammels, and to facilitate the residence of Levantine Christians.[63]

Having sketched the salient features of his hero's political, moral, and cultural programme, Ghurbāl returned to his main theme. He underlines the stark conditions of a land without 'a master'. He manages to expurgate the Mamlūks by pointing to 'their reduced numbers' and the Porte's decision to prohibit 'the exportation of young boys', which made it impossible for the Mamlūks to reassert their authority or expel the Ottomans. The situation presented itself not as a political equilibrium of forces, with no single party possessing sufficient power to assert itself, but as sheer anarchy. It was an anarchy which could have resulted in 'no other outcome than foreign occupation, or the coming to power of an adventurer'. Foreign occupation was excluded and warded off. The hour of deliverance was at hand: 'the adventurer was already on the scene .... His part consisted rather in availing himself of opportunities than in making them.' With the appearance of Muḥammad 'Alī on the stage, the reader is treated to a vivid description of his physical and psychological attributes:

> Physically, he was rather below the average height, was dark complexioned, with a reddish beard. His air was defiant and his eyes were restless. He had none of the sedateness and composure of a Turkish grandee, but all the agility of his race; was sober in habit and simple in attire.[64]

How did this adventurer avail himself of political and other opportunities? Between 29 April and 2 May 1803, the Albanian troops under the command of Ṭāhir Pasha were in open mutiny demanding the payment of their arrears. Khosrev, the Viceroy, was consequently banished, and the leader of the mutiny was proclaimed acting Viceroy (and not 'a new Pasha', as Ghurbāl contends). Al-Jabartī attributed the mutiny to the secret machinations of Muḥammad 'Alī. Ghurbāl, however, dismisses the whole idea as 'unwarrantable'. He bases his firm conviction on the mere fact that 'a rising of undisciplined and irregularly paid soldiers was a very common occurrence in Turkey'. Sensing the weakness of his rather sweeping statement, he adds in a footnote that al-Jabartī was 'very hostile to Mehemet Ali'. By the same method of logical deductions, one may retort that Ghurbāl, being very sympathetic to Muḥammad 'Alī, absolves him of any responsibility in the rebellion. More importantly, we have it on the authority of none other than Ghurbāl himself that his hero loved power, and saw in it a means of achieving 'great things'.[65]

Ṭāhir did not live long to enjoy the trappings and fruits of his newly acquired position. The Janissaries, the Ottoman infantry troops, saw in him a direct threat to their livelihood. Whenever they asked him for payment or provisions, he would refer them to the deposed Viceroy. They therefore decided to murder him and succeeded in so doing. Nevertheless, before his murder he had opened negotiations with the Beys in order to bolster his status. Muḥammad 'Alī went a step further and invited the Mamlūks to enter Cairo. 'Thus began the coalition of the Mamelukes and the Albanians which ultimately turned to the profit of Mehemet Ali.'[66] Ghurbāl chooses this particular event to reveal his hero's 'love of power' and implicitly underlines its contrast with events in which 'the means of satisfying lust' are employed, such as Ṭāhir's mutiny.[67] Nevertheless, the new Albanian chief was still the junior partner in the coalition, shunning 'undue prominence', as he was uncertain of the Porte's attitude towards his relationship with a rebel force. Having duped the Ottoman authorities about his real intentions, Muḥammad 'Alī approached Major Misset, the British representative, and declared his desire to return to Albania on one of His Majesty's ships. The stratagem was most effective, as it lulled the suspicions of his potential enemies. On the other hand, al-Bardīsī and Ibrāhīm Bey, the two Mamlūk chiefs, were now basking in the limelight. Furthermore, al-Bardīsī, in the absence of his more able comrade, al-Alfī Bey, who was in London, gained a paramount influence among the Mamlūks. His policy was to build up his full authority, and reduce that of any future Ottoman viceroy to a nominal presence. However, it is hard to detect 'perfidy' or 'intrigue' on al-Bardīsī's part towards his new partner and ally. On the contrary, it was Muḥammad 'Alī who went to great lengths to demonstrate his 'love of power'. Ghurbāl concedes as much. He blames the Mamlūk chief for being 'short-sighted enough not to see that the safest course would have been to make such arrangements as would extricate him from the Albanian Alliance'. His retrospective advice to him is that he should have reinstated the deposed viceroy, instead of arresting him. However, such a step would have meant turning his back on Muḥammad ʻAlī, the deadly enemy of Khosrev. When the Porte appointed ʻAlī Pasha, as a new Viceroy, Muḥammad ʻAlī applied all his persuasive skills, ʻand succeeded in persuading the foolish Bardissy to destroy ʻAli'. Ghurbāl's hero moved one step up the ladder of power, with his reputation intact:

> The Pasha was, accordingly, decoyed into a trap and assassinated, and his small army dispersed in all directions. Mehemet Ali had kept studiously in the background and the odium fell on Bardissy. The Bey had thus burnt his boats and put himself more and more at the mercy of his ʻally'.[68]

In all these manoeuvres Muḥammad ʻAlī is presumbly exonerated of the stigma which stains those who use power as ʻthe means of satisfying lust'. Since no material transactions were involved, the adventurer, or the creative personality in his Toynbean dimensions, has finally consummated ʻhis movement of Withdrawal-and-Return'.[69]

In narrating these events, Ghurbāl confines himself to a graphic description of the direct engagements between prominent individuals. Consequently other social and political forces are lost sight of. Had the historian adopted a different approach, he would have come face to face with an Egyptian society far removed from his curt comments and dismissive generalizations. The same episodes were narrated by al-Jabartī with unsurpassed accuracy and careful attention to minute detail. Yet Ghurbāl insists on restricting his sources to the dispatches of Major Misset, whose political shortsightedness he cites with sarcastic satisfaction.[70] He overlooked the evidence furnished by al-Jabartī in order to avoid coming into contact with the ʻ*ulamā*' and religious orders who had emerged as a political force in their own right, as well as the Mamlūks' legitimate standing in the eyes of the Egyptians.[71] The barriers between foreigners and natives, slaves and freemen, which Ghurbāl postulated as a natural order of a static society, were simply an intellectual smoke-screen devised to justify his hero's ability ʻto play fast and loose' with every kind of Egyptian.

Nevertheless, Ghurbāl's narration of the subsequent intrigues deployed by Muḥammad ʻAlī to gain ultimate power does not differ in its substance from that of al-Jabartī. They both see his hand in the major events which eventually led to his assumption of the Viceroyalty. They agree that he engineered the two main incidents which enabled him to chase the Mamlūks out of Cairo, namely the destruction of al-Alfī upon his return from London, and the demonstrations which the inhabitants of Cairo organized against al-Bardīsī.[72] However, where Ghurbāl and al-Jabartī differ is in their evaluation of al-Alfī's political and military role.

Muḥammad al-Alfī presented an obvious embarrassment to Ghurbāl. His relatively enlightened ideas, consistent political conduct, and firm convictions contradicted our historian's thesis about the degenerate and treacherous character of the Mamlūks. To him, they were a doomed force incapable of entering the new world which was about to emerge through Muḥammad 'Alī's efforts. If al-Alfī seemed to violate this stereotyped pattern, Ghurbāl's task became rather daunting. Moreover, it was not possible to ignore this Mamlūk chief, as he was the main rival of the historian's hero. Ghurbāl seems to have solved his dilemma by resorting to a deliberate suppression of evidence, and a selective method of presenting facts. In so doing he managed to cast doubt on al-Alfī's abilities and turn him into a savage villain, like the rest of his race.

One of the preconditions that Ghurbāl postulated for the birth of Egypt as a modern nation was the propagation of a real or imaginative link between the Pharaonic past and its present. This step was highly crucial for detaching Egypt from 'Pan-Islamic trammels' and the Ottoman Empire. Ghurbāl considered al-Alfī one of those who would hamper such a historic change since he did not possess a scientific mind to understand the origin and significance of the Pyramids and the old monuments of Egypt.[73] This deficiency was compounded by al-Alfī's flagrant lack of real attachment to Egypt. Ghurbāl goes to great lengths to highlight this last defect, pointing out that al-Alfī was thinking only of his own materialistic interests when he left in the company of General Stuart to sail to London in March 1803. Reporting his departure he announces, 'That Bey had been thinking for some time of "emigrating", and his brethren were anxious to rid themselves of a masterful colleague by sending him to London as their official representative'; he then continues in a footnote:

As early as Dec. 1801, he asked Hamilton[74] what percentage interest he could obtain from investments in England, and was disappointed when told 6 per cent, for the Egyptian peasantry would give him 30 per cent on loans and consider it a good bargain.[75]

In fact the conversation between Hamilton and al-Alfī can hardly be construed as indicating a serious contemplation on the latter's part of leaving his country and settling in another. Hamilton merely says:

our conversations with Elfi at Farshiout [Farshūt, Upper Egypt] turned as usual, on the plans he was to adopt for regaining the Säid [Ṣa'īd] from the Turks; the probability of the Mameluke cause being cordially espoused by England; the necessity to which he might eventually be reduced of seeking an asylum in this country; the advantage he would derive from living here, and the treatment he would receive.[76]

This sounds more like an offer from Hamilton rather than a definite decision taken by al-Alfī. Moreover, Hamilton was in no doubt about al-Alfī's future plan:

But it was evident he only looked forward to the departure of the English for an opportunity of attacking the Ottoman troops, and driving them for ever from the Province. For this object, he had already begun negotiating on the frontiers of Nubia for an army of mercenaries to assist him.[77]

As for the anxiety of the Mamlūk chiefs to free themselves from their domineering colleague by sending him to London, there is no evidence to support this assumption. Ghurbāl bases his unqualified statement on a letter which the Beys addressed to General Stuart. It is dated 25 Rajab 1217 (21 November 1802), and signed by Ibrāhīm Bey and al-Bardīsī.[78] The bearer of the letter was al-Alfī himself. At that time the two Mamlūk chiefs, who had escaped from their detention by the Grand Vizier a year earlier, were still being harassed and chased by the Ottoman forces. Neither of them was thinking of sending a representative to London at the time. No such plan is alluded to in their letter. They simply entreat General Stuart to intercede with the Sublime Porte in their favour, and place themselves under his protection as a sincere ally of the Sultan. What they say about al-Alfī is that he enjoys their full confidence, and is authorized to reach whatever agreement or compromise on their behalf.

After being detained in Malta for some months, 'because it was necessary', as *The Times*[79] correspondent put it, 'to apprize the English Government of his intended visit', al-Alfī was finally allowed to proceed to England in the frigate *Experiment*. He arrived on 3 October 1803 at Portsmouth. Upon his arrival the British press published similar items of news relating to the purpose of his visit, his career, and peculiar habits. Ghurbāl picked out one particular passage and through it reduced al-Alfī to a debauched maniac. We are told that *Gentleman's Magazine*[80] gives this description. Elfi had a suite of 17, drank two bottles of Champagne or Burgundy after dinner, was fascinated with everything, especially the ladies'.[81] Had Ghurbāl been neutral towards his subject, or slightly inclined in his favour, he would not have been so selective in paraphrasing only what suited his purpose. The same magazine presents a more balanced picture of the Bey, and alludes to his alcoholic and amorous disposition in a way that is not intended to slight his character or prejudice him in the eyes of his hosts. Moreover, the identical pieces on al-Alfī appeared verbatim in other newspapers and magazines,[82] which makes one suspect that they were drafted by one of al-Alfī's partisans in either the Foreign or War Office anxious to advance his cause. The *Gentleman's Magazine* introduces the Bey to its readers thus:

> This day arrived in London, on a diplomatic mission, Mehemet-Bey- Elfi Murad, one of the Mameluke Chiefs who fought so bravely at Alexandria. He was wounded in the side with a musket-ball, and concealed it for two days, lest, if known, his danger should produce a cabal among the other rival chiefs, and dismay among his troops.[83]

While al-Alfī was still waiting in Malta, the Ottoman Porte and the French authorities began to voice their displeasure at his reception as a fully credited ambassador of the Mamlūks. The British Foreign Secretary hastened to counter 'any unfounded rumours', and deemed it necessary to inform Constantinople 'that this Mamluk Chief has arrived in this country without the knowledge or sanction of His Majesty's Government, whose fixed determination it is, not to listen to any proposals from him, which may affect the interest or the rights of the Ottoman Porte in Egypt'.[84] Shunned by Downing Street, al-Alfī was getting restless in spite of the visits he received from various officials, and the attention accorded to him by the press. After the intercession of one of his admirers, Sir G.C. Braithwaite Boughton, who recommended in a private letter the 'very high character of Alfy Bey, both as a soldier, and as a man of uncommon frankness and loyalty in all his dealings', the British Government authorized Lieutenant-Colonel J. Moore to see him and report on his views.[85] More importantly, news of the Mamlūks' ascendancy, their almost complete control of Egypt and the apparent acquiescence of the Ottoman Porte began to reach London. The Government calculated it would be in its own interest to drop any misgivings it had about dealing with 'a masterful Bey'.

Ghurbāl, however, sees things differently. He concerns himself with rebutting the statement of the French historian, Felix Mengin, who claimed that al-Alfī was 'first well-received, then entirely neglected, but when the news of the entry of the Mamlukes into Cairo reached London, Elfi suddenly returned to favour'. What evidence does Ghurbāl offer for his rebuttal? He simply asserts, 'As a matter of dates, the return of the Beys to power took place in May and was known in London long before Elfi reached it'.[86] However, the question which he is reluctant to ask does not concern the date on which the British Government had knowledge of the Beys' resurgence, but rather the views and attitude of the Ottoman Porte towards their return to power. The British Government had an explicit treaty with the Porte upon the evacuation of Egypt and wanted to know whether the Mamlūks were still rebels in the eyes of the Sultan before committing themselves publicly. Al-Alfī was shunned by the British Government when the Porte protested at his reception as an official representative. Their change of heart came with the gradual softening attitude of the Ottoman authorities. By the first week of November, al-Alfī had learned of the Porte's decision to pardon the Beys and restore their former privileges. He did not delay in exploiting this decision to his advantage. The London *Morning Post* carried on 7 November 1803 the following item:

> It is said that Elphy Bey, the Mameluke Chief, received by the last Hamburgh Mail the pleasing intelligence that the

Porte, since the surrender of Alexandria,[87] and the other towns in Lower Egypt, has written to all the Foreign Powers, expressing a desire to come to terms of accommodation with the Beys, and re-establish them in all their ancient privileges. If this report be true, it is probable that Elphy Bey will be received at St. James's with all the dignity of his mark.

Moreover, the British Government came to the conclusion that in their refusal to allay the fears of al-Alfī of not being accorded a 'proper' or official hearing, they were unwittingly delivering the Beys into the hands of the French. Having observed that the Beys were 'at present in possession of every part of the country except Alexandria', Downing Street instructed the British Ambassador at Constantinople to work for a lasting accommodation between the Porte and the Mamlūks. This was spelled out as an urgent task which required the Ottoman authorities to forgo their hopeless plans of scoring a complete victory. On the contrary, it was stressed that the inevitable failure of such a futile exercise would 'drive the Beys into a connection with France, by which Egypt may be open to another invasion and ultimately become subject to the French Government'.[88]

It is true, as Ghurbāl maintains, that the French were deceived in taking al-Alfī to be nothing but an agent, or a stooge, of the British. According to Captain Hallowell, who conveyed al-Alfī back to Egypt, the Bey stated that he would be 'glad to encourage the importation of English manufactures but never wished to see an English soldier in the country'.[89] Such a statement, according to Ghurbāl, refutes the accusations of the French historians, and proves al-Alfī's determination to defend his country against any invader, be he French, Russian, or British. The positive aspects of such a statement and their indubitable implications run counter to the dogmatic theory as regards the Egyptian Mamlūks and their character, and to which our historian constantly alludes.

However, the malignancy which Ghurbāl harbours against his subject does not end here. He is anxious to assure his readers that al-Alfī was a mere barbarian whose journey to London did not affect him either politically or culturally. Al-Alfī spent almost three months in England, a relatively long period during which a visitor is expected to avail himself of this rare opportunity and endeavour to discover the secret behind the success of Britain as a world power. But how did our Mamlūk spend his time? 'British reports', Ghurbāl asserts, 'do not show that Elfi had greatly benefited from his visit to London. The only net gain seemed to be his developing a pronounced taste for milk-punch.'[90] This comical and sarcastic remark captured Toynbee's attention in his preface to the book, and he hailed it as one which contributed 'to the interest and entertainment of the play'.[91]

Having dealt his hero's enemy a mortal blow, Ghurbāl turns his sarcasm against the Egyptian historian al-Jabartī, who was an admirer of al-Alfī and a ruthless critic of Muḥammad 'Alī's policies. Al-Jabartī, as Ghurbāl concedes, 'pictured an Alphi sobered by experience and struck by all that he had seen in London — order, prosperity, absence of begging, and all this in spite of "infidelity".' How is Ghurbāl to explain and reconcile two diametrically opposed statements — his own and that of al-Jabartī? The only expedient is to show al-Jabartī as an emotionally disturbed and superstitious character whose judgements are not to be trusted. 'The chronicler was', Ghurbāl extrapolates, 'rather partial to Elfi, partly through detestation of Bardissy, and the Albanians, and partly through common interest in astrology.'[92]

It has already been observed that Ghurbāl quotes the British press reports out of context in order to buttress his argument. When these reports prove difficult to manipulate, he simply ignores them, leaving the impression that what the English newspapers had to say about al-Alfī did not go beyond his drinking habits, and the manner in which he gulped his milk punch within the walls of his hotel suite. How far is this exotic description an objective representation of the facts?[93]

Four days after his arrival in London, we are informed that 'the Mameluke Chief took a ride in coach, accompanied by Lord Blantyre, yesterday morning, through the squares and principal streets at the West end of the town, to view the Buildings, and was highly gratified'.[94] Another newspaper reported that 'Elphy Bey proves himself to be a man of sense, by the eagerness which he manifests in visiting every thing worthy of the attention of a foreigner in this metropolis'.[95] The same newspaper carried on 17 November this significant and highly indicative report:

Elphy Bey is pleased with the splendour and magnificence

displayed in this Metropolis, so far exceeding any idea that he could have formed of it, and so very different from the tawdry, tasteless stile [*sic*] of the East, that it is said he intends to introduce some of our useful and elegant arts into his country; and that in case he obtains permission from our Government, he will invite a numerous train of literati, Astronomers, Geographers, Physicians, Surgeons, Artists, etc to accompany him to Egypt.

It is a remarkable fact that al-Jabartī, who was a pious Muslim and enormously proud of his country's glorious past, could so easily and intimately defend and embrace the views and general attitude of a Mamlūk *amir* such as al-Alfī. Unlike Ghurbāl, the Egyptian chronicler was a faithful observer of events and a keen reporter of the various developments that he witnessed or was able to verify.[96] This fact is demonstrated in the way he treats al-Alfī's political and military activities. There is no attempt on his part to either conceal or embellish the record of a person he so obviously admired and supported. Al-Alfī's virtues are paraded along with his defects and misdeeds. He situates his career in the wider sociopolitical context of Egypt, the Ottoman Empire, and the European power struggle.[97] Confining such an attitude to mere partiality and a common interest in one hobby is an outright distortion of the real relationship which united and brought together an Egyptian ʿ*ālim* and a Mamlūk leader. Such friendships or political alliances were not a peculiar state of affairs in the late eighteenth and early nineteenth centuries. It was a spontaneous phenomenon cutting across a variety of social groups, owing to the decline of the position and authority of the Ottoman Porte, and the emergence of a new economic and political order in which the Mamlūks had almost regained their former status as the dominant military power.[98] This ascendancy was, however, accompanied by the rise of the ʿ*ulamā*ʾ and other religious clerics who acted as effective mediators between the military rulers and their subjects, be they fellahin, artisans, or merchants. The ʿ*ulamā*ʾ, in addition to their religious and moral status, shared and participated in the accumulation of wealth and material benefits as *multazims* and supervisors of *awqāf* (religious endowments). They even started to imitate the Mamlūks in their lifestyle, a fact which did not escape the critical eye of al-Jabartī.[99] Along with the ʿ*ulamā*ʾ, the merchants were acquiring *iltizāms* and playing an active role in the life of their community. The French occupation did not change the overall structure of Egyptian society. It nevertheless contributed to a relative decline of the power of the Mamlūks, who had to compete with other military forces for the control of Egypt. The Mamlūks, moreover, resumed their old internal feuds which served to decrease their effectiveness. As a result, the '*ulamā*' wielded more influence and enjoyed wider prestige among the population. Al-Alfī saw correctly the hopelessness of relying on a narrow base, and tried to widen his alliances and involve England in his diplomatic and military confrontations with the Ottomans or the Albanians.[100]

When Muḥammad 'Alī expelled the Mamlūks from Cairo in March 1804 and installed Khurshīd, the Governor of Alexandria, as the new Pasha, a fresh phase opened in the struggle for power. The Albanians were now in control of Cairo under an Ottoman viceroy, considered to be their stooge. However, the Porte was seeking to expel the Albanians, and remove Muḥammad 'Alī from the scene by appointing him to the governorship of Salonika or Jedda. The English agent, Misset, exerted all the influence he had to thwart the ambitions of the Albanian chief. Napoleon, on the other hand, was trying to win the Mamlūk Beys to his side,[101] the same Mamlūks whose power he was supposed to have shattered a few years previously.

The Mamlūks at last decided to unite their forces, albeit on a temporary basis. They laid siege to Cairo, and defeated all the forces sent against them, which included a body of 2,000 cavalry, dispatched as reinforcements from the Ottoman Porte to the Viceroy, and 1,000 Albanians, under the command of Muḥammad 'Alī. Misset explained to Lord Hobart:

> That in the recent union of their respective means Elfi Bey and Osman Bey Bardissi have only had in view the momentary purpose of driving the Turks from Cairo, cannot be for one moment doubted. If they succeed in that object, each of them will then exert himself to destroy his rival, in order to remain alone at the head of the government.[102]

However, Misset was pinning his hopes on the Viceroy to drive out the Albanians. He subsequently gave al-Alfī a vague non-committal answer when the latter requested his 'advice as to the measures he is to pursue'.[103]

With the sudden rise of the Nile, the Beys were obliged to lift their siege of Cairo and head for Upper Egypt. Muḥammad 'Alī, sensing his inability to score a military victory against the Mamlūks, resorted to outright bribery. He instructed 'his banker at Constantinople to spare no expense in endeavouring to procure him the dignity of Viceroy'. His other course of action was to seek the mediation of the French Ambassador, General Brune, 'to induce that Minister to recommend him to the Divan for the situation to which he aspires'.[104]

Ghurbāl omits to mention this second step taken by his hero, and conflates the first move with another separate development in order to remove any remote connection between him and the French Ambassador at Constantinople.[105] He highlights Muḥammad 'Alī's 'recourse to new allies, the sheikhs and inhabitants of Cairo',[106] as 'a stroke of genius'. He discovered in them 'a source of strength' which had been untapped. His adoption of the cause of the 'contemptibles' marks him off and places his character in a different category. While the Turks and the Beys were busy 'kicking and fleecing' the Egyptians, he thought of them as honourable human beings worthy of joining his glorious march towards the summit of power.[107] The latter events took place in May 1805, while his practice of 'corrupting' the Ottoman officials was launched as early as 1804. Between these two dates the Albanians were terrorizing the city and its contemptibles,[108] while the Mamlūks were replenishing their diminishing ranks by recruiting Arab tribes. Major Misset calculated the numerical strength of the Bedouins who rallied to the various Mamlūk Beys to be no less than 10,000.[109] In the meantime, the Ottoman Porte sent a reinforcement of several thousand 'Turkish' cavalry,[110] along with strong detachments of infantry and artillery. They started pouring into the environs of Cairo, intent on the destruction of both the Mamlūks and the Albanians.[111]

Muḥammad 'Alī quickly realized the intentions of the Porte, and quitted the battlefield in Upper Egypt. He met the Commander of the Delhis at the outskirts of Cairo, and managed to win his confidence. They agreed on a by now familiar strategy. Muḥammad 'Alī duly 'sent one of his officers to demand of the Viceroy four millions of Turkish piasters, the amount of six months pay to his men'.[112] He then entered Cairo at the head of about 4,000 Albanians and other armed groups, thus swelling the number of troops quartered in the city to no less than ten thousand. As for the Delhis, his new allies, they fulfilled their undertakings and went on a rampage.[113]

On 9 May 1805 Khurshīd, the Viceroy, read before the *Divan* a firman of the sultan, conferring the Pashalik of Jedda on Muḥammad 'Alī. The latter pretended to accept his new investiture, knowing full well what was in store for the Viceroy. Relying on his past experience and the way he had succeeded in chasing the Mamlūks out of Cairo, 'Alī waited for Khurshīd to make his next move and became embroiled with the inhabitants of Cairo. With the presence of hordes of unruly troops in and around Cairo, and the prospect of new taxes being imposed to meet the demands of the Albanians and the Delhis, the stage was set for yet another popular rising led by the '*ulamā*' and the artisans' guilds.

The revolt erupted in the main against the wild Delhis who were wreaking havoc on the lives and properties of the Cairenes. 'Umar Makram, who acted as the leader of the various quarters and groups, called on Khurshīd to resign his viceroyalty. However, Khurshīd refused to budge 'declaring that he was Pasha by order of the Grand Signior and would not relinquish his position at the demand of the "fellaheen"'. Drawing on al-Jabartī's narration of these events, Ghurbāl proudly announces:

> The Pasha was promptly declared deposed, was besieged in his palace, and Mehemet Ali allowed himself to be elected governor pending the pleasure of the Sultan. The scene in Cairo reminded Frenchmen of the enthusiasm which reigned in the early moments of the Revolution.[114]

Thus, dropping his contemptuous attitude towards the obscurantist '*ulamā*', he could not resist the temptation of linking the resurrection, which led to the definitive rise of Muḥammad 'Alī, to the ideal type of all revolutions. Nevertheless, the 'Frenchmen' Ghurbāl refers to are actually one single person: the French agent Bernardino Drovetti, who was in this particular instance describing the psychological and emotional state of the population. His political evaluation of the nature of the whole revolt is included in another dispatch. In it he compares the movement to that of the Sicilian Vespers who revolted in 1282 against the French authorities on the island.[115] More importantly, Ghurbāl refers the reader for the whole episode to al-Jabartī's chronicle. A close scrutiny of this chronicle, particularly al-Alfī's biography, would yield information which has hitherto gone unnoticed by a number of scholars. The salient fact which stands out relates to the direct involvement of al-Alfī in the revolt. Not only did he move his camp closer to the outer suburbs of Cairo once the resurrection was under way, but he also was in direct communication with 'Umar Makram, and channelled through him funds and provisions to sustain it.[116] Al-Jabartī informs us that it was in the last stages of the revolt when Muḥammad 'Alī finally struck a deal with 'Umar Makram, whereas the latter had first assured al-Alfī that 'this revolt is for your sake and in order to chase out these riff-raff'.[117] Moreover, Muḥammad 'Alī, contrary to common belief, was not declared governor or viceroy, but rather a *qā'immaqām* or acting-viceroy. This was a traditional practice inaugurated by the Mamlūks whenever the viceroyalty became vacant or its occupant was deposed.[118] The '*ulamā*' were simply treading in the footsteps of their recent masters. Had they elected Muḥammad 'Alī as a full viceroy, such an act would have meant their renunciation of the sultan's sovereignty over Egypt — a step which was difficult to contemplate. 'Umar Makram justified his choice of Muḥammad 'Alī as acting-viceroy by the sole fact that the candidate was one of *al-qawm*,[119] i.e. an Ottoman representative. Furthermore, what seems to have tipped the balance in Muḥammad 'Alī's favour had nothing to do with his discovery of the strength of the Egyptian masses — or his willingness to treat them as allies. It was the enormous military forces under his command or influence which in the final analysis concentrated the minds of the '*ulamā*'. His election was thus a desperate act dictated by the immediate needs of the Cairenes to relieve themselves of extortions and widespread destruction. One may even go further and consider the decision as the reluctant capitulation of a movement which had reached the point of sheer exhaustion. After all, one has only to recall the countless military revolts and popular uprisings which the Cairenes had either witnessed or initiated, and all the material devastation, human sacrifice, and financial ruin entailed, ever since the Ottomans attempted to regain their supremacy in 1786.[120] It was these factors which facilitated Muḥammad 'Alī's rise to power and its consolidation. Far from being a lone adventurer, as Ghurbāl would like us to believe, Muḥammad 'Alī relied on the Albanians and the

Delhis[121] to relegate the Egyptians and their religious and other leaders to an adjunct of his strategy. Once confirmed in his position by the sultan, he resorted to a systematic campaign of intimidation and manipulation against the same 'source of strength' he had so ingeniously discovered. New taxes were imposed. The Mamlūks' *iltizāms* were confiscated. The '*ulamā*' gradually lost their privileges and tax exemptions. When 'Umar Makram decided to make a stand and voice his disapproval of the new measures, he was sent into exile. The majority of the Mamlūks were lured into a trap in the Citadel and ruthlessly massacred in cold blood. All these steps were prerequisite conditions for the birth of Ghurbāl's modern Egypt. Hence he narrates the episodes with a proud tone. However, his boundless excitement blinds his vision and leads him to indulge in contradictory evaluations. It seems that once Muḥammad 'Alī was firmly in the saddle, the historian no longer feels obliged to apply his strict moral and political code. Admitting the failure of his hero to 'obtain a decisive victory over' the Mamlūks, he simply declares with apparent satisfaction: 'The result was treachery and the massacre of the major part of them in March, 1811.' Ghurbāl then tries to explain Muḥammad 'Alī's various activities by focusing attention on his 'hoarding of treasure'. This was a categorical necessity, and the trait of 'Near Eastern adventures — be they Jewish or Turkish'. Hence the new viceroy had to amass large quantities 'of precious stones, ornamental daggers and swords, costly stuffs, snuff-boxes, pipes and species'. Even scientific thinking, which al-Alfī lacked, is mysteriously removed for the sake of an adventurer: 'Astrologers, divines and prophets seconded his operations'. What was the motive behind this feverish activity?

> He had to feed the cupidity of the Porte. He had to bribe the Mamelukes into submission in the years preceding their destruction. But it was his Albanians who devoured his treasure. He was at their mercy but was unable to do without them. In 1809 they numbered 10,000, but received the pay of 30,000. Three years later, they increased to 15,000 and the troubles of the Pasha rose in proportion.[122]

Having destroyed the material and moral power of the Mamlūks and the '*ulamā*', he began to establish the new order and a putative modern national identity. Thus the land passed 'into the hands of the Viceroy, who distributed it among members of his family, officers, favourites and the peasants'. Egypt was violently and unscrupulously turned 'into a vast personal estate'. It now had one master and spoke with one voice. The inhabitants, superstitious, apathetic, and horribly traditional, were dragged into the modern world. The national identity could at long last crawl out of its hiding place and bless the estate and its sole owner. The historian thus delivers his final judgement and proclaims: 'Mehemet Ali made modern Egypt'.[123]

It was the disruption of this society and its transformation which al-Jabartī condemned and abhorred. It was a society built on intimate and clearly defined roles and social categories. His emphatic disapproval and strictures had nothing to do with the introduction of new modern techniques or the improvement of the economy. They rather relate to the new social relations, the political authoritarianism and the denigration of the Egyptian Muslims, be they Mamlūks, religious leaders, or merchants. He correctly observed that the Pasha had pushed aside all the indigenous Egyptians and their natural rulers. The economic, political, financial, and administrative organization of the country was usurped and controlled by Albanians, Greeks, Armenians, Turks, Levantine merchants, and finally French and Europeans in general.[124] Judging from al-Alfī's career, his ambitions and alliances, and al-Jabartī's illuminating allusions to Egypt's long history and the tension he experienced between the old and the new, one is struck by the development of a natural feeling of belonging to one Egyptian territory. This almost spontaneous affiliation was not at that stage encumbered with the European notion of the nation-state. It is revealed, for example, in the way al-Jabartī castigates the Mamlūk Bey 'Alī al-Kabīr (1760–73), who as *Shaykh al-Balad* aimed at wresting Egypt from Ottoman control. He is strongly rebuked not for his inclination towards independence, or his anti-Ottoman activities, but rather for his expansionist policies in trying to annex Syria and al-Ḥijāz, instead of satisfying himself with governing the whole of Egypt, a fact 'which former Kings and Pharaohs used to boast of before other Kings'.[125]

MUḤAMMAD 'ALĪ REVISITED

During the Second World War Ghurbāl published in Arabic a full biography of Muḥammad 'Alī.[126] In it he excels himself in his adulation and unswerving admiration. Only his hero's virtues are allowed to shine through. Even the scope of his ambitions is widened to embrace the regeneration of the Ottoman Empire and the Muslim world as a whole.

While in the first version Muḥammad 'Alī's love of power is flaunted as a positive trait, and the steps of accomplishing his lofty dream are meticulously noted, the Arabic biography postulates a diametrically opposite view. Here we are informed that the adventurer did not seek the position of viceroy, nor did he betray the slightest inclination towards that purpose. It was rather coincidence which led him to assume the viceroyalty, and he had it thrust upon him. He, as an accomplished Ottoman gentleman, hated power, politics, personal squabbles, and intrigues. He did not plot the massacre of the Mamlūks — they fell victim to the demonic machinations of the Albanian clans and their leaders. Muḥammad 'Alī, being of pure Turkish origin, was above the Albanians and their wild deeds. He only acquiesced in the treachery in order to appease these unruly troops and convince them of marching away to fight the Wahhābis in the Arabian Peninsula.[127]

When Ghurbāl revisited his hero he had been on bad terms with the Wafd Party headed by Muṣṭafā al-Nahḥās. The contemporary politics of his country made yet another incursion into his life. He was now drawn closer and closer into the circle of the Royal Palace. King Fārūq was toying with the idea of declaring himself as a new caliph of all Muslims.[128] A number of Azharite '*ulamā*' and politicians rallied to the King's cause and launched a widespread campaign in his support. Furthermore, the Egyptian intellectuals at that time had begun to re-evaluate their negative attitude towards Islam. Gone were the days of extolling liberalism, nationalism, the Pharaonic past, and European civilization. While the latter movement can be considered as either a regressive step or a restating of old beliefs, depending on the observer's philosophical point of view,[129] Ghurbāl's case was rather unambiguous. He joined the debate on a more personal level, and did not conceal his faith in the future or Muḥammad 'Alī's dynasty. His passionate and highly subjective defence of his hero leaves us in no doubt about his political and ideological loyalties. In stressing the Ottoman dimensions of Muḥammad ‘Alī’s strategy he was rehabilitating Islam and tying its fortunes to a particular monarch at the same time. His previously harsh judgement of Islam as an impediment retarding the birth of modern Egypt, was dropped and implicitly renounced as a naïve idea. It is true Ghurbāl did not become a fervent Muslim fundamentalist, nor did he look at the west with the eyes of a fanatic. However, he gave up much more than he cared to concede. We are told: ‘Muḥammad ‘Alī started off, lived and concluded his career as an Ottoman Muslim. His task was, as he defined it from the beginning to the end, the revivification of the Ottoman power in a new form’.[130] Egypt as a result loomed in his horizon as a mere base, a launching pad for greater and more fulfilling adventures. He refused to confine himself to ‘a small narrow corner of the world whose horizons were narrow and its aspirations limited’. Muḥammad ‘Alī, therefore, never entertained the equally destructive ideas of independence and nationalism. He realized that by adopting one or the other he would precipitate the disintegration of the Ottoman Empire, and make it an easy prey to western states.[131] The national identity was prudently sacrificed on the altar of Islam, and Egypt traded its dead past for a promising future.

How did Muḥammad ‘Alī set about accomplishing his new task? The answer about which Ghurbāl expatiates covers the familiar policies of creating one single authority, reforming and reorganizing the agricultural system, building a new army, founding a firm industrial sector, developing the foreign trade of Egypt, and overhauling the educational system. These reforms went hand in hand with his military campaigns in the Arabian Peninsula, the Sudan, Greece, Syria, and finally his attempts to reach Constantinople, which were thwarted by the concerted efforts of the European powers. Thus the ambitious plans did not materialize. Ghurbāl, notwithstanding his disappointment, manages to console himself with his moral platitudes. Muḥammad ‘Alī’s ‘conquests are gone, his navy has disappeared, and his army has shrunk, but he is still an imposing figure, of high repute, his forehead glowing with the dignity of the whiteness of his hair, and the light of glory’.[132]

However, Ghurbāl’s biography is far from being a hagiographical account of his hero’s achievements and sorely lamented failures; it is shot through with the Toynbean concept of the role of creative minorities and individuals. He consecrates a whole chapter to elucidating Muḥammad 'Alī's genuine endeavours to create an élite charged with a laudable mission. This élite is frankly identified as 'the Turkish-speaking aristocracy'. Its emergence expresses the belief of its patron in the European idea of 'movement' in opposition to that of stagnation and immobility. Moreover, while the Europeans thought that the mission of Islam was no more, Muḥammad 'Alī was 'realizing one of the old laws of the Islamic nation's development'. Ghurbāl's concept of the élite as a new impetus revitalizing the inherent forces of his new nation suffers from apparent weaknesses. He points out, for example, that to all the members of this Ottoman aristocracy Muḥammad 'Alī was 'le maître des faveurs'. His relationship with them was modelled on that of a father and his sons: 'A father who was generous and firm, endeavouring to turn them into men able to understand his intentions and assist him in achieving his aspirations'.[13] These two practices are hardly conducive to the creation of a new political society, be it western or Islamic. At best, they reproduce a higher form of slavery and serve to perpetuate it until it extinguishes itself.[134]

THE PHARAOHS OR THE ARABS?

The *coup d'état* of 1952 brought about the demise of the Egyptian monarchy as well as Ghurbāl's cherished theories and historical expositions. During the first years of the new regime General Muḥammad Najīb appeared to the outside world as the leader of the revolution and a father-figure to whom the younger army officers expressed their loyalty and respect. He was an old-type politician who held some enlightened ideas, particularly in his declared adoption of a multi-party system. Moreover, Najīb was a traditional Egyptian who believed in his country as a nation with a clearly defined character. Ghurbāl did not wait long to jump on the bandwagon. He briefly relapsed into his Pharaonic obsessions and delivered a series of radio broadcasts on the history of Egypt in 1954.[135]

A clue to his new approach is disclosed by the title of his talks: 'The formation of Egypt'. Hence, the evolution of Egyptian society is seen as a long-term process, unfolding in accordance with certain underlying trends which over-ride specific individuals and prominent leaders. His main theme involves the permanent interaction in the history of Egypt between the two principles of continuity and change, the factors of social cohesion, the position of the individual in society, and the differences between the city and the countryside. Egypt in this perspective is not, as Herodotus maintained, ‘the gift of the Nile’, but rather ‘the gift of the Egyptians’. Using Toynbee’s model of ‘challenge and response’, he stresses the way the ancient Egyptians responded to the opportunities offered by geography and refashioned it to develop their own peculiar way of life. This first creative confrontation between man and nature gave birth to a nucleus. It was this nucleus that made it possible for Egypt to establish a balance between continuity and change, and led to the formation of a nation in its interaction with all the races and cultures of the ancient world down to the nineteenth century.[136]

In the course of Ghurbāl’s analysis and delineations the names of certain leaders, associated with this controlled development, crop up. One figure is conspicuous by his absence: Muḥammad ‘Alī. Only the system he left behind, the Khedivate, is mentioned and in such disparaging remarks as to turn it into the worst political regime Egypt has ever known. Instead of drawing its inspirations and policies, Ghurbāl informs us, from the triple revolutions of Europe — the scientific, the industrial, and the French — the Khedivate subjected the Egyptians to barbarian methods and concepts. Under it the people suffered from an oppressive power which did not recognize ‘the rule of the law’ nor the necessity of justice. The educational system suffered from mediocrity and narrow utilitarian aims. The long-awaited birth of ‘a virtuous élite’ was thus thwarted and Egypt witnessed the cancerous growth of ‘corrupt administrative tools’, woefully incompetent in carrying out their duties. The greed of a local and foreign minority prevailed with disastrous consequences. In 1882 Britain occupied Egypt and Sir Evelyn Baring, Lord Cromer, attempted to turn the clock back and govern the country in the traditional style of the Middle Ages. He overlooked one essential fact which stipulated that the final settlement of Egypt’s destiny would be with its people. The revolt of 1919 implied this significant fact. However, ‘a new national renaissance’ was not achieved. The Egyptian leaders satisfied themselves with limited measures and cautious policies. The whole system was bound to fall and be replaced with an Egyptian republic. Ghurbāl’s hopes, dreams, and theoretical beliefs are summed up in a quotation from Burke's *Reflections on the Revolution in France*:

> But the state ought not to be considered as nothing better than a partnership.... It is a partnership in all science; a partnership in all art; a partnership in every virtue, and in all perfection.[137]

Hence Egypt was still a nation, but the state had to be created *ex nihilo.*

However, Ghurbāl's relapse into the Pharaonic past and its ever-evolving nucleus was brief and temporary. Najīb was soon manoeuvred out of his position and Nasser emerged as the effective and charismatic leader of the new republic. By 1958 Egypt had adopted Arabism as its official ideology and political culture, joined Syria in forming the United Arab Republic, and launched a socioeconomic programme with clear socialist orientations. Ghurbāl at that time had retired from his university and governmental posts and replaced Ṣāṭi' al-Ḥuṣrī as the Director of the Institute of Higher Arab Studies at the Cairo-based Arab League. In 1961, he delivered at the Institute a series of lectures on 'the historical factors' which led to 'the formation of the Arab nation'.[138] By and large, his general survey of the history of the Arab World conforms to the selective methods and historicist approach of a number of Arab nationalist intellectuals in Syria and Iraq. He chronicles the local and international conditions and conjunctures which facilitated at first the autonomy of various Arab countries and their eventual independence in the twentieth century. The basic concepts he had already applied to his study of the emergence of a new Egypt[139] are now generalized to illuminate the history of each Arab country. The rise and decline of the Ottoman Empire receive extensive treatment, and the fate of the Arabs is closely related to developments within the institutions and political life of the Ottomans. Three national units are seen to have come into being and slowly evolved since 1516: Iran, the Arab nation, and Turkey. From the sixteenth century to the end of the eighteenth, the Ottoman Empire was governed along traditional Islamic lines, in addition to some peculiar administrative and political innovations. Only with the challenge of European economic, scientific, military, industrial, and cultural superiority, towards the beginning of the nineteenth century, did the

Ottomans respond by implementing military and other reforms.[140] Muḥammad ʻAlī's policies fall within the same pattern and constitute one facet of a wider movement in the Ottoman Empire as a whole. However the aims of his forgotten and then resurrected hero are no longer the same. The eventual rise of Arabism has to be accounted for. Precedents, potentialities, and portents have to be grasped and underlined. We now learn that 'historians disagree amongst themselves as to the real aims of Muḥammad ʻAlī'. Nevertheless, Ghurbāl ventures to offer his own opinion and states that ʻAlī's aims were twofold: the independence of Egypt and the unification of most of the Arab World. According to Ghurbāl, Muḥammad ʻAlī perceived the geographical connections and natural integration of the Arab countries and the fact that their inhabitants belonged to 'the Arab nation'.[141] Ottomanism and Islamism were not the central preoccupations of this new Arab leader; those were the twin cornerstones of the strategy of Sultan ʻAb dal-Ḥamīd II (1876–1909). It was this Ottoman sultan who sought to revitalize the Empire and re-establish his control over its vast territories. However, he did so at a time when nationalism and the drive for independence had already made permanent inroads into his domains. Even various Turkish reformers and army officers were no longer convinced of the imperial unity and the implicit equality of all its races, religions, and sects. The synchronization of these trends with European expansionism resulted in the final disintegration of the Ottoman Empire and the dawn of new Arab policies and political movements. International boundaries were demarcated, the native inhabitants were recruited into national armies, slavery was abolished, a modern education system produced new groups of administrators and technicians, and finally the nomadic tribes were settled on agricultural lands which paved the way to their reintegration into the structures of the Arab states. Although these phenomena developed separately and on a purely local basis, the Arab identity constituted a common denominator between one fatherland and another. The Second World War inaugurated a new era — the era of Arabism proper. All Arabs, in their various independent states, began to contribute towards the building of an Arab society based on solidarity and close cooperation.[142]

Thus, between 1920 and 1960, Egypt emerged as a nation-state at the hands of Shafīq Ghurbāl under four different perspectives. First it was firmly rooted in a wonderful drive towards westernization carried forward by the genius of Muḥammad ‘Alī. It then changed course under the same adventurer and donned an Islamic flowing robe until the advent of a republican regime. Egypt suddenly discarded its outworn garment and entered the modern world with a self-reproducing nucleus. The Suez Crisis of 1956 and the rise of Nasser finally injected the hereditary code of the nucleus with a permanent Arab identity, or so it seemed to the historian in the last stage of his career.

NOTES

1. Published in 2 vols (Paris, 1919–21).
2. Jack Crabbs, Jr, ‘Politics, history, and culture in Nasser's Egypt’, *IJMES*, vol. 6 (1975), p. 389.
3. See, for example, Kāmil's book, *al-Mas'ala al-sharqiyya* (Cairo, 1898).
4. One example of this type of literature is Mohamed Fahmy, *La vérité sur la question d'Égypte* (Saint-Imier, 1913).
5. M. Sabry, *La question d'Égypte* (Paris, 1920).
6. A personal communication from Ghurbāl's son, Dr Murad Ghorbal, 18 August 1985.
7. Ahmad ‘Izzat ‘Abd al-Karīm, ‘Nadwat Muḥammad Shafīq Ghurbāl’, *al-Majalla al-Tārīkhiyya al-Miṣriyya*, vol. 19 (1972), p. 28.
8. Dr Muḥammad Anīs, ‘Shafīq Ghurbāl’, *al-Majalla*, no. 58 (Nov. 1961), pp. 12–17.
9. A personal communication from Professor Aḥmad ‘Abd al-Raḥīm Muṣṭafā, 2 May 1983.
10. ‘Izzat ‘Abd al-Karīm *op. cit.*, p. 30.
11. Shafīq Ghurbāl, ‘Makān al-thawra al-miṣriyya’, *al-Hilāl*, vol. LXII (July 1953), p. 33.
12. *Ibid.*, pp. 33–5.
13. It seems what Ghurbāl had in mind was not English historiography in general, but rather the views of historians such as Herbert Butterfield in *The Whig Interpretation of History* (London, 1931).
14. Shafīq Ghurbāl, ‘Aḥkām al-mū'arrikhīn ‘alā al-rijāl’, *al-Hilāl*, vol. LXIII (April, 1955), pp. 40–3.
15. Shafīq Ghurbāl, *Tārīkh al-mufāwaḍāt al-miṣriyya-al-briṭāniyya*, vol. I (Cairo, 1952), pp. i–ii.
16. Shafīq Ghurbāl, ‘Ḥurūb Miṣr fī Filasṭīn’, *al-Kitāb*, vol. VI (June 1948), pp. 189–94. The Caliph ‘Umar had the honorific title *al-Fārūq* — he who distinguishes truth from falsehood.
17. Shafīq Ghurbāl, ‘Markaz Miṣr al-Sīyāsī’, *al-Kitāb*, vol. X (Jan. 1951), pp. 22–3.
18. *The Beginnings of the Egyptian Question* (London, 1928). Hereafter *BEQ*.

19. *Ibid.*, p. xiii.
20. *Ibid.*, pp. ix–x.
21. *Ibid.*, p. xiii.
22. *Ibid.*, p. 284.
23. On the significance of the Mongol defeat in Palestine see the interesting article by J.J. Saunders, 'Islam and the Mongols: the battle of Goliath's spring', *History Today*, vol. XI, no. 12 (Dec. 1961), pp. 843–51.
24. The recruitment of the Mamlūks encompassed a much wider area than Georgia.
25. Given the fact that the sultanate was not established on a clear hereditary basis, some Mamlūk sultans did reign for quite long periods, such as Baybars (1260–77), al-Nāṣir Muḥammad (1310–41), and Barsbay (1422–38).
26. I.e. homosexuality.
27. *BEQ*, pp. 1–2. Napoleon Bonaparte, who invaded Egypt in 1798 under the pretext of defending Islam against the 'injustice and greed' of the Mamlūks, was fully aware of the peculiar characteristics of the 'slavery' institution in Islam. He clearly saw that 'slavery neither is, nor ever was, in the East what it was in Europe'. Two eighteenth-century Mamlūk chiefs 'Murad-Bey and Aly-Bey had been sold to some of the Beys at a tender age, by merchants who had purchased them in Circassia. They at first performed the meanest offices in their masters' household. But their personal beauty, their dexterity in bodily exercises, their bravery or intelligence, progressively raised them to the principal situations. It is the same with pachas, viziers, and sultans. Their slaves are promoted in the same manner as their sons.' Somerset Declair (ed.), *Napoleon's Memoirs* (London, 1946), p. 318.
28. *BEQ*, pp. 2–6.
29. *Ibid.*, pp. 47–8.
30. It is not clear to which of al-Jabartī's chronicles Ghurbāl was referring. The only chronicle used by him, '*Ajā'ib al-āthār* . . ., is silent on both the style and contents of Bonaparte's proclamation. However, al-Jabartī's first chronicle, *Tārīkh muddat al-Faransīs bi-Miṣr*, edited and translated by S. Moreh (Leiden, 1975), pp. 2b–3b, does criticize the spirit and letter of the Proclamation.
31. *BEQ*, p. 50.
32. *Ibid.*, p. 51.
33. However, when the French convened the first *divan* and asked the '*ulamā*' to appoint a new chief of police and a market superintendent, they immediately chose Mamlūk officials. 'This after a long argument in which the French said no one of Mamlūk stock could hold a position. The Shaykhs replied that the people of Cairo feared only the Mamlūk race', al-Jabartī, *Tārīkh muddat al-Faransīs bi-Miṣr*, p. 8b.
34. *BEQ*, p. 73.
35. *Ibid.*, pp. 74–5.
36. The revolt is recorded in chilling detail by al-Jabartī, '*Ajā'ib al-āthār*, vol. II (Beirut, n.d.), pp. 322–42.
37. *BEQ*, pp. 103–18.
38. However, al-Jabartī, '*Ajā'ib al-āthār*, pp. 390–1, had no

hesitation in doubting the sincerity of Menou's conversion.

39. But this was what Napoleon had already conceived and delivered.

40. *BEQ*, pp. 120–2.

41. *Ibid.*, pp. 122–5.

42. 'Abdul Raḥīm 'Abdul Raḥmān and Nagata, Yuzo, 'The iltizām system in Egypt and Turkey', *Journal of Asian and African Studies*, no. 14 (Tokyo, 1977), pp. 170–6. Cf. Claude Cahen, 'Féodalité', *JESHO*, vol. III (1960), pp. 15–16.

43. *BEQ*, pp. 125–6.

44. *Ibid.*, pp. 137–8.

45. Al-Jabartī, '*Ajā'ib al-āthār*, vol. II, p. 426. Murād died in April 1801.

46. *BEQ*, p. 159.

47. *Ibid.*, pp. 158–62.

48. *Ibid.*, p. 163.

49. *Ibid.*, p. 164.

50. G. Douin and E.C. Fawtier-Jones (eds), *L'Angleterre et l'Égypte: la politique Mamaluke*, vol. I (Cairo, 1929), pp. 30–3. It was perhaps such statements by Ghurbāl which led Toynbee to hail him 'so thoroughly detached' and objective. However, apart from not being objective, Ghurbāl was echoing his belief in the fairness of western civilization and its representatives in contrast to the savagery and duplicity of the Mamlūks and Ottomans. To him, both France and Britain were responding to the beckoning gestures of an unhappy mistress. Their failure owed a great deal to a breakdown of communications. Destruction by inundation could not therefore be accommodated within this process of courtship.

51. *BEQ*, pp. 155 and 165–7; G. Douin and E.C. Fawtier-Jones, *L'Angleterre et l'Égypte*, pp. 50–4.

52. *Ibid.*, p. 165.

53. According to J.C.B. Richmond, *Egypt 1798–1952* (London, 1977), p. 138, 'The Dufferin report clearly illustrates the falsity of the position which made British rule over Egypt the least admirable of our imperial undertakings. Having just destroyed a genuine, if embryonic, Egyptian nationalist and constitutionalist movement, the British proposed to establish constitutional institutions which were given no effective power to control the Khedive's autocracy'.

54. *BEQ*, pp. 165–6.

55. *Ibid.*, p. 125.

56. *Ibid.*, pp. 167–8.

57. *Ibid.*, pp. 168–71. This was Muḥammad al-Alfī.

58. *Ibid.*, pp. 171–83.

59. *Ibid.*, p. 211.

60. *Ibid.*, pp. 207–9.

61. Ghurbāl's method of propagating history reminds one of the education that Plato thought would be most suitable for a healthy upbringing of his imaginary guardians. This education would include true and fictitious stories since 'we don't know the truth about the past but we can invent a fiction as like it as may be'. See Plato, *The Republic*, trans. and intro. by Desmond Lee, 2nd edn (Harmondsworth, Penguin,

1974), pp. 377a and 382d.

62. This is what Ilyās al-Ayyūbī, in *Tārīkh Miṣr fī 'ahd Ismā'īl*, vol. I (Cairo, 1923) pp. 331–34, thought Khedive Ismā'īl (1863–79) had accomplished by founding a school of Egyptology.

63. *BEQ*, pp. 209–10.

64. *Ibid.*, pp. 210–11. Cf. Ghurbāl's portrait of Menou, p. 119, 'He was fat and bald, had the face of a *bon viveur*, and was uneasy on horseback.' One of the sources which Ghurbāl culled for his hero's description was Ali Bey, *Travels*, vol. II (London, 1816), p. 13. Ali Bey (pseud) Domingo Badia y Leblich, who was in Cairo in 1806, tells us that, after receiving and returning the visits of the leading '*ulamā*', he

> paid one to Mehemed Ali, accompanied by Seid Omar ('Umar Makram) ... and he received me with every sort of politeness. This prince, who is very brave, is still young; he is thin, and is marked with the small pox; he has quick lively eyes, and a certain air of defiance. Although he is possessed of good sense and wit, he wants education, and is frequently embarrassed; it is then that Seid Omar, who has a remarkable influence over him, renders great services to the Pacha and the people.

65. Al-Jabartī, '*Ajā'ib al-āthār*, vol. II, pp. 570–1; *BEQ*, p.211.

66. *BEQ*, p. 211. The 'coalition' lasted for almost ten months (May 1803–March 1804).

67. Ghurbāl seems to imply that great men do not concern themselves with mundane matters, such as arrears of payment or shortages of provisions, particularly during the period which immediately precedes their rise to power. At that stage they are either in a trance, or they temporarily withdraw from the world.

68. *BEQ*, pp. 212–13.

69. Toynbee explains this movement as follows: 'The disengagement and withdrawal make it possible for the personality to realize individual potentialities which might have remained in abeyance if the individual ... had not been released for a moment from his social toils and trammels.' He goes on to say: 'The return is the essence of the whole movement, as well as its final cause.' *A Study of History*, vol. III (Oxford University Press, 1962), p. 248. (First published 1934.)

70. Ghurbāl's negative evaluation of Misset sprang from the latter's espousal of the Mamlūk cause and his constant intrigues against Muḥammad 'Alī. In assessing the second British invasion of Egypt in 1807, which ended in fiasco, Ghurbāl blames Misset for the whole enterprise and delivers this gloating remark: 'This was Misset's last effort. He had to leave the country and retire to Italy. The Mamelukes as a political body, he had discovered, were now extinct. When he came back in 1811 on a second spell of office, it was his fate to see them literally extinct and himself a helpless cripple.' *BEQ*, p. 261. For other remarks see pp. 212, 216, 225–6, 248, and 260.

71. Al-Jabartī, '*Ajā'ib al-āthār*, vol. II, pp. 561–97.

72. *Ibid.*, pp. 609–39; *BEQ*, pp. 221–2.

73. *BEQ*, p. 210, n.1. To what extent was Ghurbāl scientific in

demanding the creation of this connection, particularly when he goes on to say, 'real or fictitious did not matter'?

74. William Hamilton, British antiquarian and the Secretary of Lord Elgin. He was sent by the latter to Egypt in 1801 to gather 'first-hand information'.

75. *BEQ*, p. 183.

76. William Hamilton, *Ægyptiaca* (London, 1809), pp. 252–3.

77. *Ibid.*, p. 22.

78. For the full text of the letter see G. Douin and E.C. Fawtier-Jones, *L'Angleterre et l'Égypte*, vol. I, pp. 329–31.

79. 10 October 1803.

80. October 1803, p. 972.

81. *BEQ*, p. 216, n. 10.

82. See, for example, *The Morning Herald*, 12 October 1803.

83. It goes on to say: 'He is a great epicure, and drinks two bottles of Champagne or Burgundy after dinner ... He appears to be fascinated with the customs of this country. Of the English ladies he speaks in terms of the most enthusiastic admiration'. Moreover, his 'enthusiastic admiration' was not one-sided. On 27 October, 1803, *The Morning Post* reported the following, 'Elphy Bey is already a great favourite with the Ladies. Indeed, *bey* is such a pretty mincing half-word, so proper for the blushing lips of a young bride'. Cf. Georges Douin, 'L'ambassade d'Elfi Bey à Londres (Octobre–Décembre 1803)', *Bulletin de l'Institut d'Egypte*, vol. VIII, (Cairo, 1925), pp. 95–120.

84. Georges Douin (ed.) *L'Angleterre et l'Égypte*, vol. II (Cairo, 1930), p. 37. Hawkesbury to Drummond, 18 October 1803.

85. *Ibid.*, pp. 36–7.

86. *BEQ*, p. 219.

87. This was an apparent exaggeration since the Mamlūks had failed in their repeated efforts to capture the city.

88. Douin (ed.) *L'Angleterre et l'Égypte*, vol. II, p. 71.

89. *BEQ*, p. 220.

90. *Ibid.*

91. *Ibid.*, p. xi–xii.

92. *Ibid.*, pp. 220–1.

93. Although no attempt is being made to set up al-Alfī as a perfect gentleman, or a progressive statesman, redressing the balance helps to explore the feasibility of Muḥammad 'Alī's enterprise, and sheds a new light on the configuration of the various social forces in Egypt on the eve of their subjugation to one political authority, embodied in the person of an Ottoman viceroy.

94. *The Morning Herald*, 12 October 1803.

95. *The Morning Post*, 7 November 1803.

96. For a revealing description of his historical method, see his *'Ajā'ib al-āthār*, vol. III, p. 315, cf. D. Ayalon, 'The historian al-Jabartī and his background', *BSOAS*, vol. XXIII (1960), pp. 231–2.

97. Al-Jabartī, *'Ajā'ib al-āthār*, vol. III, pp. 147–73.

98. André Raymond, *Artisans et commerçants au Caire au XVIIIe Siècle*, vol. I (Damascus, 1973), pp. 1–16.

99. Afaf Marsot, 'Political and economic functions of the 'Ulama in

the 18th Century', *JESHO*, vol. 16 (1973), pp. 130–54.

100. The reorganization of his forces along French lines, his recruitment of Arab tribes, Nubians, and Maghribis indicate that the old Mamlūk option was no longer available on its own. Georges Douin and E.C. Fawtier-Jones, *L'Angleterre et l'Égypte*, vol. I, pp. 336–8.

101. Douin, *L'Angleterre et l'Égypte*, vol. II, p. 185.

102. *Ibid.*, pp. 173–5.

103. *Ibid.*, pp. 175–7.

104. *Ibid.*, Misset to Hobart 16 June 1804.

105. *BEQ*, p. 227.

106. Ghurbāl is here referring to Muḥammad ʻAlī's alliance with ʻUmar Makram, who was the most popular and influential religious leader.

107. *BEQ*, p. 227.

108. Al-Jabartī, *ʻAjā'ib al-āthār*, vol. III, pp. 5 and 27.

109. Douin, *L'Angleterre et l'Égypte*, vol. II, p. 220.

110. These were the Delhis known as the madmen.

111. *Ibid.*, p. 221.

112. *Ibid.*, p. 221–2.

113. Douin, *Mohamed Aly, Pacha du Caire 1805–1807* (Cairo, 1926), pp. 14–15 and 21.

114. *BEQ*, p. 227.

115. Douin, *Mohamed Aly*, p. 33. For the Sicilian revolt, see S. Runciman, *The Sicilian Vespers* (Cambridge University Press, 1958).

116. Al-Jabartī, *ʻAjā'ib al-āthār*, vol. III, pp. 157–8.

117. *Ibid.*, p. 157. The riff-raff were meant to be the Albanians and Delhis.

118. P.M. Holt, *Studies in the History of the Near East* (London, 1973), pp. 184–5.

119. Al-Jabartī, *Ajā'ib al-āthār*, vol. III, p. 158.

120. *Ibid.*, vol. I, pp. 620–50.

121. In fact new contingents of the Delhis continued pouring into Cairo long after Muḥammad ʻAlī was firmly in power. See al-Jabartī, *ʻAjā'ib al-āthār*, vol. III, pp. 275, 304, 328, and 331.

122. *BEQ*, p. 280.

123. *Ibid.*, pp. 281–4.

124. Al-Jabartī, *ʻAjā'ib al-āthār*, vol. III, pp. 371–4, 549–50.

125. *Ibid.*, vol. I, pp. 432–4.

126. Shafīq Ghurbāl, *Muḥammad ʻAlī al-Kabīr* (Cairo, 1944). Hereafter *MAK*.

127. *Ibid.*, pp. 9–60.

128. See Y. Porath, *In Search of Arab Unity 1936–1945* (London, 1986), pp. 158–9, 258, and 270.

129. For different evaluations of this intellectual development see Nadav Safran, *Egypt in Search of Political Community* (Cambridge, Mass., 1961), pp. 125 ff; Charles D. Smith, 'The "crisis of Orientation": the shift of Egyptian intellectuals to Islamic subjects in the 1930's', *IJMES*, vol. 4 (1973), 382–410.

130. *MAK*, p. 62.

131. *Ibid.*, p. 63.

132. *Ibid.*, p. 157.

133. *Ibid.*, pp. 73–82.

134. Ghurbāl returned to his theme in two lectures which he delivered in French in February 1951. See, Shafik Ghorbal Bey, 'La contribution de Mohamed Ali à la solution de certains problèmes méditerranéens de son époque', *Annales du Centre Universitaire Méditerranéen*, vol. IV (Nice, 1950–51), pp. 9–28.

135. Shafīq Ghurbāl, *Takwīn Miṣr* (Cairo, 1957). The broadcasts were first delivered in English and later translated into Arabic by the author and his colleague, the Egyptian historian Muḥammad Rif'at.

136. *Ibid.*, pp. 1–20.

137. *Ibid.*, pp. 90–3.

138. Shafīq Ghurbāl, *Minhāj mufaṣṣal li-dars al-'awāmil al-'asāsiyya fī binā' al-umma al-'arabiyya* (Cairo, 1961).

139. Such as the creation of a central authority based on the rule of the law, the establishment of permanent institutions, and the western concept of citizenship.

140. Ghurbāl, *Minhāj* pp. 69–90.

141. *Ibid.*, pp. 91–3.

142. *Ibid.*, pp. 130–51.

5

Kamal Salibi and the History of Lebanon: the Making of a Nation?

On 1 September 1920 the French High Commissioner in Syria and Cilicia (better known to the Arabs as the province of Iskenderun, and which constituted the north-western district of French-Mandated Syria), General Henri Gouraud, held a ceremony in Beirut to proclaim the creation of Greater Lebanon. Among the invited guests was an American diplomat, Paul Knabenshue. In a dispatch to his Secretary of State he described this historic event and made the following observations:

> The ceremony was held at 5.30 pm, at the Park[1] in Beirut, in the presence of the Consular Corps, high government officials, the Maronite Patriarch and other ecclesiastics, Syrian notables,[2] and a crowd of people numbering many thousands.... The Greater Lebanon, as constituted by the proclamation of General Gouraud, extends from Nahr-el-Kébir in the North to the boundary of Palestine in the South and to the summits of the Anti-Lebanon in the East. Thus the Lebanon is enlarged by the addition of the cities of Beirut, Tripoli, Sidon, Tyre, Jebel Aamel, Hasbayah, Rashaya and Baalbeck, and the rich Plains of The Bikaah.[3]

The General was not simply engaged in a purely technical exercise. He was re-creating the past, fusing history with geography, and relaunching a time-honoured cultural and commercial enterprise.

> At the foot of these majestic mountains which have been the strength of your country and remain the impregnable

> stronghold of its faith and freedom, on the shore of this sea of many legends that has seen the triremes of Phoenicia, Greece and Rome and now, by a happy fate, brings you the confirmation of a great and ancient friendship and the blessings of French peace …, I solemnly salute Greater Lebanon in its glory and prosperity in the name of the Government of the French Republic.[4]

The High Commissioner was, throughout the delivery of his emotive speech, flanked by the Maronite Patriarch, Ilyās Ḥūwayyik, and the Sunni mufti of Beirut, Muṣṭafā Najā. The first stood at his right side listening intently and approvingly, while the other, a little further to the left, gazed silently into the unknown.[5] Gouraud's message was clear, articulate, and exclusive. His flattering reference to the impregnability of Mount Lebanon, his invocation of the glories of ancient empires, and his emphasis on France's manifest destiny, constituted material and cultural symbols which animated the spiritual and temporal domain of the Maronite Patriarch. The latter was indeed witnessing the concrete realization of official assurances pledged to him by the French government. Almost one year earlier he had been in Paris at the head of a Lebanese delegation, appealing to the Delegates of the Peace Conference to restore Lebanon to its 'historical and natural boundaries' and place it under a French mandate. One month later, on 10 November 1919, Georges Clemenceau, the French Prime Minister, wrote to the Patriarch promising the full support of France.[6]

However, the 'Syrian notables' of the American diplomat, both Muslim and Christian, found themselves in an anomalous and ominous situation. Many of their co-religionists had extended an ecstatic welcome to another liberator, Prince Fayṣal, the son of al-Sharīf Ḥusayn of Mecca. When he visited Tripoli and Beirut in November 1918 jubilant Muslim youths hailed him as their new sultan.[7] He counted amongst his supporters numerous Christians, including some Maronites. They rallied to his cause as an Arab leader who made no distinction between Muslims, Christians, or Jews. Even a Maronite priest from Mount Lebanon, Père Ḥabīb Isṭifān, travelled to Damascus and, in an eloquent speech on Arab unity and national independence, delighted and bewildered his Muslim audience.[8] A stream of committees, organizations and various representative societies made the pilgrimage to

Damascus, and were among the members of the General Syrian Congress which declared Syria a United Kingdom under its first constitutional monarch, 'His Majesty King Faisal I'.[9]

Thus people who had never thought of themselves as Lebanese, or announced their allegiance to a wider national entity, were suddenly told to shed and renounce whatever identity they had adopted, and embrace a new one. Gouraud's phraseology would have left them either unmoved or utterly outraged. The deliberate choice of words, designed to blot out thirteen centuries of their Arab and Islamic heritage, indicated the subsidiary role assigned to them in the new state. It was a state to be run by the French in association with one particular sect and those prepared to accept the French Mandate.

Over the next two decades, Lebanon was to embark on a new phase of its history, fraught with mutual suspicions, ingrained doubts, and perpetual conflict. The partisans of a purely Lebanese entity confronted and clashed with the upholders of Syrian unity. By the middle of the 1930s the initial disagreements had crystallized into two diametrically opposed poles. The history writings of this period faithfully reflect the tensions and contradictions inherent in the structures of the new polity. Two histories, which were textbooks intended for primary schools, exhibit wide divergences on almost every event or historical development connected with the past of Lebanon. The first was written by two Sunni teachers who taught Arabic literature and history, respectively, at the Islamic College al-Maqāṣid. The other text was co-authored by al-Bustānī, a Maronite professor of Arabic literature at the Jesuit St Joseph University, and Asad Rustum, a Greek Orthodox professor of Near Eastern history at the American University of Beirut. Asad Rustum, however, repudiated the contents of this text and claimed that he collaborated in its composition with al-Bustānī as a result of political and financial pressures exerted by the pro-French President of the Republic, Emile Eddé. He also stated that the specific chapters he had to draft were later altered while being printed at the Catholic Press in Beirut.[10] Al-Bustānī depicts Lebanon as a multilingual society, an impregnable fortress, and a refuge for all Near Eastern religious and racial minorities. He boasts of the Maronites' alliance with the Crusaders, blames the Ottomans for instigating its civil wars, castigates the Maronite peasants for revolting in 1858–59 against their equally Maronite feudal lords, praises France for safeguarding Lebanon's independence, and, finally, singles out the Maronite Patriarch's endeavours for special mention, quoting Gouraud's proclamation as a conclusive vindication.

Farrūkh and Naqqāsh, on the other hand, treat Lebanon as an integral part of the Syrian nation. They fail to see any peculiar characteristics in its history, and which might serve as a justification for its separation from the mother country. Their narrative highlights the political, commercial, and economic motives behind the Crusades, exonerates the Ottomans of direct responsibility for Lebanon's sectarian strife, and discovers the enlightened aspects of the peasants' uprising. They hold Europe responsible for dividing Syria into various states, and remind the Allies of their unkept promises to the Arabs.

In 1929, barely a few years after the declaration of Greater Lebanon, Kamal Salibi, the future historian of its national identity, was born in Bḥamdūn, a resort town overlooking the coast of Beirut. He was brought up as a Protestant, his grandparents having adopted Presbyterianism during the nineteenth century. His branch of the family produced a number of educationists, with a keen interest in establishing local schools and raising funds in Britain for their upkeep.[11] After receiving his primary and secondary education in a local school, he entered the American University of Beirut (AUB), graduating with a degree in history and political studies. Lebanon in the meantime had become independent and a full member of both the Arab League and the United Nations. In 1953 he was awarded a doctorate degree by the University of London for his thesis 'Studies on the Traditional Historiography of the Maronites on [sic] the Period 1100–1516'.[12] Bernard Lewis, who was his supervisor, is credited by Salibi for suggesting the topic of his dissertation. Ten years later, after his appointment as Associate Professor at the American University, he was asked by Bernard Lewis to write a history of Lebanon for a London publisher.

Salibi was probably the first historian to join the History Department of AUB, whose main academic and political pursuits were strictly Lebanese. This institute of higher education, despite its foreign-sounding name which it adopted after 1920, continued to exercise a crucial local influence in its own way. In 1919, its President, Daniel Bliss, had actually championed the cause of Syrian unity in his capacity as adviser of President Woodrow Wilson.[13] One of its former students, the medical doctor 'Abd al-Raḥmān Shahbandar, was a prominent leader of the 1925–27 Syrian revolt against the French Mandate. In 1932, it was mainly from its students that Anṭūn Sa'ādah recruited the members of his clandestine organization, the Syrian Nationalist Party.[14] Other organizations, with Arab nationalist ideologies, flourished on its campus throughout the 1940s and 1950s.

During the same period its history department became a focal point for all those historians, of Arab origin, who believed in either Syrian or Arab unity. The Maronite Philip Hitti produced a series of historical studies on Syria, the Arabs, the Near East, and Islamic civilization, long before he published his *Lebanon in History* in 1957. Asad Rustum started his career as a historian of Syria, particularly under the rule of Ibrāhīm Pasha in the 1830s. He was the first historian in the Arab World to publish in Arabic a manual dealing with various aspects of the western historical method of research.[15] Other historians, such as Constantine Zurayq, Nabīh Amīn Fāris, and Nicola Ziadah, were more inclined towards Arabism, and edited and composed various histories of the Arab World.

A NEW HISTORY

It is against this background that Salibi launched his career, anxious to advance a new interpretation of his nation-state. His history of modern Lebanon is presented as a pioneering study 'based on original sources: traditional histories, family histories, memoirs, books of travel, documentary material, and contemporary accounts of events'. He seems to imply that his was the first history to propound a coherent and meaningful analysis of Lebanon's development as a polity and a distinct society. Thus Philip Hitti's *Lebanon in History* is considered to be no more than a general survey 'from pre-historic to modern times'. Its main defects are its rapidity, and the way it concerns itself 'more with the general regional history in which Lebanon was involved than the intimate history of the country'.[16] In an earlier review of Hitti's book, Salibi blames the author for neglecting the history of his own country until well into the last days of his writing career. Hitti is also reminded how he had concentrated, or probably dissipated, most of his scholarly labour on the history of Syria and the Arabs. However, the incubation period was fruitful and somewhat promising. It is at least reassuring to observe that he does not treat Lebanon 'as part of Syria or a mere member of the Arab community, but as a fatherland with a distinctive historical character'. Be that as it may, Hitti's history still falls short of Salibi's strict requirements. Its main theme is confined to narrating what happened in Lebanon rather than 'the historical development' of the events. Hence, another title is suggested for the book: *History in Lebanon.* This curious proposition is postulated as an inevitable conclusion resulting from Hitti's failure to present a meaningful and connected story of Lebanon's history. One gains the impression, Salibi maintains, that Lebanon is like 'an empty vessel', whereby the link between the history of ancient Phoenicia and that of the modern Republic is not clearly delineated,[17] nor is the development of the Emirate during the Mamlūk period shown to be the nucleus out of which Greater Lebanon was a natural extension. Hitti, however, is excused for his shortcomings, on account of the scattered sources of Lebanon's history and the difficulty of collecting and sifting all the available materials. As a final gesture of condescension, he is thanked for his 'scholarly contribution' which constitutes 'the first testimony given by a remarkable scholar on the historical identity of Lebanon and its continuity' throughout the ages down to the present time.[18]

Salibi as a result approaches the writing of Lebanon's history with a serious outlook and a reverent posture. Any historian, particularly of Lebanese origin, who undertakes this enormous task, must adhere to certain principles and come up with a meaningful story. Despite the numerous obstacles, the scarcity of primary sources, and the gaps in the historical record, one ought to exert all humanly possible efforts and salvage Lebanon's national identity from the debris of the past. His is not only the Lebanon that is, or was, but also the one that ought to be. That he is fascinated with Lebanon and its history goes without saying. However, this fascination is tempered with a somewhat strict historical method and a desire to accommodate the interests and views of various religious sects which make up the Lebanese mosaic.

He looks at the writing of history as two separate stages. First, the historian collects his data and establishes the facts; only then is he to proceed to the second phase and begin his interpretation and analysis. The initial step is a totally objective operation, executed with the precision of a purely scientific method. Its parameters encompass a natural ability derived from long training and an intimate knowledge of the subject under scrutiny. Once this is accomplished, the historian is given free reign to offer his personal opinion and exhibit his mastery of the sources. If two historians disagree in their respective explanations, each is entitled to his own opinion provided they both use and rely on the same facts. Furthermore, a historian has to keep an open mind, so that when new facts are brought to light, he has to show the willingness to alter his conclusions and acknowledge any mistaken deductions.[19]

This method, which may seem slightly arbitrary, is posited as a *sine qua non* for all historians. Nevertheless, nowhere is the nature of the presumed facts explained or the range of their operation defined. One would have liked to know how in practice such a separation between the two stages exists. How does one go about finding facts, always remembering to keep this dichotomy in mind? Is the historian's mind supposed to be a *tabula rasa* on which are impressed raw or undiluted facts, and by means of some mechanical device or unseen hand? In what precise manner can the detached historian differentiate between factual and normative statements?

These questions become more pertinent as the motives behind Salibi's fact-finding mission are revealed. What did make our historian decide to study Lebanon's history and extricate out of its labyrinth a truly wholesome work of art? Were the facts he unearthed so overwhelming in their relevance that he had no choice but to register their significance, and analyse their relentless march towards a national consummation? The answer is simple: 'the possession of historical truth by both the élite and common people is in the final analysis the best foundation on which a sound society is built'. Moreover, no one has so far managed to offer a satisfactory account of what really happened, and it is incumbent on a good Lebanese citizen to remedy such an anomaly. Lebanon's historical development has been subjected to blatant distortions and submerged in strident theories. The ordinary Lebanese deserves to be told the truth, as he himself is basically capable of distinguishing between what is true and what is false. Consequently, the objective historian has a powerful ally in 'the good and innate nature' of the common man. Lebanon's history has so far been presented in the form of myths. These myths 'divide the Lebanese' and set them against each other. The indulgence in creating legends about the past is perhaps 'one of the most important causes which still fragments and tears asunder Lebanese society'. These views were aired after the eruption of the 1975 civil war in Lebanon. Salibi is clearly shocked and frustrated. He turns his anger against all the mythmakers who persist in their destructive activities. 'Stating the simple historical truth, with all the frankness that goes with it, while fully recognizing the limits of correct judgements, may turn out to be the best remedy for the damage which so far has resulted ... from distorting history.'[20] Sooner or later the combatants have to lay down their arms and heed the voice of reason, embodied in the historian with a true story to relate.

The image of Lebanon as depicted by its historians can be reduced to two broad myths or political formulas. There is, on the one hand, the Maronite idea of Lebanon as a *sui generis* national entity deeply rooted in its Phoenician past, and a cultural experience which transcends its Arab or Islamic surroundings. This formula assumes a variety of theoretical and historical constructions, depending on the background of a particular historian, his general education and social position. The Muslims of Lebanon, on the other hand, look at Lebanon as part of a larger whole, be it the Arab nation or geographical Syria.

Salibi believed that both images, or myths, had failed to create a healthy national idea and engender the requisite consensus for building a stable society. After the declaration of Greater Lebanon, one Lebanese Roman Catholic banker and writer, Michel Chiha (Shīḥā), whose Assyrian family originally hailed from Iraq, advanced a theory for the new Lebanon modelled on its ancient history. He thought that it had 'a character all its own, recognizable in all the stages of its history'. The Lebanese as a Mediterranean people were destined to resume and perform the role of their ancestors and compatriots, the commercially minded Phoenicians. The function of the modern Lebanese was to maintain and refine that of Phoenicia, both as a trading nation and a cultural intermediary between the west and the east. However, 'the Phoenicianist idea' appealed to limited social groups, namely, 'the predominantly Christian middle class' and 'the Lebanese emigrants', the overwhelming majority of whom were Christian, and particularly Maronite. Another formula, hatched under the benign wing of the French Mandate, was that of the Jesuit missionary and orientalist, Henri Lammens. He made Lebanon into a refuge for religious minorities as well as a haven and a fortress warding off the onslaughts of oppressive, especially Muslim, oriental despots. Foreign occupation was legitimized as an inevitable consequence for the sake of all those who had fled from the interior of Syria and the Ottoman Empire into 'l'asile du Liban'. Salibi sees in this myth lineaments capable of attracting a wider audience. It certainly finds positive echoes in the midst of 'the Shi'ites and Druzes who were historically acquainted with persecution'. The Maronite community, as the embodiment of all suffering minorities, would also embrace the formula and welcome its ingenuity.[21]

Nevertheless, both images were rejected and considered unacceptable to the Sunnites. Chiha's formula was 'seen as part of a French imperialist conspiracy against Arab nationalism'. Sunni scholars reiterated the Canaanite semitic origins of the Phoenicians, who joined other migratory waves from the Arabian Peninsula in the Fertile Crescent. Hence they were Arab in descent and culture. Lammens's theory was also dismissed as it explicitly assigns to the Sunnites the unedifying honour of being the real culprits and persecutors.

The thesis of the Maronites and their theorists has clearly encountered fierce opposition. It gave rise to an antithesis no less vehement in its opposite ingredients. What is the historian to do? Can he reconcile two conflicting views while keeping his objectivity and academic reputation intact?

No one can dispute, Salibi explains, that 'Lebanon was undoubtedly Arabic in speech and traditional culture. Its history in Islamic times, until certainly the seventeenth century, could be clearly separated from the history of Syria (if not from Arab and Islamic history in general) only by lame artifice.' But no matter how essential 'this historical and cultural connection between Lebanon and Arabism' is, the latter smacks of a distinct 'Islamic flavour'. This dilution precludes its adoption by the Maronites and other Christian minorities. The Arab nationalist formula is, moreover, dangerous and sinister. When its adherents try to apply its tenets and work out its connotations, they immediately infringe the sovereignty of Lebanon and threaten its existence as 'a separate entity'. This was demonstrated in 1958 in the wake of the union between Egypt and Syria: 'Lebanon was thrown into a crisis verging on civil war as its Arab nationalists clamoured for the country to join the union'.[22] The Muslims have shown at regular intervals an alarming attitude which violates the sovereignty of the state and raises strong doubts over their loyalty to the state. What is the verdict of the historian so far? The Christian myth is 'intellectually untenable', and the Muslim formula brands its supporters willy-nilly with high treason.[23] Impartiality does not mean flinching from passing a severe judgement on the guiltier party. However, the fact remains that, *mutatis mutandis*, both camps are antagonistically opposed, and no good citizen can accept such alarming difficulties.

Fortunately these myths reflect and express the vested interests of contending groups whose real purpose is not difficult to identify. The impartial historian is in an ideal position to expose the subterfuges and their perpetrators.[24] A synthesis is then called for. A true Hegelian process, or a dialectical progression, through which the ultimate absolute idea is finally grasped and assimilated.[25]

A new political formula is needed which accounts for all the local, regional, and external factors that led to the creation of Lebanon in its present boundaries. Where does the story begin? How was it that Lebanon became a sovereign state? The only approach is to find out how minor or major events, certain specific features and their conjunction, had the potentiality of coming into being and developing over time. Some of these factors may go back to the times of the Crusades, others to the period of the Arab conquest. Then, starting with the seventeenth century, a cluster of developments finally detached Lebanon from Syria and launched it on a course of its own. Lebanon was not created at the dawn of history, as the Maronites contend, nor has it kept its unaltered character ever since. Nor was it, as the Muslims insist, a mere artificiality, willed by some European power. Its modern structure and identity have to be understood historically. One has to discover what intrinsic forces made its separate existence possible, and at what particular juncture the latent characteristics merged into the mainstream of European culture and nationhood. How and when did one particular Lebanese group or community succeed in proclaiming itself the embodiment of a defined recognizable national polity? The Lebanese historians, Sunnite and Maronite, have not yet managed to view their past in this multilayered perspective. Once again, there are extenuating circumstances which lessen the deficiencies of Christian historiography. The Maronites have at least endeavoured to prove that 'ce pays, tel qu'il existe aujourd'hui, est le résultat d'un processus historique profondément enraciné dans le passé, plutôt que celui des décisions fantaisistes de la Conférence de la Paix de 1919, ainsi que le suggère la théorie nationaliste arabe'.[26]

IN THE BEGINNING …

Salibi tirelessly carried the torch for the Maronites, at least in the first phase of his career. His dilemma was to convince them of his version of their past, and turn their myths into a historical structure with a solid base in reality. He conceded that Lebanon was different — more than a mere Arab country. His first writings on the subject reveal a purely Christian approach to the Lebanese past and present. Although he handles his sources with a critical mind and meticulous attention to details and dates, his premises do not in essence deviate from the imagery and broad outlines of the Maronites. He even indulges in the art of glorifying the same characteristics which constitute the bewildering welter of the Maronites' image of themselves and their mountain.

The idea of Lebanon as a haven, a crossroad, a frontier region, a school, a backwater, and a resort is described in great detail and anchored in historical illustrations and geographic settings. The crossroads results from the position of the country as 'a geographical highway', linking 'the Near East to Europe by way of the Mediterranean'. The end product is a merchant republic. It is an oasis of liberal policies and traditions. This liberalism stretches back into the late sixteenth century, at least in its economic principles. Salibi is not blind to the defects of his merchant republic. He acknowledges the existence of malpractices or 'irregularities and a certain lack of scruples'. Nevertheless, all things considered, the advantages stand out in their wider implications. They have a direct bearing on the essence of the *Volkgeist.* The business spirit engenders qualities of a superior nature which are instantly recognizable, and serve to set Lebanon apart from its Arab surroundings. The Lebanese merchant is endowed with a feeling of mild patriotism which is a far cry from 'nationalist fanaticism', the trademark of neighbouring Arab countries. Pragmatism, realism, the graceful acceptance of the inevitable — these are some of the qualities which infuse the merchant republic with an amazing degree of stability.

The liberal multilingual republic has also been a refuge, a fact which makes the Lebanese proud of their history. However, this pride is imbued with 'a traditional politeness' which one persecuted community exhibits towards the other. Moreover, a rare phenomenon grows out of these graceful attitudes and acts 'as a social cement' which welds the heterogeneous inhabitants facing outside aggression and dangers. Maronites, Druzes, Jacobites, Greek Orthodox, Shi'ites, Armenians and Assyrians, and many others, 'infiltrated or immigrated into Lebanon from other countries to escape some form of intolerance: tyranny, persecution, discrimination, or pressure'.

As a frontier region Lebanon has developed into a cultural centre for Europe and the Middle East and a political arena, reflecting and condensing the conflicting interests of regional and world powers. Admittedly tensions are bound to appear. But the resultant divisions between the communities are always short-lived and occur infrequently. In this sense no permanent damage is caused. Viewed positively, these tensions are almost a blessing in disguise. One cannot fail to appreciate the opportunities offered to a country occupying the point of contact and interaction of outside forces. The country becomes 'a school and a forum for the exchange of ideas'. While as a backwater Lebanon can intentionally avoid the limelight, it is an aspect resting on a deliberate decision and calculated either to escape the revenge of greedy neighbours or to protect economic prosperity. Finally, as a resort, which is the only modern aspect, the Lebanese encourage tourism and know how to derive full pleasure from the beauty and facilities of their country.

To a superficial observer, Salibi points out, these various aspects may seem contradictory and discordant. However, the historian's discerning eye sees things differently. These aspects not only complement and reinforce each other but they also 'blend in unexpected harmony'. In other words, they form a rhythmic succession of single tones organized as an organic and aesthetic whole, or simply, a harmonious melody. It is, moreover, a melody handed down over the centuries from one generation to another: composition sheets, instruments, singers, and all the paraphernalia of a national identity which 'clearly keeps its roots'.[27]

So far the Sunnis are still absent. The Maronites occupy the centre stage. All these aspects, blending, interacting, or merely coexisting, describe one unique characteristic which lends the

Maronite polemic literature its unity of means and ends. This partial image is hardly found in other non-Maronite literary, religious, and historical writings, with the possible exception of some Catholic theoreticians. One looks in vain in the literature of the Druzes, the Shi'ites and the Greek Orthodox for such reiterations and exclusive allusions. However, one notable aspect of the Maronite political formula is missing, and gives us a clue to Salibi's reconciliatory synthesis. This is the military or militant dimension in the war cry of a mountainous community.[28]

In the beginning was the Refuge, and the Refuge had another aspect, that was the feudal system. And the hereditary nature of land tenure in the Lebanon of the Middle Ages is a myth tirelessly stressed and retold. Another myth, not unrelated to the first is how a passing contact between a Druze or Muslim notable and the Maronites always yields beneficial results. The Druze notable is miraculously converted from a despotic narrow-minded bigot into an enlightened humanitarian prince.

Salibi embraced, in his first phase of Lebanese nationalism, these conceptual frameworks and added to them an impressive armour of scholarship. Notwithstanding these replenishments, one feels a certain uneasy suspicion about the absence of qualifying adjectives and adverbs, the refusal to suspend judgement or offer a final opinion. We are told

> The Druzes of southern Lebanon developed a distinct political talent. Between the twelfth and the sixteenth centuries their leaders, who served the successive Moslem states and administrations of Damascus, acquired a number of distinguishing privileges. While the Mamluk military–feudal system was never hereditary, the Druze feudal families, led by the Buḥturids, succeeded in getting their hereditary hold over their land recognized; and this recognition became official as early as 1314.[29]

A historic event or phenomenon is only a sign. It is a prelude to another, more propitious development. It signifies and points in the direction of a course it is bound to travel. Seen as an isolated, separate incident, with no latent energy for movement and maturation, it becomes dull, lifeless, and insignificant. Hence, the theory of a hereditary feudal structure was later amplified, and the system it denoted was stamped and dispatched whirling down through the centuries. The teleological qualities were no longer in doubt:

> The Maronite feudality, which appeared after the Ottoman conquest and replaced the older Maronite village and district chieftainships, was an offshoot of Druze feudalism, organized in its manner and remaining ancillary to it until the breakdown of the Lebanese feudal regime towards the middle of the nineteenth century.[30]

The pre-Ottoman period witnessed the consolidation of a hereditary nucleus, confined to a small stretch of hills, lying to the south-east of Beirut. Out of this nucleus, and as a result of a long process of mutations and metamorphoses, a definite autonomous Lebanon emerged. 'The Buḥturids were the forerunners of the Ma'nids and ... without them the history of Lebanon under the Ottomans might well have taken an entirely different direction.' For over four centuries, before the rise of the Ma'nid dynasty which coincided with the Ottoman conquest of Syria, the seeds were planted in a unique agricultural experimentation no other Arab country had known or approximated. Other Syrian regions, in particular, were complete strangers to a new world emerging on their doorstep.

> The Buḥturids succeeded in maintaining, in an important region of southern Lebanon, a considerable measure of local rule that made it essentially different from other regions in Syria. By opposing Mamluk attempts at centralization, they preserved in southern Lebanon a hereditary feudal system that was to serve later as the basis of autonomy under the Ottomans.[31]

The main source for Salibi's conclusions was Ṣāliḥ ḅ Yaḥyā's *History of Beirut*,[32] written in the first half of the fifteenth century (*c.* 1437). The chronicler was himself a Buḥturid *amīr*, anxious to defend the interests, reputation, and paramountcy of his family. The documents he produces in his chronicle to show the Buḥturids' entitlement to their *iqṭā'* are of a dubious nature. One of the earliest scholars to use this chronicle and consider the documents it contains as possible forgeries was A.N. Poliak. He also pointed out how the same technical terms used in the charters for confirming or assigning titles to lands underwent considerable change. 'After the Mamluk conquest', Poliak explains, 'the native chieftains tried to claim the lands granted to them by the Crusaders as *mulk* in the Islamic sense of the word, but the government (though tolerating the use of this term in regard to them) regarded them as ordinary feudal lands.'[33]

Salibi's argument, on which Lebanon's distinct development over the centuries is built, revolves round his interpretation and translation of one single sentence in Ṣāliḥ ḅ Yaḥyā's text. The historian's task is rendered more daunting by the fact that this same sentence is written in corrupt and broken Arabic.[34] Any conclusions based on it must, therefore, remain tentative and preliminary. Furthermore, the controversial sentence is not part of an official copy of grant issued by the Mamlūk authorities; it is no more than an argument contained in a pleading letter by the Buḥturid *amīr* Nāṣir al-Dīn al-Ḥusayn (1269–1350), addressed to the governor of Damascus. Thus what we have is the Buḥturid version of the story and not what the Mamlūk officials had to say. Salibi does not attempt a literal translation of the sentence, given its doubtful meaning, but only what he thought it meant: 'and the greater part of their *iqṭā'* was legal private property honoured by the Šarī'a'.[35]

Bearing in mind that the Buḥturids were charged with guarding the harbour of Beirut and thus their *iqṭā'* duties embraced an area larger than their Gharb base, it is more likely that the sentence means the following: most of their freehold properties are situated in the *iqṭā'* for which they do their service.

These properties (*amlāk*, plural of *mulk*) denote in this context small orchards and houses or buildings rather than the whole arable land or the harbour of Beirut (or the city itself for that matter, which was no more than a small town at the time). This interpretation tallies with what H.A.R. Gibb and H. Bowen had to say about the meaning of *mulk* in Ottoman terminology.[36] This assumption is further strengthened when in the same text of the letter these properties are referred to as 'the dwellings' of the Buḥturids (*masākinuhum*).[37]

Consequently, the whole argument of an ever-expanding autonomy, having as its base a hereditary feudal system, rests, to say the least, on meagre evidence and weak logical deductions. What is more intriguing, Salibi himself demolished part of his theory a few years later. We now learn that

> Ordinary Islamic feudalism was based on the non-hereditary *iqṭā'*, the revocable right to the revenue of a village or district, granted by a sovereign to a civil or military officer as part of his pay. Under such a system it was difficult for local feudal aristocracies to develop, for the *iqṭā'* frequently changed hands, and remained throughout under the direct control of the central government. In the Druze mountains, however, as in northern Lebanon, *Transjordan, and othcr rugged parts of Syria,*[38] the *iqṭā'* system did not regularly apply. Even during the Mamlūk period, when Islamic feudalism was not strictly organized and centralized, the Druzes, along with other isolated Syrian communities, maintained their peculiar feudal traditions with the tacit recognition of the Mamlūk government.[39]

The tenor of a considerable chunk of an exclusive *sui generis* feudal system has been reduced to a faint echo. Lebanon is, after all, not different from other parts of Syria, other than in one, highly crucial aspect. In 1979 the hereditary principle of the land tenure was still held to be valid, but it was confined to the Mamlūk period, or at least until the *Ḥalqa* was abolished during the days of the Burji Mamlūks.[40]

AN ENLIGHTENED PRINCE?

Another shift of emphasis, which Salibi's interpretation of Lebanon's national identity underwent, relates to the role of the Ma'nid dynasty in the whole enterprise, and particularly that of its leading Prince, Fakhr al-Dīn II (1585–1635).

The emergence of this *amīr* was first considered as the beginning of a new era, during which Lebanon took a definite step towards acquiring 'a permanent political identity'. His other function was to hold the fort for the Maronites. Under his tolerant and enlightened rule the Maronites entered into an alliance with the Druzes, and the two sects went on collaborating and working side by side until the Maronites abandoned their erstwhile allies and embarked on a course of their own.[41]

The legacy of Fakhr al-Dīn as the founder of modern Lebanon has been claimed by Sunni, Druze, and Maronite historians. His deliberate decision to keep the 'Lebanese ' guessing as to his true religion lends these claims and counter-claims an air of authenticity. However, when he commissioned or requested one of his close aides, al-Shaykh Aḥmad b. Muḥammad al-Khālidī al-Ṣafadī (d. 1625), to write his biography[42] the matter was different. He is presented throughout the chronicle as a loyal Ottoman governor, a Sunni Muslim who builds mosques, endows charities, and ensures the safety of the pilgrims' road from Damascus to Mecca. More importantly, no mention of an autonomous or independent Lebanon is even hinted at. Lebanon itself, as a name designating a certain territory, is nowhere to be found, which makes the title conferred on it by its editors a travesty of accuracy.

The Maronite historians, starting with the nineteenth century, stress the special and intimate relationship which developed between the *amīr* and his Maronite subjects and advisers. The Khāzin family is singled out as the inspiring power behind the tolerant attitude of the *amīr* towards the Christians. His reforming zeal and positive collaboration with the Pope, France, and Tuscany are ascribed to the influence of certain Maronite members of his entourage. Salibi opts for this version. We are told:

> The Khāzins of Kisrwān, perhaps the most powerful Maronite feudal family at the time, did not allow their religion to prejudice their political activities. In earlier times they had been responsible for the upbringing of a Druze emir, Fakhr ad-Dīn of the Ma'ns.[43]

The reader is then informed of how Fakhr al-Dīn responded to the sound advice of his Maronite loyal supporters and turned to Europe as a promising Christian in disguise.[44]

The story that Fakhr al-Dīn was smuggled into Kisrwān by his mother in order to escape the revenge of the Ottomans, who accused his father of having a hand in plundering a tribute caravan, is taken seriously only by Maronite historians.[45]

Salibi does not go as far as Chebli or Ismail in idolizing the *amīr* of the Druze mountain. Instead of eulogizing his hero and thus freezing the development of Lebanese history within watertight compartments, he is always conscious of a historical process which gathers momentum in its constant movement. Fakhr al-Dīn is a stepping-stone towards a distant goal.

The *amīr* did not enunciate the identity in its full completeness; he only acted as its prefiguration. Having discarded his assumptions about the feudal system, the historian resorts to another notion in his scholarly armoury. From being a feudal chieftain, he is transformed into a living personification of 'the Protestant ethic' in its Weberian dimensions.[46] Salibi contrasts the career of Yūsuf Sayfā (1579–1625), the Turkoman chieftain of the 'Akkār region and Pasha of Tripoli, with that of Fakhr al-Dīn in the southern areas of modern Lebanon and the adjoining territories. The first, an Ottomanized *beylerbeyi*, a Sunnite, and a chieftain of the traditional type, represented the epitome of 'a rapacious tax collector'. Being subservient to the Porte, 'he lacked the imagination and energy' to develop Tripoli and make its port a prosperous harbour teeming with the ships of European traders and Frankish adventurers. The Maronites of his *eyalet* mistrusted him, no matter how hard he tried to protect their interests and appease their notables. 'As a local chieftain anxious to promote his regional popularity, he may have treated the Maronites in his *eyalet* with a measure of kindness and clemency; yet they certainly felt at his hands, as a *beylerbeyi*, the full rigour of the Ottoman state.' The loyalty of the Maronites depended on a number of inter-related factors, not the least of which was the relationship with Catholic Europe. The acceptance of European intervention or occupation on the part of a local Muslim governor becomes an index of modernity and prosperity.

> No agent of the Ottomans, Faḫr al-dīn Maʻn was actually an ally of the Sultan's chief enemies in Christian Europe, who were at the same time the sponsors and benefactors of the Maronites in Mount Lebanon. No wonder that Pope Paul V himself, in 1610, wrote to the Maronite Patriarch Yūḥannā Maḫlūf urging Maronite support for the Maʻnid emir.[47]

Upon the adoption of this trustworthy attitude, other concomitant attributes follow in accordance with the iron law of national identity. Fakhr al-Dīn, Salibi tells us, 'was a born adventurer who combined military skill and eminent qualities of leadership with a keen business acumen and unusual powers of observation'. Then, to seal his argument, he quotes the impression of Fakhr al-Dīn formed by the English clergyman and traveller, Henry Maundrell: 'A man above the ordinary level of a Turkish genius'.[48] The Buḥturids, his mother's family, gave him something much more important than a hereditary feudal system; they 'had lived since the late thirteenth century in Beirut and were well acquainted with commercial enterprise'. Another laudable quality was his miserliness and prudence, while 'the bigoted' Yūsuf Sayfā 'appears to have been a spendthrift who maintained a sumptuous court and patronized poets'.[49] This last vice was formerly considered by our historian a significant virtue when practised by the Buḥturids whose 'hereditary hold over their land' set Lebanon on the right track towards eventual independence.[50] Furthermore, nowhere are we made fully aware of the devastating effects of Fakhr al-Dīn's repeated military campaigns against Sayfā's territories, nor of the deliberate destruction of his fortresses, farm lands, and residences, in addition to acts of burning, looting, or confiscating properties, provisions, treasures, cattle, and money. Al-Khālidī, Fakhr al-Dīn's biographer and henchman, relates these deeds in his chronicle with relish and extreme frankness. Both Yūsuf Sayfā and Fakhr al-Dīn come out as two traditional Ottoman chieftains, using the same military organization and methods, and each coveting the territories of the other by means of entering into an alliance with local tribal leaders and Ottoman officials, or by trying to appear more useful to the Porte and thus gain its direct support. Fakhr al-Dīn went a step further and attempted to solicit direct European intervention in his favour. Sayfā was more circumspect. His suspicious attitude towards the Frankish traders was not primarily a function of his bigotry, but rather the result of his political alignments and his fear of an imminent European Crusade to reconquer the Holy Land.[51]

Only someone with preconceived notions, and who is anxious to explain contemporary trends by tracing distant origins, may end up with such a one-sided evaluation of Fakhr al-Dīn II. Muḥammad 'Alī's ambitions and horizons, for example, were much wider and encompassed a whole range of innovations. Yet, Salibi insists on seeing him in a different light. 'The ultimate goal of Muhammad 'Alī's reforms was neither social nor cultural.' His sole purpose, we are told, was 'to establish his own power and to perpetuate the rule of his dynasty in the Nile Valley, and if possible in Syria and Arabia'.[52]

Even when an element of detached observation is injected into Salibi's assessment of Fakhr al-Dīn's achievements, the result is still almost the same. In another article the Ma'nid *amīr* is considered 'a rapacious tyrant who weighed his subjects down with taxes'. Nevertheless, the national identity is not lost sight of. He describes his enlightened ideas, his innovations and reforms of agriculture and commerce, and the way he promoted 'the political union between the Maronites and Druzes which was to be of great importance in the subsequent history of Lebanon'. Then the evolution of Lebanon as a physical organism, bereft of its hereditary land system, is stated in its inherent potentiality and ceaseless struggle to realize itself:

> Fakhr al-Dīn II, indeed, is regarded by the Lebanese today as the father of modern Lebanon, for it was under his rule that the Druze and Maronite districts of the Mountain became united for the first time, with the adjacent coastlands and the Bikā, under a single authority.[53]

Thus the burden of the real truth is placed on the shoulder of the Lebanese themselves. The historian, despite his doubts, nods his head with a reluctant approval. The *amīr*'s whole career, if examined objectively, may turn out to be a myth, but it is a useful one, provided it is used with circumspection. This conclusion forms the gist of a lecture which Salibi delivered in front of a Maronite audience in 1970. In it the concocted stories about Fakhr al-Dīn are demolished, one after the other.

First, the genealogy of the Ma'nids as related in traditional chronicles, particularly by al-Shidyāq in his *Akhbār al-a'yān fī Jabal Lubnān*[54] is a pure legend, full of contradictions and false assumptions. Second, between 1584 and 1591 Fakhr al-Dīn II is supposed to have taken refuge with the Khāzins in Kisrwān. Is this story true?, the historian asks his audience, and begins by raising his doubts about the whole episode. He basically agrees with Adel Ismail that it was a nineteenth-century invention. He identifies the inventor as al-Shaykh Shaybān al-Khāzin (died *c.* 1850). This particular Khāzin was perhaps the first to give credence to the story (and for reasons not hard to find) in a chronicle which was not printed until 1958. Salibi makes clear that the Ma'nid *amīr* did not enter into any relationship with the Maronite Khāzins before 1598, when he was fully established in his authority as a Druze chieftain. Third, his alliance with the Maronites was purely political, based on advancing his self-interest in the struggle for power with Yūsuf Sayfā. The historian even asks the following question: If Fakhr al-Dīn was the Maronites' friend, which is not in doubt, was Yūsuf Sayfā their enemy? Whatever Sayfā did was related to political expediencies, he being a loyal Ottoman Pasha.[55] Fourth, the extent of Fakhr al-Dīn's rule as a tax-farmer appointed by the Ottoman Porte was not confined to Lebanon, but included Galilee (al-Jalīl), Palestine, the Syrian interior as far as Palmyra, the Nusayri mountains, and the areas to the north. Thus the *amīr* was not bent on unifying the Lebanese region 'in one single state'. He only tried to exploit the weakness of the Ottoman Empire and its preoccupation in its wars with the Persians. His close allies among the Maronites were the inhabitants of Kisrwan, and not those of North Lebanon. After his downfall in 1633 the Ma'nid Emirate reverted to its former base in the tiny corner of the Shūf, south of Beirut.[56]

The myth of Fakhr al-Dīn emerged in the nineteenth century, when it grew out of all proportion until he became 'the pioneer of Lebanese independence and the symbol of national unity'. Nevertheless, this myth is today 'more eloquent than reality'. For all that national unity was not achieved, the unity of interests between the sects came into being and continued after his disappearance. 'Even if Fakhr al-Dīn was not the originator of the Lebanese idea, which is a fact, there is no doubt that this amir laid the foundation-stone of the Lebanese entity which emerged after him.'[57] Myth and reality are two sides of one coin. The legitimacy of the Lebanese state as it stands today is shrouded in mysterious origins. It is a new synthesis whereby the Maronites keep the present and the Muslims satisfy themselves with a scholarly past.

A CHRISTIAN NATION AND A GREEK ETHOS

Salibi launched his academic career as a student of Maronite historiography and intellectual life, particularly in its religious dimensions. His *Maronite Historians of Mediaeval Lebanon* is a study of three chroniclers, who are elevated to the position of representing three historical moments in their sect's development.

Their works are considered worthy of perusal for a number of interrelated reasons. They offer rare information on the history of a country often neglected or ignored by Arab and Eastern Christian chroniclers. Moreover, no history of Lebanon in the later Middle Ages is possible without recourse to these sources. Only by an extensive examination of these Maronite sources is the historian able to discover the origins of Lebanese autonomy and its growth into a modern national entity. They furnish the modern scholar with the basic tools to unravel 'the foundations of Lebanese feudalism . . . , the earliest relations between Christian Lebanon and Western Europe', and to grasp the way 'the tradition of Lebanese autonomy first developed'.[58] An understanding of the Lebanese personality is unthinkable without comprehending the self-image of the Maronites as it evolved over three centuries.

The reader is cautioned at the outset that

> the present work is not a study of Maronite historiography, nor is it a survey of the Maronite literature on mediaeval Lebanon. It is an analysis of the history of Lebanon under Crusader and Mamluk rule (1099–1516) as presented by three leading Maronite historians of the traditional school: Ibn al-Qilā'ī (d. 1516), Duwayhī (d. 1704), and Tannūs ash-Shidyāq (d. 1861).[59]

Salibi's analysis operates at two parallel and overlapping levels: factual and interpretative. At the first level facts are revised, dates corrected, myths discarded, and local events placed in their proper and wider historical context. Here his scholarly method is revealed at its best. Against the Maronites' claim of their constant orthodoxy and perpetual attachment to Rome, he highlights their initial Monothelitism and heretical origins as a religious community.

Ibn al-Qilā'ī, one of the first Maronites to study in Rome, returned from Italy in 1493, after an absence of twenty-three years, during which he studied Latin, theology, science, and other subjects, having completely avoided coming into contact with the humanist currents of the Italian Renaissance.[36] Once in Lebanon he was disturbed to observe a great number of Maronites flocking to join the Jacobite Church. 'As a Franciscan priest, full of Catholic zeal', it was his vocation to admonish the heretics and redeem their souls lest the entire Maronite community be consumed by the fires of hell or the swords of its enemies. Ibn al-Qilā'ī did not write proper history to combat the heresies of his day. His best-known work, studied by Salibi, *Madīḥa 'alā Jabal Lubnān*, is a long poem written in broken colloquial Arabic, some time after 1495. It is 'a sermon in verse' which remained in manuscript until 1937. It was, however, widely used by other Maronite clerics and chroniclers as an authentic source. Confusing legendary with historical events, its main theme is not historical but openly theological. Nevertheless, he related certain events in a chronological order and had to use documentary materials. It is for this reason that Salibi holds the *Madīḥa*, in spite of its shortcomings, to be 'a most important source for the history of the Maronites during the period of Crusader and Mamluk rule', and attempts to correct some of its glaring inaccuracies.[61]

With the appearance of Patriarch Istifān al-Dūwayhī, Maronite historiography made a new departure. He was the first chronicler of his sect to consult a wide range of primary sources. Having studied theology and philosophy at the Maronite College in Rome for a period of fifteen years, he was selected as a missionary by the College of Propaganda to serve in Lebanon, Aleppo, and Cyprus. By the time he was elected as Maronite Patriarch of Antioch in 1670, he had already established himself as an eloquent preacher who 'converted many Melchites, Nestorians, and Jacobites to the Catholic faith'.[62]

The histories and religious tracts he produced had the same aim as those of Ibn al-Qilāʿī: the religious and historical origins of the Maronites and how their union with Rome and Orthodoxy was never broken. But there were marked differences. He wrote in prose, trying to adhere to the idioms of classical Arabic. Nevertheless, 'there is much colloquialism in his style, except for the passages copied or paraphrased from classical Arabic sources'. However, he was conscious of mentioning his sources, including Ibn al-Qilāʿī, Muslim and Druze annalists and the chronicles of the Crusader period.[63]

Dūwayhī's *Tārīkh al-ṭā'ifa al-mārūniyya* 'is written in the ponderous style of dignified polemics'.[64] Another work of his, *Tārīkh al-azmina*, is a chronicle modelled on the traditional Islamic school as represented by the annals of al-Ṭabarī. Salibi first introduced this particular work as 'a general chronicle of the history of the Near East with special reference to Lebanon and the Maronites'.[65] A few years later he was more specific:

> Duwayhī ... was a well-travelled and well-read scholar who had visited various parts of Syria and become acquainted with the better-known Arabic chronicles and histories; and he seems to have been impressed by the fact that the history

> of his community and that of Mount Lebanon were inseparable from the general history of Muslim Syria. . . . In a chronicle entitled *Ta'rīkh al-muslimīn* (History of the Muslims) or *Ta'rīkh al-azmina* (History of the times) . . . Duwayhī lays particular stress on the history of the Druzes and the Maronites of Lebanon in the context of the general history of the region of which Mount Lebanon forms part.[66]

From the seventeenth century the historian jumps to 1850 and lands on Ṭannūs al-Shidyāq busily scribbling his chronicle on the notables of Mount Lebanon.[67] One immediately senses the inexorable movement of history and the birth pangs of the national identity. The chronicler lived at a time when Lebanon had become entangled in the international struggle and politics of European powers. After Napoleon's expedition at the turn of the century and Muḥammad 'Alī's occupation of Syria in the 1830s, Mount Lebanon was turned into an arena of conflicting western interests. Its traditional structures began to crumble, while the simmering conflict between Druzes and Maronites was continuously stirred up by outside forces.

In the meantime, al-Shidyāq worked as a clerk, a political emissary, an agent, and a spy for various Shihabi *amīr*s. He also participated in the civil wars of the 1840s, championing the cause of the Maronites, with a particular sympathy for their traditional notables.[68] As a Maronite, his first interests were geared towards his sect's history. Thus in 1833 he wrote an abridgement of the first part of Dūwayhī's history of the Maronite sect, and then summarized another work by the same author, *Tārīkh al-azmina.* In 1848 his interests widened, and he composed a book on the history of the rulers of the Arabs and Islam (*Tārīkh mulūk al-'Arab wa al-Islam*). Unfortunately, the manuscript is no longer extant. Next, the history of his family claimed his attention in 1850. However, his reputation as a chronicler largely rests on his *Akhbār al-a'yān*, published under the supervision and editorship of the well-known Buṭrus al-Bustānī.[69]

Salibi devotes the third chapter of his study to an examination of this last work. Unlike the writings of the previous Maronite chroniclers, it was a history by a Maronite layman, and devoid of open theological polemics. Its author, moreover, wrote 'as a Lebanese and not as a Maronite'. It is secular, reflecting the fact that 'Maronite and non-Maronite Lebanon,

Christian and Druze Lebanon, were no longer entities apart'. How did al-Shidyāq manage to create out of the Lebanese chaos an orderly significant unity? Salibi explains

> He did not treat his subject chronologically and divide it into periods, but took every family of *a'yān* [notables] separately, relating its history from its origin to the date of its extinction, or to his own day. Families which had served as governing dynasties (*wulāt*) in Lebanon were dealt with twice. The first time Shidyāq only considered their genealogy and family history; the second time he considered the history of their *wilāya* (period of governorship).[70]

Unless Salibi had told us that al-Shidyāq was expressing a new development in Lebanon seeing it as one political unit, we would not have dared to put forward such a postulate and risk being accused of anachronism. Not even zealous Maronite historians ever dreamt of producing such a skilful interpretation. Philip Hitti, for example, was unaware, while using *Akhbār al-a'yān* for his *Lebanon in History*, that al-Shidyāq was more than 'a judge under the Shihāb amīrs and compiler of the annals of the feudal families of Lebanon'.[71] Asad Rustum described the same chronicle in 1924 thus: 'in a way, Shidyāk's history is scarcely anything but an account of the Emir's[72] efforts to rid himself of his rivals'.[73] This is certainly the impression one gains from reading the chronicle, or deciphering Salibi's verdict on it: 'He [Shidyāq] was essentially a compiler; and his history is an uncritical and confused collection of material from a number of sources. . . . Besides, Shidyāq did not try to interpret the material he compiled'.[74] How are we to reconcile two contradictory evaluations of the same chronicler by the same historian?

Salibi does not confine his study to correcting dates and facts, or trying to re-create historical events in medieval Lebanon in a connected narrative. This is only one aim of his work and was accomplished in an almost impeccable manner. Nevertheless, it seems a secondary one when placed beside his other major preoccupation. All his efforts to polish, recast, and verify events appear an incidental exercise once his interpretative level is brought into focus.

His study of Maronite historiography evoked in one of his reviewers this picturesque depiction: 'the history of Lebanon, like that of Iceland, will not have many lovers, but those who have once been attracted by it are enthralled forever.' Then the reader is informed of the importance of Salibi's analysis which goes beyond medieval history and 'throws light ... on the modern development of historical writing in Lebanon, and the growth of the Lebanese national consciousness'.[75] However, Salibi was not thinking of Icelandic sagas and histories. Nor did he have Iceland in mind when he surveyed the development of Maronite historiography. It was rather Greece, its poetry and culture, which captured his imagination. This assertion, it must be pointed out, does not rely on direct, concrete evidence. Nowhere does Salibi mention Greece or Greek historians. Yet the labels he attaches to his chroniclers, who are designated as historians throughout his book, afford us with ample clues as to his implicit analogy.

Ibn al-Qilāʻī's longest poetical work, *Madīḥa*, written in the Lebanese vernacular, is referred to as 'the one which most nearly approaches the epic'. The partial likeness is then explained that 'not only in size that the *Madīḥa* ... resembles the epic, but also in its poetic conception and its theme.' It is, moreover, 'heroic in tone'. It begins with a description of 'a golden age in Mount Lebanon. . . . It may refer to no historic age, but merely to an imaginary past when Maronite military success was coupled with orthodoxy and religious unity'.[76]

The age of the epic with its interest in origins, the heroic past, and the pure foundations of the community, gave way, in due course, to the rise of proper history. Isṭifān al-Dūwayhī represents this new phase in its full and complete growth. The scholar Georg Graf is quoted in a statement which considered Dūwayhī 'the father of Maronite history'.[77] Salibi appropriates this statement towards the end of his chapter on Dūwayhī, whose history is said to be 'a remarkable work revealing the diligence and critical powers of its author and his ability to compile a co-ordinated and intelligible history from fragmentary information. It is for this reason that Dūwayhī fully deserves to be called "the father of Maronite history".'[78]

Since Maronite historiography is held by Salibi 'to have originated as an expression of national pride', it was inevitable for it to culminate in a concrete manifestation of its reality. By the middle of the nineteenth century, the Maronites had become aware of a new dimension of their identity, and started to see their community's history in a wider context. 'It was now that the lay Maronite historian first appeared, not so much interested in the religious history of his own community as in the history of Lebanon, which he considered as a political unit composed of religious and feudal parts'. Ṭannūs al-Shidyāq embodied in his *Akhbār al-a'yān* this trend of Lebanese consciousness. His history heralded the birth of secular Maronite historiography, and Lebanon, consequently, assumed the attributes of a new entity.[79]

The analogy with Greek historiography can hardly be lost on the western reader. Salibi's neat classification of Maronite historians is explicitly modelled on a direct European view of the peculiarity and specificity of its own heritage. Ibn al-Qilā'ī is none other than the Homer of the Maronites, al-Dūwayhī is definitely their Herodotus, and al-Shidyāq is almost a faithful reproduction of Ephorus of Cyme. J.B. Bury had this to say about the last Greek historian:

> We must always remember that the Greeks had never formed a nation ... they had no national history in the proper sense of the word. . . . Now the novelty of the work of Ephorus lay in this, that, recognising this unity of culture which contained potentialities of a real Hellenic nation, he brought together the particular histories of all Greek-speaking communities, and thus produced what might be called a quasi-national history.[80]

There is no need to show that Salibi was consciously aping Bury's scheme of classifying Greek historians. This model is not an exclusive invention of one single western scholar, nor is it alluded to in Salibi's text. Rather, it is an implicit theme directly connected with a constant effort to clothe the Lebanese entity in western garb. Since this entity was assumed to be based on a distinctive feudal system of landownership, its cultural heritage had also to be differentiated and affiliated to a clear western tradition. Moreover, the absence of the epic in Arabic literature has become a cliché hackneyed by almost every orientalist. The mere allusion to the existence among the Maronites of an inherited pattern of epic poetry is a self-evident declaration, and an eloquent proof of what the historian had set out to demarcate and underline.

Thus Maronite historiography is distorted beyond recognition. Its immediate, intimate problems are dislocated, and the historical context is disrupted and shuffled. From being a sectarian, traditional, or antiquarian enterprise, it is transformed into a national and humanistic movement. Instead of situating any originality it had in its local environment and Near Eastern historical background, Salibi transposes his subject into a living western legacy, pulsating with the rythmical throbbing of a vigorous Greek heart. While the perpetual orthodoxy of the Maronite Church is subjected to severe scholarly criticism, and its legendary figures are dislodged from their rostrum, another orthodoxy, no less flagrantly concocted, is installed in their place and made the object of reverent adulation.

Ibn al-Qilāʻī's *Madīḥa* does not differ in substance from a tribal war poem. It sings the praises of the Maronites as a defiant sect united under the leadership of their chief, the Patriarch. It is, moreover, shot through with an exclusive, highly alarming, and narrow-minded outlook. The Jews, the Jacobites, and the Muslims are all considered enemies or heretics to be either exterminated or banished from the Kingdom of the Maronites.[81] It took Salibi almost two decades, and two Lebanese civil wars, to see the same poem in a different light. In 1979, after the close relationship between the Maronites and the Israelis had become common knowledge, the *Madīḥa* was pronounced to be no more than an attempt to depict the Maronites 'as a chosen people selected by God . . . to uphold the true Christian faith in its impregnable Lebanese stronghold'.[82]

As for Dūwayhī, his world consisted of three concentric circles. Any effort to isolate, or disentangle, one from the other would constitute an arbitrary act dictated by anachronistic notions. It is true, as Salibi observes, that the most original part of *Tārīkh al-azmina* is the one which deals with the history of the Maronites. However, these original items are integrated into the history of Syria and the Islamic world at large. Dūwayhī never loses sight of his three circles as interdependent units, arranged in the best Islamic traditions of annalistic chronology. Thus under the year AD1400 (803 H), for example, he mentions the reign of the Mamlūk Sultan al-Nāṣir Faraj, the Patriarch Dāwūd Yūḥannā and his bishops in Mount Lebanon, Tamerlane's invasion of Syria, the reluctance of the Egyptians to defend Damascus and resist the spread of locusts, the appearance of infectious diseases, and the steep rise in prices in various Syrian towns.[83]

Al-Shidyāq belongs to the same tradition: his historical

horizon embraces his sect, family, the Arab and Islamic World. Nowhere does he betray in his chronicle of Mount Lebanon a national preoccupation with or an understanding of Lebanon's history as a political entity, or a fatherland. The structure of his work, which has the notable families as its units of study, precludes the possibility of such an outcome. Furthermore, he wrote at a moment when Druze ascendancy in Mount Lebanon was already on the wane. He proclaimed his personal allegiance to that branch of the Shihābi dynasty which had abandoned Islam and joined the Maronite Church. Hence, the metamorphosis, which Maronite historiography is supposed to have undergone, is more apparent than real. More importantly, al-Shidyāq's underlying assumptions have the ring of antiquarianism rather than the quality of a modern patriotic concept. Salibi tells the reader that al-Shidyāq 'dealt with the origins and genealogies of the feudal families of Lebanon and with the internal political history of the country under their leadership. This he did at a time when the Lebanese feudal system had already matured and was approaching its downfall.'[84] In other words, al-Shidyāq thought he was canonizing and commemorating permanent features and structures, possessing the capacity of self-preservation and self-regeneration.

By 1966 Salibi began to shed most of his political formulas which were assumed to explain the origins and development of the Lebanese national identity. He discarded his cherished feudal system, the image of Lebanon as a refuge, the Phoenician contribution to the making of the modern polity, and his belief in laissez-faire liberalism represented by the merchant republic. However, his admission of the deficient nature of the Maronite myths as regards the history of Lebanon did not lead him to question the validity of the sectarian political system within which these images flourished and operated. Whether the myth was Christian or Muslim, it was considered something different and detached, transcending the contradictory interests and social milieux of various sects. The national identity was held to be basically sound and well-adjusted to meet new needs. What we are left with, as a result, is the emergence of the Maronites as a sociopolitical and cultural community with a clear national identity. Lebanese nationalism, and not the Lebanese nation, was therefore born out of the energy and highly positive traits of the Maronites and other Christians who chose to follow the same course. The Maronite identity arrogates and appropriates to itself other subcultures and social groups within Lebanon and infuses them with a national character which is its own. The other communities are evaluated, and their contributions noted, once some of their members display an inclination to enter the system and adhere to the prior rules of the game. Both his article 'The personality of Lebanon in relation to the modern world',[85] and his *Modern History of Lebanon* express this new approach. Lebanon is considered essentially a Christian creation, closely allied with Europe and its civilization.

Salibi firmly believed in the present and future of Lebanon as a polity dominated by its presumed Maronite majority. Its Muslim inhabitants were to be tolerated, educated, coaxed and cajoled, and finally won over. Although no reliable statistics exist about the exact proportional distribution of the sects in Lebanon, its population was by 1950 almost evenly divided between Muslims and Christians. However, two decades later, the former had overtaken the latter in numerical strength.[86] Even as early as 1933 the French mandatory authorities, who were naturally inclined towards the Maronites, were voicing their fears about the rapidly growing imbalance of the sects. They were particularly aware of the political dangers and social repercussions of the steady Christian emigration from Lebanon to various western and African countries.

> This emigration caused France, in 1920, to grant more area to the Lebanese state, thus creating Greater Lebanon. That move, however, did not successfully check emigration and at the present moment (1933) the Christian population of Lebanon may be placed at less than half of that of the Moslem.[87]

It never occurred to Salibi to question the doctored figures of the Lebanese government until his own political views had undergone yet another change. The Maronites still perceive Lebanon as a Christian country. Its raison d'être is solely highlighted as a homeland dreamt up and carved out for their safety and protection. Salibi shared and rationalized this view.

Intricately balanced, singularly structured, minutely arranged, the personality of Lebanon is singled out by Salibi for its unique characteristics amongst the Third World countries. A comparative study between Lebanon and other Asian and African countries is conducted to bring out the stark realities and contrasts. A rapid glance at most oriental states, for example, reveals the prevalence of slums, the existence of streets littered with dirt, and uncovers poor municipal services wide divergences between rural and urban areas, cultural incongruities, social contradictions, inferiority complexes manifested in outward arrogance towards the west, and misguided perception of their real problems. The list of deficiencies and woeful ignorance is endless. Having wrongly associated progress with power, they concentrate on building up their armed forces. Hence they end up with military dictatorships aided and abetted by their own anti-democratic intellectuals. Islam, confronted with a superior western civilization, responded by throwing up new defences. Muslim leaders, eager to stem their decline, contrived to manage and regulate the transition to a modern westernized order. But to no avail; a wide cleavage opened up between the upper rich strata and the traditional down-trodden masses. Their despair of parliaments and constitutional systems as effective instruments of rapid material progress made them fall victim to a series of coups d'état which rendered their goals more difficult to attain. A sombre present and a bleak future face the reckless leaders of the Third World. However, Lebanon is an exception. Its Christian community has escaped the fate of a backward country, in spite of its geographical location.

> Lebanon presents a striking contrast to the general pattern of westernization in the Arab Middle East. Because of the influence of its Christian population, this country stands apart from its surroundings, displaying those marked Western tendencies by which it is chiefly distinguished.[88]

Unlike their neighbours, the Christians in Lebanon have unlocked the secret of the west, and experience no difficulty in identifying with its culture and ideals. They know that the underlying factor of western civilization is not primarily power or technology, but rather the idea and practice of 'civic freedom' and democratic responsibility. Such a comprehension leads to the existence of a harmonious society, propelled in its forward movement by a large middle class. Its intellectual stratum forms an integral part of the wider community. The organic unity of Christian intellectuals extends into other sections of society, creating a political bond around which all classes tend to adhere. They constitute the élite that determines the 'general goals' of others and set their 'unity of purpose'. Their homogeneous nature functions as a direct reflection of firm social roots and complete immersion in a familiar environment.[89]

The Muslims, who form the other half of Lebanon, lack all these positive qualities. Salibi thought that they still dissipated their energies on non-Lebanese causes, such as pan-Arabism. This glaring anomaly disqualifies them from sharing power on an equal basis with their Christian compatriots. Thus the latter have no choice but to assume the onerous task of national leadership and guidance. Lebanon and its Christians are inseparable. Their adherence to its independence is an act of faith and a perpetual belief in its inviolability. In opposing pan-Arabism, they nurture their democracy and ward off the evils of 'Arab authoritarianism'. However, an enlightened Christian should endeavour to minimize and neutralize the negative aspects which the Muslims' attitudes entail and reinforce. Only by turning the neglected Muslim masses into good Lebanese citizens can the national identity be saved. Once again Salibi pins his hopes on the leaders of the political system to steer Lebanon into safe waters:

> Christian Lebanese leaders are beginning to realize that a free Lebanon can be better secured against pan-Arabism if its masses are more closely associated in active citizenship. To be good citizens, these masses must first be helped to share in the national and cultural advantages which ordinary Christians have for a long time enjoyed. For this reason, Christian parties and social organizations are now becoming increasingly interested in Muslim Lebanon. Government departments, acting often under Christian inspiration, are tending to concentrate more of their efforts on the development of Muslim regions.[90]

Salibi concludes his complacent diagnosis with a eulogy which culminates in his desertion of the real world. He takes refuge in the supernatural forces of nature or some invisible archangel. The Lebanese, our historian speculates, 'are conscious of their firmly rooted democracy, which, as authoritarianism continues to spread in the surrounding regions, appears to them daily more and more of a wonder'.[91] Yet this complacency did not last long. The social, political, and economic changes which the Lebanese entity underwent impelled the historian to retrace his steps and arrive at a new synthesis.

THE POLITICS OF HISTORY

It has become abundantly clear that Salibi's historical method of interpreting the characteristics of the Lebanese identity, and its development, witnessed drastic revisions and transfigurations. One may well ask how it is that these shifts of emphasis take place. Does the historian hint at, or inform the reader of, a new stance replacing an old one? Is there a pattern which accounts for these sudden intellectual reverses?

As a matter of fact, nowhere does Salibi explicitly refer to his adoption of new notions or his abandonment of certain conclusions. Only once does he perform this mundane chore, and in a manner which hardly violates his vows of silence. This solitary gesture was contemplated when Salibi noticed some odd discrepancies in the genealogy of the Ma'nid dynasty, namely the identity of the Ma'nid emir who ruled as chieftain of the Shūf region of Lebanon in 1516–17, and is supposed to have made his submission to the Ottoman Sultan Selim I at Damascus. Salibi allows himself to indulge in self-criticism for the sole reason that other eminent scholars[92] committed the same blunder.[93] Be that as it may, the shifts of emphasis do occur and require more than a passing remark.

Salibi's historical narration and methodology gain their proper signification when his political beliefs are fully spelled out. Holding the *a priori* conviction that Lebanon was different from other parts of Syria, the historian embarked on his search for facts and data to prove his case. This conviction remained relatively static and dogmatic, whilst its scholarly reaffirmations and life-support system were subjected to three major innovations. It seems that our historian is rarely convinced by the sheer force of a counter-argument to his established mode of thought. Unless other external factors impinge on his orderly academic pursuits, the temptation to examine the same problems in a different light is almost non-existent. Between 1950 and 1960 Salibi approached the history of Lebanon from a purely Maronite standpoint. The ideological assumptions, which did not have to correspond to the minute details of

Maronite self-image, bred in the historian a marked aloofness and a tendency to ignore the pitfalls of such a narrow view. His involvement with the past of the Maronites went beyond academic theorization and enmeshed him in direct political participation. He is reputed to have acted as an adviser and intellectual patron to a generation of Maronite student activists – a role not unknown to other AUB dons. After 1958, the year of the first Lebanese civil war in the twentieth century, the historian began to respond to the new circumstances. The traditional politicians of the old school of the Lebanese merchant republic lost their glamorous veneer and loomed as faded images of another age. A new type of leadership claimed his attention and devotion. No sooner had Fū'ād Shihāb, the former commander-in-chief of the armed forces, been elected as President of the Republic than Salibi rushed to rally to his cause. As a military man with fixed ideas of his own, the new president was in an ideal position to break fresh ground. The rise to power of military officers in Egypt, Syria, and Iraq could not have escaped his notice. His main programme consisted of two aspects: reaching a *modus vivendi* with the Egyptian president, Nasser, as the undisputed leader of the Arab masses, and implementing essential socioeconomic and administrative reforms calculated to appease and enhance the living conditions of the Muslims in Lebanon. However, Shihāb thought he could accomplish his goals without touching the foundations of the Lebanese system or reducing the supremacy of the Maronites.

The 1958 civil war is seen by Salibi as a watershed in the history of Lebanon. Fundamental changes took place which constitute no less than a 'true revolution'. The hallmarks of this revolution are manifold and herald the beginning of a new Lebanese entity with the President of the Republic acting as its *deus ex machina.* 'The prestige enjoyed by President Chehab today, which gives him the supreme power, is based not on his management of an oligarchy but on his being the only leader to whom all Lebanese factions can be loyal.' He, unlike former Maronite presidents, arbitrates between the Lebanese and refrains from wielding the enormous powers conferred on his office. The Maronite presidency is consequently 'confessionally neutralized', along with the Maronite army command. 'The one-time commander-in-chief of the Army is himself the President, and the Army that was once a body apart has been integrated in the State.' Other laudable developments are clearly noticeable. Organized political parties, be they Sunni or Maronite, have started to replace the old type of politicians who dominated Lebanese politics since the Second World War. 'In this manner, the political Lebanon of today may be regarded as the Lebanon giving the least possible offence to Nasser, while maintaining the most possible of her original character.'[94]

When President Shihāb's term of office ended in 1964, Salibi volunteered to offer a general assessment of his hero's internal reforms and external policies. He shows himself as an admirer and enthusiastic supporter of a president who saw the necessity of promoting a sense of national unity in Lebanon, and displayed a keen interest in 'the neglected parts of Lebanon, which were predominantly Moslem'. The rampant and haphazard policies of the old regime gave way to the planned and measured reorganization of the administration and the economy. The eventual failure of these reforms is deemed to be no fault of the former General's honest character and good intentions. The blame belongs to the Lebanese 'inefficient and corrupt' administration. Even Shihāb's excessive reliance on his security and army intelligence forces, a fact which partly accounts for the shortcomings of his rule, is pronounced by Salibi a positive achievement which made 'the country safe for the ordinary citizen'.[95]

Salibi's *Modern History of Lebanon*, published in 1965, bears the hallmarks of the author's Shihābist image of his country's past and present. It opens with a fairly long introduction which offers a sociological analysis of the various sects, and boldly proclaims a new political theory, designed to legitimate the fundamental structures of the state.[96]

The Lebanese sects are turned at the hands of the historian into independent individuals, endowed with a personality of their own, and a specific set of psychological and social traits. The history of each sect, the date of its entry into Lebanon and the particular qualities and aptitudes are carefully ascertained and emphasized. Their different histories, divergent characteristics, and cultural diversities lead to an imperative hierarchy of functions and contributions. Their association in one body politic over a period of long or short duration, depending on individual cases, evolved into a workable formula which stamped Lebanon with its distinct identity:

Coming from diverse origins and established in the country

> under different circumstances, the various religious communities of Lebanon grew as distinct groups, each with its special social character. The Shi'ites, Druzes, and Maronites developed as rebel mountaineers, hardy and clannish, with a staunch particularism and a strong spirit of independence.

On the other hand, 'the Sunnite and Melchite communities of Lebanon differ from the Shi'ites, Druzes and Maronites in being essentially townsmen, with none of the ruggedness and particularism of the mountaineers'. Then a list of political and psychological categories is drawn up, and each sect is assigned its proper position in society. The Druzes, as the first sect to assert itself politically in Mount Lebanon, 'tend to be reticent, secretive, and urbane, masters of the ruse in politics and of the stratagem in war'. However, the Maronites, as the most numerous sect in Lebanon, were destined to replace the Druzes as the natural leaders of the country. They are 'notoriously forward and outspoken, their habitual indiscretion contrasting sharply with the Druze reserve. Headstrong individualists, the Maronites have generally been the more adventurous and enterprising people, greatly excelling the Druzes in economic and cultural achievement'. The Sunnites, as loyal subjects of the Ottoman state, were rather submissive and dependent on the sultan's favour. 'They never developed the self-reliance of other Lebanese sects', and became a source of disorder and instability under the French mandate and continued to be a disruptive element after Lebanon had gained its independence. The Shi'ites are even less qualified to represent the Lebanese spirit and true personality. 'A prolonged history of persecution and repression has reflected itself in the community's characteristic political timidity, and its seemingly haphazard organization.' Finally the Greek Orthodox and Greek Catholics are affable, enterprising, and self-effacing. 'Politically shy, they still excel in those fields where there is least government interference, and are economically and culturally the most active communities in the country.'[97]

How did these sects, with all their apparent dissimilarities, manage to live together in one civil society? Salibi resorts at this point to the political theory of John Locke and offers the history of Lebanon as its best illustration. He concedes that under the rule of the Shihābs (1697–1840) the Lebanese did not 'constitute a nation, united in purpose and consciousness of identity, nevertheless, they did stand out as a distinct community of sects, organized according to what has been perhaps the nearest known approximation to a "Social Contract".'[98]

Salibi's history of Lebanon is a prolonged discussion of the way this 'social contract' developed and affected the political process of the Lebanese civil society. However, in doing so, he implicitly introduces another political theory in order to account for the ascendancy of one sect and the inevitable decline of another. From being independent individuals, who had consented to join the body politic in accordance with the terms of a social contract, the sects are alternately considered as political élites. These élites have their own myths, cultural symbols, social programmes, and economic ambitions. Only one single élite may become predominant and wield the reins of power in a particular historical period. The explicit domination of one sect and the tacit recognition of all other sects of their subordinate position ensure the stability of the national identity, and open the way for its evolution into a nation-state. An élite, or its Lebanese counterpart, manages to keep its hegemony as long as it possesses the ability to co-opt and absorb into its ranks elements of other sects. It thus replenishes its strength and maintains the privileges it enjoys. Knowing no way of adapting itself to changed circumstances and new developments, the dominant sect gradually becomes obsolete and is replaced by a more vigorous one.[99] This was the fate of the Druzes in their vain attempts to preserve their political power and their outmoded social structure at the same time.

Consequently, his history narrates the steady ascendancy of the Maronites to power in the late eighteenth century. The Lebanese identity is henceforth interlocked with the fortunes of that particular sect. Along with the gradual and sustained rise of the Maronites, the country itself begins to change its name. Whereas Mount Lebanon previously designated a restricted area of the northernmost section of the Lebanon range, it now embraces the domain of the Druzes, after whom it was formerly called, i.e. *Jabal al-durūz*.

All major and minor events taking place inside or outside Lebanon conspired to place the Maronites in the most propitious position. As their *muqaddams* became subservient to the Mamlūk and later on Ottoman local governors, the clergy identified themselves with the cause of their flock, the Maronite peasants. Their patriarch slowly emerged as the spiritual and political leader of his community, while the Druze religious leaders fell under the dominance of their feudal lords and lost their independence and prestige. 'By the mid-eighteenth century the growth of the Maronite community in numbers and importance had become a matter of political consequence'.[100]

The defeat of the Yemenite Druze faction at the Battle of 'Ayn Dārā in 1711 marked a new chapter in the history of Lebanon. Although the victors were the Qaysite Druze forces led by Ḥaydar Shihāb, the Maronites benefited from the growing rift within the Druze ranks. The Qaysite–Yemenite sanguinary struggle for power and economic resources was soon replaced by that of the Junbulāṭī–Yazbakī. This factional division became the landmark of the Lebanese political scene, and involved the leading families of different sects. Eight families of *muqāṭā'jiyya*, or tax-farmers, ruled over the various districts of Mount Lebanon. Their duties and rights were regulated by a Shihābī *amīr* whose tenure of office was renewable on a yearly basis by the Ottoman governor of Acre or Sidon. The Druzes boasted five tax-farming families who controlled the most extensive and fertile districts. The three Maronite families, the Khāzins, the Ḥubayshes, and the Daḥdāḥs, shared between them the rocky district of Kisrwān and its adjoining areas. However, the Khāzins received the lion's share of Kisrwān and its revenues. The Druze districts were flooded with Maronite peasants seeking employment and new opportunities in the more prosperous regions. Soon the sectarian balance began to change in their favour. Amīr Mulḥim, a devout Sunni encouraged his children to embrace the Maronite creed. By 1770 the Emirate had its first Maronite Shihābī Emir.[101]

It was not only the demographic strength of the Maronites that advanced their supremacy. Other factors were at work. Their association with silk production, sold to European traders, the influx of immigrant Greek Catholic families into Lebanon from inner Syria, their special relationship with France, and the reorganization of their church under the supervision of Roman Catholic missionaries gave them a decided advantage over the other sects. Economically, politically, and culturally the signs of their inevitable preponderance were unmistakable. Moreover, these auspicious portents coincided with the decline of Ottoman power and influence. Various European states exhibited a heightened interest in the fate of the sick man of Europe. When Bashīr II (1788–1840), another Christian prince, outwardly professing Druzism and Islam, was appointed governor of Lebanon by Jazzār Aḥmad Pasha of Acre, the underlying changes in the internal structure of the Emirate were given a new impetus. By that time, Mount Lebanon had become a vital link in the entangled chain of the Eastern Question.[102]

Bashīr II proceeded to destroy the power of the 'feudal' families one after the other. He consequently weakened the position of the Druzes even further, and by 1825, when he crushed the most powerful Druze Shaykh Bashīr Junbulāṭ, the Druze political dominance in the country was dealt 'a last blow'.[103]

Ibrāhīm Pasha's invasion of Syria led to the total emancipation of Christians. The Druzes sided with the Ottoman army. Their successive revolts against Ibrāhīm Pasha made them the target of severe punitive actions. While Bashīr II remained faithful to the cause of his old ally, Muḥammad 'Alī, the Maronites finally turned against the Egyptians. The great powers intervened in 1840 and put an end to the Egyptian occupation. With the fall of Bashīr II and the accession of Bashīr III, a new phase in the development of the Lebanese entity began to unfold. 'The Maronites, after 1840, sought to assert their supremacy', and Mount Lebanon plunged into civil strife which lasted until 1860. This prolonged crisis expressed the rapidly changing internal balance of forces. However, despite the Maronite bid for power, in which the Church and the Patriarch played a crucial role, the socioeconomic changes in Lebanon failed to reflect themselves at the military and political level. In order for the Maronites to translate their numerical strength, and economic and cultural supremacy into concrete and permanent features, an outside power was urgently required. Defeated by the Druzes and the connivance of the Ottomans their aspirations were time and again thwarted and blocked.[104]

At this juncture Salibi interrupts his narrative and poses the following question: 'What was the secret behind the flagrant temerity of the Druzes at the time, and the seemingly inexplicable Christian cowardice?' The answer he gives is substantially that proffered by Charles Henry Churchill a hundred years earlier.[105] The Christians lacked discipline, organization, and competent leaders. The antagonism between Muslims and Christians throughout the Ottoman Empire had assumed a new political dimension. Whatever cowardice the Maronites revealed was linked with a fear sweeping the ranks of all Christians in the area. Having amassed fortunes, and established 'close commercial, cultural, and sometimes also political contacts with Europe,' they gradually aroused the jealousies and fanaticism of their Muslim neighbours. The Druzes capitalized on these prevailing conditions and succeeded in presenting their cause in the context of general Muslim grievances. Foreign intervention by European powers was the only expedient which could salvage the Maronite cause and settle the future of Lebanon.[106]

The remainder of Salibi's narration of events is largely devoted to a persistent justification of European interference and direct involvement in the internal affairs of Lebanon. He is particularly anxious to demonstrate the positive outcome of this controversial aspect. The new entity which emerged after 1860 under the auspices of European powers is considered a step in the right direction. Notwithstanding the fact that the country was governed by a foreign *mutaşarrif*, albeit a Catholic Christian, and directly responsible to the Ottoman Porte, Salibi uncovers praiseworthy accomplishments which ensured the continuity of the national identity. One such was the birth of 'an administrative aristocracy' whose members were descendants of the old leading families of middle Lebanon. It was this group which developed the ideology of Lebanese nationalism, and thought of France as the ultimate custodian of their aspirations. 'It was therefore amid wide Christian rejoicing, especially among the Maronites, that the French in 1918 occupied Lebanon, bringing to an end the period of Ottoman rule.'[107]

After a long chapter, entitled 'The Lebanese awakening', which turns out to be a breathtaking panorama of the Maronite–Catholic renaissance in the fields of culture and education, Salibi resumes his political narrative, and he has a surprise in store for the reader. He casually announces that 'the history of modern Lebanon may be said to have begun in 1918 with the French occupation',[108] and goes on to sketch this history in no more than forty-two pages using his memory and secondary sources. However, the underlying message is still the same. Lebanese independence is awkwardly equated with the military presence of France as a mandatory power. The latter had to be in Lebanon so as to act as a shield against the pan-Arab claims of the non-Maronite Lebanese. In due course Greater Lebanon acquired a constitution in 1926 and it 'served to provide Lebanon's political life with a firm basis'. Other desiderata were soon fulfilled, including 'a workable system of government' which made Lebanon 'a modern state'. Independence was finally achieved by 1943 and Lebanon became a full and responsible member of the free world. Weathering the storms of its reticent Muslim inhabitants and greedy Arab neighbours, the young republic is seen to have passed its hour of trial. Salibi ends his narrative on this cheerful note:

> In the early summer of 1960, barely two years after Shihāb took over power, the eleventh general elections since 1920 were held in Lebanon. Considering the general situation in the surrounding Moslem World, the event was particularly significant. In a region where military dictatorship had become the rule, the Lebanese Republic, because of its peculiar nature and problems, could still afford the free practice of constitutional life.[109]

By 1970 Salibi was so confident of the future of his national identity that he no longer felt the need for a political theory to justify its existence. The pace of Lebanese nationality has outstripped any theoretical construction. By the mere fact of living together, the Lebanese have become conscious of their distinct national character. Sectarianism is rapidly declining and being replaced by the rise of new social configurations. 'The steady growth of the Lebanese middle class, which has come to include an increasing proportion of Moslems and Druzes, has broadened the meeting-ground for the various Lebanese communities.'[110] This process is irreversible and presages the advent of a truly western nation.

Nevertheless, with the eruption of the 1975–76 civil war in Lebanon Salibi became sceptical of his optimistic approach, and entered a third phase in his search for Lebanon's identity. In his appraisal of Shihāb's policies he had injected a cautionary note about the pitfalls of corrupt administrators and selfish leaders. Having observed the utter failure of various reforms, he now reached another conclusion. Keeping in mind his theory of the circulation of the élites in governing Lebanon, and the way one sect secures hegemony and domination, it slowly dawned on him that the Maronite ascendancy was coming to an end. The logic of events invites the promotion of another sect.

Between 1970 and 1975 the Shi'ites, his politically timid community, had emerged as an organized political force with social and economic demands under the leadership of their energetic Imām, Mūsā al-Ṣadr. They were also claiming to be the largest religious sect in Lebanon. When Salibi produced his instant history of the first stages of the civil war, which still rages unabatedly, he refrained for the first time from quoting the figures of official censuses, lending his implicit support to the Shi'ite claims.[111] Being a specialist in Lebanese medieval history, he therefore felt compelled to revise his earlier description and theory about the 1305 Mamlūk campaign against the Lebanese district of Kisrwān. In his pro-Maronite phase he showed this campaign to be directed against the Maronites, along with the Shi'ites and Druzes. But he had no doubt that the Maronites bore the brunt of the punitive expedition as their monasteries, churches, and forts were destroyed. An anonymous history of the ancient churches of Lebanon, still in manuscript, is then quoted to back up his conclusions and seal the argument.[112] In the updated version the Shi'ites are squarely acclaimed as the main, if not the only, victims of the same Mamlūk expedition. Maronite sources are alluded to in a noncommittal statement, which is a far cry from his previous unequivocal belief in their reliability, while an Arabic biographical dictionary which he had occasion to peruse and consult as early as 1955 is referred to in support of the new theory.[113] Thus the Shi'ites are assured of a deeply rooted position in the annals of Lebanese history and provided with a well-groomed image befitting their prescribed role.

Hence, Salibi's *Crossroads to Civil War* serves both as an obituary notice of the Lebanese sociopolitical system and a sad recognition of his failure to redeem it. He observed the fragility and dubious nature of the democratic institutions. His middle class proved to be a factitious and fickle contrivance. No individual, be he bourgeois, aristocrat, or proletarian, existed as a citizen or an independent human being outside the life cycle of one sect or another. The state itself appeared as a ramshackle assemblage of disparate, mutually exclusive religiopolitical communities. The political notables and leaders shielded their own sectarian constituencies against the penetration of the state. No one, as a result, dealt directly with a national institution. The clash of self-images did not erupt in a vacuum of abstract thought. Concocting a historical balance sheet on which the sharp disparities are jotted down and reconciled seemed a superficial solution and a futile exercise. The myths obviously expressed legitimate grievances and firm convictions arising out of the relative subordination or dominance of one sect or another, and in response to real issues and concrete conditions. It was the multiplex system itself which reinforced and injected these political formulas with a new lease of life.

In the same way as Ṭannūs al-Shidyāq clung to a past which was crumbling before his own eyes, Salibi followed suit in another context, and with the added advantage of someone embracing destiny with a smiling face. Al-Shidyāq did not pretend to offer an alternative to his intimate world, nor did he possess the vision or drive to project a new image for the future. His was an antiquarian mind unperturbed by the roaring winds of change. He was a chronicler who revelled in piling up one unconnected event upon another, relishing and conveying his exhilaration at the brief skirmishes and almost mediocre battles of his notables and chieftains. Salibi's tragedy is compounded by his awareness of the interplay of forces beyond his control. He first believed himself to be swimming with the tide of history, kept afloat by the best scientific instruments. When obstacles were encountered and unexpected setbacks occurred, he brushed them aside as momentary difficulties to be tolerated and later surmounted. Civil wars, foreign interventions, complete collapses of public order, the rise of new social and political forces, rapid economic changes and sectarian upheavals were all subsumed under the magic functioning of an essentially sound 'social contract'. It is no wonder that, at the moment of his society's dismal disintegration, the yearning for salvation should reverberate with the memory of a vanquished adversary: Arabism. His obituary of the Lebanese political system ends with this passage:

> At a time when many Arabs were turning away from Arabism and barely managing to conceal their sympathy for the Christian Lebanese position, Arabism found itself making a last stand in Lebanon. . . . What the outcome of the contest will be … remains to be seen. However, only in an Arab world where the bond of Arabism remains significant can a country like Lebanon retain its special importance.[114]

By adopting Arabism when it had become a shadow of its former self, he was reclaiming two lost worlds — that of Lebanon and his tattered architectonic synthesis. Whether the Shi'ites are the ideal candidates to shoulder the burden of

Arabism, as the Maronites were once charged with that of democracy, is a question still awaiting the verdict of a new phase of history.

More importantly, the internal sectarian conflict in Lebanon has ceased to possess its own momentum or dynamism. Without the broader context within which it operates, sectarian violence has often degenerated into meaningless death and destruction. Thus, the political and socioeconomic contradictions between one sect and another gain their significance in so far as they are articulated in the wider field of the Arab World, or in their immersion in the protracted confrontation between Israel and the Arabs. Since 1969, both the Palestinian and Syrian factors have become entrenched as two internal dimensions on to which were grafted various Lebanese grievances and ambitions. The old divisions, which pitted Druzes against Maronites, or Muslims in opposition to Christians, have given way to the new political, military, economic, and demographic transformations effected by the penetration of the Syrian and Palestinian elements into the Lebanese balance of forces. By seeking to create the widest possible political alliances, the Palestine Liberation Organization and the Syrian state have prevented the Lebanese social contradictions from assuming the character of pure sectarian strife. Accordingly, it is no longer possible to reconstitute the Lebanese institutions along the lines of the old formula. Moreover, the viability of Lebanon itself as a state is almost totally dependent on the direction of developments generated by the advent of its new elements.[115]

NOTES

1. This ‘Park’ is the Pine Forest in which Gouraud’s Residence was located.

2. The American diplomat is here referring to notables from the newly annexed cities and areas which are enumerated in the last sentence of the quoted section of this despatch.

3. Walter L. Browne (ed.), *The Political History of Lebanon, 1920–1950. Documents on Politics and Political Parties under French Mandate, 1920–1936*, vol. I (North Carolina, 1976), pp. 12–13.

4. Quoted in Philip K. Hitti, *Lebanon in History* (London, 1957), p. 489.

5. The ceremony was commemorated by a painting which still hangs at the entrance of the French Embassy in Beirut.

6. Edmond Rabbath, *La formation historique du Liban politique*

et constitutionnel (Beirut, 1973), pp. 284–6 and 351–3. General Gouraud pointed out, in the course of his proclamation, how the soldiers of France, five weeks earlier, had crushed the remnants of the Arab Government in Damascus, and saved the Lebanese from enslavement.

7. Zeine N. Zeine, *The Struggle for Arab Independence* (Beirut, 1960), p. 51.

8. Rabbath, *op. cit.* pp. 300–6.

9. Zeine, *op. cit.* p. 138.

10. See Zakī al-Naqqāsh and 'Umar Farrūkh, *Tārīkh Sūriyya wa Lubnān* (Beirut, 1935); Dr Asad Rustum and Fū'ād Ifrām al-Bustānī, *Tārīkh Lubnān al-mūjaz* (Beirut, 1937); and 'Umar Farrūkh, *Tajdīd al-tārīkh* (Beirut, 1980), p. 96. Farrūkh indicates that this information was reported to him by Asad Rustum himself, and points out that the same repudiated textbook was still reprinted as late as 1957.

11. Salibi was obviously proud of his family's activities in the educational field. He, accordingly, dwells at length on the various aspects of these activities. See Kamal Salibi, *The Modern History of Lebanon* (London, 1965), pp. 134–7.

12. It was later published as *Maronite Historians of Mediaeval Lebanon* (Beirut, 1959).

13. Zeine, *op cit.*, pp. 69–71.

14. Labib Zuwiyya Yamak, *The Syrian Social Nationalist Party* (Cambridge, Mass., 1966), p. 55.

15. Anwar G. Chejne, 'The concept of history in the modern Arab world', *Studies in Islam*, vol. IV (1967), pp. 18–21. The manual, *Muṣṭalaḥ al-tārīkh*, Asad Rustum (Beirut, 1939), was however, largely based, even in its division of chapters and general themes, on that of Langlois and Seignobos, *Introduction aux études historiques* (Paris, 1898), a fact which Chejne fails to mention.

16. Salibi, *The Modern History of Lebanon*, pp. 215–16.

17. As we shall see, Salibi was later to drop his insistence on a continuous link between Phoenicia and Lebanon, and for reasons other than the discovery of some new evidence or the result of archaeological excavations.

18. Kamal Salibi, *al-Abḥāth*, vol. XIII (1960), pp. 488–90.

19. Kamal Salibi, *Munṭalaq tārīkh Lubnān* (Beirut, 1979), pp. 11–12.

20. Ibid., pp. 14–15.

21. Kamal Salibi, 'The Lebanese identity', *Journal of Contemporary History*, vol. 6 (1971), pp. 80–5.

22. However there is no evidence that Sunni leaders 'ever planned to overthrow the existing political arrangement or to attempt to re-unite the Muslim areas of Lebanon with those across the border'. Roger Owen, 'The political economy of Grand Liban, 1920–1970', in Roger Owen (ed.), *Essays on the Crisis in Lebanon* (London, 1976), p. 29.

23. Salibi, 'The Lebanese identity', pp. 84–6.

24. Salibi, *Munṭalaq tārīkh Lubnān*, p. 14.

25. Salibi's impartial historian with his scrupulous task bears a striking superficial resemblance to Karl Mannheim's 'relatively classless,

socially unattached' intellectual. The latter is able, with the aid of his refined cultural attachment, to achieve 'an intimate grasp of the total situation' and formulate 'a dynamic synthesis' of mutually opposing theories which correspond to the interests of specific social groups. See Karl Mannheim, *Ideology and Utopia* (London, 1976), pp. 130–65. First published in England 1936.

26. Kamal Salibi, 'L'historiographie libanaise: histoire de vanité', *L'Orient*, 23 May 1965.

27. Kamal Salibi, 'Six aspects of Lebanon', *Middle East Forum* (March 1960), pp. 30–3.

28. This aspect is examined below, pp. 142 and 163 n. 81.

29. Kamal Salibi, 'Lebanon in historical perspective', *Middle East Forum* (March, 1959), p. 19.

30. Kamal Salibi, 'The Buḥturids of the Garb. Mediaeval Lords of Beirut and of Southern Lebanon,' *Arabica*, vol. VIII (1961), p. 74.

31. *Ibid*, p. 97.

32. *Tārīkh Bayrūt wa akhbār al-umarā' al-Buḥturiyyīn min banī al-Gharb* (published by Louis Cheikho, Beirut, 1927). However, Cheikho, a Jesuit scholar, who was anxious in the early years of Greater Lebanon to defend the inclusion of Beirut in the new state against the claims of the Sunnis and others, altered the original title of the chronicle in a subtle manipulation which turned it into a history of the city instead of a particular family. The original title was, *Akhbār al-salaf min dhurīyyat Buḥtur b. 'Alī amīr al-Gharb bi Bayrūt.* The same work was later edited by Kamal Salibi and Francis Hours (Beirut, 1969). This time the editors had the courtesy to add the original title as a subtitle to Cheikho's. It is to this edition references are being made here. The first edition appeared in 1902.

33. A.N. Poliak, 'Some notes on the feudal system of the Mamlūks', *JRAS* (January, 1937), p. 98 cf. Robert Irwin, 'Iqṭā' and the end of the Crusader states', in P.M. Holt (ed.) *The Eastern Mediterranean Lands in the Period of the Crusades* (Warminster, England, 1977), p. 69.

34. The sentence in question reads as follows, 'wa ghālib iqṭā'ihim al-ladhī yakhdumū 'alayhā amlākuhum al-thābita bi al-shar' al-sharīf.' *Tārīkh Bayrūt*, p. 86.

35. Salibi, 'The Buḥturids of the Garb', p. 90. He then draws his own sweeping conclusions: 'the Mamlūk authorities reconsidered the case of the Buḥturid *iqṭā'*, and the old fiefs of the family were restored. By so doing the Mamlūks formalized the hereditary system of feudal land tenure which had become traditional in southern Lebanon, and which was maintained throughout Mamlūk and Ottoman times.' *Ibid*, p. 91.

36. *Islamic Society and the West*, vol. I, part i (London, 1950), p. 236. 'Thus the sites of houses in villages were private property — *mulk*, and each house had attached to it a half-*dönüm* of land that was likewise *mulk*.'

37. *Tārīkh Bayrūt*, pp. 86–7. Incidentally this plural noun is translated by Salibi as 'their home' so as to make it sound like a vast cultivated territory.

38. The italics are mine.

39. Salibi, *The Modern History of Lebanon*, pp. 4–5. See also

Salibi, 'The Lebanese Emirate 1667–1841', *al-Abḥāth*, vol. XX, no. 3 (Sept. 1967), pp. 1–16.

40. Salibi, *Munṭalaq tārīkh Lubnān*, p. 141. These shifts in emphasis will be dealt with in a separate section below. The *Ḥalqā* was a corps of free, non-Mamlūk cavalry. It had within it a unit of the sons of the *amīrs* and of the Mamlūks, known as *awlād al-nās.* David Ayalon, 'Studies on the structure of the Mamluk Army', *BSOAS*, vol. XV (1953), p. 204.

41. Salibi, 'Lebanon in historical perspective', p. 20.

42. *Lubnān fī 'ahd al-amīr Fakhr al-Dīn al-Ma'nī al-thānī*, edited by Fū'ād Ifrām al-Bustānī and Asad Rustum (Beirut, 1969), 1st edn, 1936. The original title was *Tārīkh al-amīr Fakhr al-Dīn al-Ma'nī.*

43. Salibi, *Maronite Historians*, pp. 167–8.

44. Salibi, 'Lebanon in historical perspective,' p. 20.

45. See, for example, 'Isā Iskandar al-Ma'lūf, *Tārīkh al-amīr Fakhr al-Dīn al-thānī* (Jūniah, 1934), p. 48. Al-Ma'lūf, a non-Maronite Christian historian, alludes to the fact that this particular story was not mentioned by the chronicles of two contemporaries of Fakhr al-Dīn. Neither Ibn Sibāṭ (d. 1520), nor Patriarch al-Dūwayhī (1629–1704) had anything to say on that particular incident. Adel Ismail, a Sunnite Lebanese historian and an admirer of the *amīr*, is more explicit in his refutation of the story in his *Histoire du Liban du XVIIe siècle à nos jours. Tome V: Le Liban au temps de Fakhr-ed-Din II, 1590–1633* (Paris, 1955), p. 6.

For a Maronite point of view, see Michel Chebli, *Fakhreddine II Maan, Prince du Liban* (Beirut, 1946), p. 25. Chebli quotes as an authoritative opinion the following statement by the French Consul General in Beirut, René Ristlehueber, *Les traditions françaises au Liban* (Paris, 1918), pp. 131–2,

> C'est à leur influence [the Khāzins'] et aux sentiments de reconnaissance du jeune Émir que l'on doit attribuer la large tolérance religieuse de ce dernier. Elle permit aux Maronites de collaborer sincèrement avec les Druzes dans le gouvernement de la Montagne et à l'Émir Fakhr-Eddine lui-même de faire l'unité politique du Liban en rapprochant les deux peuples.

46. According to the German sociologist, Max Weber, *The Protestant Ethic and the Spirit of Capitalism*, trans. by Talcott Parsons (London, 1930, 1974), these 'dimensions' constituted the hallmarks of western capitalism in its early stages. They include self-control, hard frugality, a rational system of life, discipline, proficiency 'in a calling', voluntary submission to religious precepts, 'shrewdness and tact in the transaction of mundane affairs', prudence and a desire to reinvest savings.

47. Kamal Salibi, 'The Sayfās and the Eyalet of Tripoli, 1579–1640', *Arabica*, vol. XX (1973), pp. 32–7.

48. Put in its proper context, this quotation would lose much of its sweeping generality. Like most Englishmen, Maundrell was fascinated with green landscapes and well-arranged gardens. On 18 March 1696,

he visited the environs of Beirut and stumbled on 'the Orange Garden' which was designed in the Italian style at the orders of Fakhr al-Dīn.

> It may perhaps be wonde'rd how this emir should be able to contrive anything so elegant and regular as this garden. . . . But Faccardine had been in Italy, where he had seen things of another nature, and knew well how to copy them in his own country. For indeed it appears by these remains of him, that he must needs have been a man much above the ordinary level of a Turkish genius.

On 27 April 1696, he crossed over to Damascus. Standing on a hill outside the city, he was once again deeply moved by the green scenery stretching before his eyes. 'On the north side of this vast wood is a place call'd Solhees (Sālihiyya) where are the most beautiful summerhouses and gardens.' Unfortunately, Maundrell was, in this last instance, reluctant to reveal the name of the genius behind these works of art. Henry Maundrell, *Journey from Aleppo to Jerusalem in 1697* (London, 1810), pp. 52–4 and 164–5.

49. *Ibid*, pp. 38–40.

50. Salibi, 'Lebanon in historical perspective', p. 19.

51. *Tārīkh al-amīr Fakhr al-Dīn al-Ma'nī*, pp. 55–80 and *passim*; N. Jorga, 'Un projet relatif à la conquête de Jérusalem, 1609', *Revue de l'Orient Latin*, vol. II (1894), pp. 183–9. It is an article quoted by Salibi himself.

52. Salibi, *The Modern History of Lebanon*, p. 132. P.M. Holt, *Egypt and the Fertile Crescent 1516–1922* (London, 1966), p. 115, states, as a historian who is not seeking to set a precedent for later developments, 'Nowadays Fakhr al-Dīn is often presented as a precursor of modern Lebanese nationalism, who sought to create a progressive, united state, independent of Ottoman rule. This is an anachronism. . . . The unity which he sought and temporarily achieved was dynastic not national'. In other words, he was no different from Salibi's Muḥammad 'Alī.

53. Kamal Salibi, 'Fakhr al-Dīn', *The Encyclopaedia of Islam*, 2nd ed., E.J. Brill, Leiden, 1983, pp. 749–51.

54. Kamal Salibi, 'Fakhr al-Dīn wa al-fikra al-lubnāniyya', in Antoine Qāzān (ed.), *'Ab'ād al-qawmiyya al-lubnāniyya* (Jūniah, 1970).

55. *Ibid*, pp. 85–104.

56. *Ibid*, pp. 108–10.

57. *Ibid*, pp. 110–11.

58. Salibi, *Maronite Historians*, pp. 13–22.

59. *Ibid.*, p. 15.

60. K.S. Salibi, 'The traditional historiography of the Maronites', in Bernard Lewis and P.M. Holt (eds), *Historians of the Middle East* (OUP 1962), p. 217.

61. Salibi, *Maronite Historians*, pp. 23–87. Dates corrected include the visit to Rome of a Maronite Patriarch and the fall of Tripoli to Qalāwūn.

62. *Ibid.*, pp. 89–92.

63. *Ibid.*, pp. 93–105.

64. Salibi, 'The traditional historiography of the Maronites', p. 221.
65. Salibi, *Maronite Historians*, p. 98.
66. Salibi, 'The traditional historiography of the Maronites', p. 222. The reader must keep in mind that Dūwayhī started writing his chronicle in 1669, almost half a century after Fakhr al-Dīn II 'laid the foundation-stone of modern Lebanon'.
67. Al-Shidyāq, *Akhbār al-a'yān fī Jabal Lubnān* (Beirut, 1855–59).
68. *Ibid*, pp. 631, 639, and 704.
69. *Ibid*, p. 200; Salibi, *Maronite Historians*, pp. 161–7.
70. Salibi, *Maronite Historians*, pp. 168–9.
71. Al-Shidyāq, *op. cit.*, p. 455.
72. The reference is to the Shihābi *amīr* Bashīr II (1789–1840).
73. Asad Jibrail Rustum, 'Syria under Mehemet Ali', *The American Journal of Semitic Languages and Literatures*, vol. XLI (Oct. 1924), p. 50, n. 4.
74. Salibi, *Maronite Historians*, pp. 232–3.
75. Albert Hourani, *BSOAS*, vol. XXIII (1960), p. 395.
76. Salibi, *Maronite Historians*, pp. 35–7.
77. George Graf, *Geschichte de christlichen arabischen Literatur*, vol. III, (Vatican City, 1949), pp. 306 and 363. In fact, Graf was merely quoting an official Maronite church journal, *al-Manāra*.
78. Salibi, *Maronite Historians*, pp. 89–160.
79. *Ibid.*, pp. 161–68.
80. *The Ancient Greek Historians* (London, 1909), pp. 162–3.
81. Cf. Buṭrus Ḍaw, *Tārīkh al-mawārina*, vol. III (Lebanon, 1976), pp. 260–1 and 284–7. Ḍaw, a Maronite priest writing during the recent civil war in Lebanon, uses Ibn al-Qilā'ī's poem to prove the military prowess of his sect and stress the exclusiveness of Mount Lebanon as 'a Maronite national homeland'.
82. Salibi, *Muntalaq tārīkh Lubnān*, p. 168.
83. *Tārīkh al-azmina* (Beirut, 1951), pp. 194–7.
84. Salibi, *Maronite Historians*, p. 18.
85. In Leonard Binder (ed.) *Politics in Lebanon* (New York, 1966), pp. 263–70.
86. According to one source, *Lebanon: A conflict of minorities* (Minority Rights Group, London, 1983), the present population of Lebanon is divided as follows: Shi'ites 1,100,000 (30%); Maronites 900,000 (25%); Sunnis 750,000 (20%); Greek Orthodox 250,000 (7%); Druzes 200,000 (5%); Armenians 175,000 (4.8%); Greek Catholics 150,000 (4%); other Christians 50,000 (1.2%). The last official population census of 1956 provides the following figures: Maronites 423,000; Greek Orthodox 149,000; Greek Catholics 91,000; all other Christian sects 122,000; Sunnis 286,000; Shi'ites 250,000; Druzes 88,000.
87. Walter L. Browne (ed.) *The Political History of Lebanon*, vol. I, p. 236.
88. Salibi, 'The personality of Lebanon', p. 265.
89. *Ibid.*, pp. 266–7.
90. *Ibid.*, p. 269.
91. *Ibid.*, p. 270.

92. Such as Ferdinand Wüstenfeld, E. de Zambaur, Henri Lammens, Philip K. Hitti, and P.M. Holt.

93. Kamal S. Salibi, 'The secret of the house of Ma'n', *IJMES*, vol. IV (1973), pp. 272–9.

94. Kamal S. Salibi, 'Lebanon since the crisis of 1958', *The World Today*, vol. 17, no. 1 (January, 1961), pp. 32–42.

95. Kamal Salibi, 'Lebanon under Fuad Chehab 1958–1964', *MES*, vol. II (1966), pp. 211–26.

96. This introduction was first published in Arabic before its incorporation in the English version referred to. See Kamal Salibi, 'Ta'rīf tārīkhī bi-Lubnān', *al-Abḥāth*, vol. XV, no. 3 (1962), pp. 364–84.

97. *The Modern History of Lebanon*, pp. xi–xxvi (hereafter *MHL*).

98. *Ibid.*, p. xxvii.

99. This theory of political élites or the ruling class was first elaborated by the Italian political scientist Gaetano Mosca towards the end of the nineteenth century. See, Gaetano Mosca, *The Ruling Class* (New York and London, 1939).

100. *MHL*, pp. 4–6.

101. It is worth noting that Salibi relegates the role of Fakhr al-Dīn II into oblivion and makes only a passing reference. The first chapter of *MHL* is entitled 'The Shihāb Emirate'. In another context, 'The Lebanese crisis in perspective', p. 370, n. 2, the reader is reminded that 'Fuad Chehab (b. 1902), a Maronite, is the scion of a family that held the emirate of Mount Lebanon under the Ottomans from 1697 to 1841'.

102. *MHL*, pp. 3–17.

103. *Ibid.*, pp. 18–27.

104. *Ibid.*, pp. 28–92.

105. *The Druzes and the Maronites under Turkish Rule from 1840 to 1860*, (London, 1862), see chapters 4 and 5.

106. *MHL*, p. 94.

107. *Ibid.*, pp. 109–19.

108. *Ibid.*, p. 162.

109. *Ibid.*, pp. 196–204.

110. Salibi, 'The Lebanese identity', p. 86.

111. Kamal S. Salibi, *Crossroads to Civil War — Lebanon 1958–1976* (New York, 1976), pp. 18 and 62.

112. Salibi, 'The Maronites of Lebanon under Frankish and Mamlūk rule (1099–1516)', *Arabica*, vol. IV (1957), pp. 299–300.

113. K. Salibi, *Munṭalaq tārīkh Lubnān*, pp. 136–8; *Maronite Historians*, p. 245.

114. Salibi, *Crossroads to Civil War*, p. 162.

115. For further details on the Lebanese civil war see Youssef Choueiri, *Bayr al-naṣṣ wa al-ḥāmish*, (London, 1988), Ch. 4. While the present work was in the press, Salibi's, *A House of Many Mansions: the History of Lebanon Reconsidered* (London, 1988) came out. The whole work constitutes yet another shift of emphasis, as well as a full scale retreat behind a smoke screen of empirical objectivity. Having read the typescript of my chapter on his works, he weaves into his new version thinly disguised layers of apologetic rebuttals and unacknowledged extractions designed to pre-empt my evaluation of Lebanese history.

6

The Panacea of Historicism: Abdallah Laroui and Morocco's Cultural Retardation

Abdallah Laroui represents a new generation of Arab historians who believed in their profession as a vocation and a prelude to political action. His intellectual preoccupations developed and matured after the Second World War. It was a period which witnessed the emergence of Arab independent states, the birth of political parties with clear ideological programmes, and the advent to power of radical army officers. Laroui welcomed and shared the various endeavours which sought to transform and regenerate the socioeconomic and cultural life of the Arabs in their individual states. Yet his writings combine and transcend the historical horizons of his generation and those of Ghurbāl and Salibi. While he asks the same recurring questions about the national identity and the conditions which occasioned its genesis, the tone and substance of his answers are more pronounced and articulated. His works are openly ideological and deliberately flaunted as a statement of political commitment. He is consequently reluctant to engage his reader in an academic debate under false pretences; nor does he enshroud his real aims in pious prologues about objectivity, detachment, or selflessness.[1] He stakes his reputation on offering a new interpretation of familiar facts and known data, culled and overworked by French and other western scholars.

Morocco, as a national entity, permeates Laroui's historical vision and constitutes his terms of reference. Through its chequered and variegated development he gropes for a comprehension of the Maghrib and the Arab World. Its past moulds his considered judgements and cogent observations. What he has to say about the Arab World is mainly theoretical and couched in highbrow generalizations; the pace of events, the political struggles, the periodization and chronology of historical phases are overtly understated. His first book, *L'idéologie arabe contemporaine*,[2] to which he owes much of his reputation, is in essence an extension of his Moroccan anxieties and aspirations, and a projection into the Arab arena of his personal experiences. It was primarily conceived as a result of his pondering 'a particular situation: that of present-day Morocco'.[3] His study of modern Arab thought was never intended to be either exhaustive or comprehensive. Moreover, it is postulated not as a straightforward objective description and classification of ideological currents, but rather as a subjective re-enactment of an inner dialogue. His systematic and almost rigid division of modern Arab intellectuals into three major categories, corresponding to three historical phases, is unabashedly declared to have been inspired by his own autobiography.[4] Exactly as Laroui the Moroccan historian and political analyst adopted three successive ideologies — Islamic, liberal, and national — so did Arab societies in progressive stages of their development. He equates the last current with 'scientific' and 'technocratic' ideas which were appropriated by nationalist leaders, such as Nasser, and incorporated in their modernizing policies. Hence Morocco's recent past and future are posited as faithful replicas of Egypt's course of development, with the first two stages telescoped into one by the career of the veteran Moroccan leader, 'Allāl al-Fāsī (d. 1974). The future is glimpsed through the ambitions of another Moroccan politician, Mehdi Ben Barka. These ideologies are, moreover, held to be direct responses to questions the Arabs ask about themselves, but which the western world formulates and imposes.[5]

Abdallah Laroui was born in 1933 in the coastal town of Azammūr, which lies about fifty miles to the south west of Casablanca. His father, who was a relatively prosperous trader, sent him to local schools and to the Lycée Moulay Youssef in Rabat for his primary and secondary education. He received his higher education at the Sorbonne and the Institute of Political Studies in Paris. Before embarking on an academic career, he worked with the Moroccan government as a Counsellor of Foreign Affairs from 1960 to 1963. In 1964 he was appointed Professor of History at the University of Muhammad V in Rabat. Between 1967 and 1970 he was Visiting Professor of North African History at UCLA, California. His academic work often overlapped with various political activities which were a cause of friction between him and the Moroccan Monarch, al-Ḥasan II. Thus in 1984 he was deprived of his university post for a few months before his reappointment in the same capacity at the University of Casablanca.[6] However, by 1985 he seemed to have resolved his differences with the royal family as he officially became the tutor of Crown Prince Sīdī Muḥammad.

In addition to the intellectual influence of French scholars and orientalists,[7] it is apparent that Ben Barka has left a lasting impression on him.[8] Ben Barka's views and wide-ranging activities form an implicit, and sometimes explicit, theme in Laroui's ideological arguments, and inform his approach to the history of Morocco and other Arab countries. Writing before 29 October 1965, when Ben Barka's fate was still unknown, Laroui calls him 'one of the purest heroes of the Moroccan people', and expresses a desire to arm his 'technocratic programme' with a cultural and historical method.[9] Moreover, upon its publication, *L'idéologie arabe contemporaine*, both in its French and Arabic versions,[10] had a mixed reception in the Arab world in general, and Beirut in particular. It was criticized for being either too simplistic, idealistic, or anti-Arab. In 1973 Laroui published in Arabic a work entitled *al-'Arab wa al-fikr al-tārīkhī*[11] (The Arabs and historical thought), which can be considered a sequel to his first book, a restatement of his ideological stance in a more defined context, and a rebuttal of his critics. In its introduction, he justifies and defends his original ambition to inject the modernizing policies of certain nationalist Arab leaders with a sociohistorical methodology, steeped in a comprehensive theory, and goes on to reveal the initial motivation behind his project. Ben Barka's failure to 'reorganize his party' or prevent Morocco from slipping into a position of 'stagnation and subordination', is highlighted as the impetus which induced Laroui to seek the roots of his country's débâcle.[12] His theoretical and historical works are accordingly practical pursuits aimed at shaping the future in the light of an arrested development of the past. To Laroui, Ben Barka broached his topics in a correct manner, asked the right questions and arrived at proper conclusions. Nevertheless, he lacked the methodological tools to endow his deductions with a sound ideological basis.

AN IDEOLOGICAL LEAP

In 1957 Ben Barka, who was then President of the Consultative National Assembly, wrote a preface to a quasi-historical book by a Moroccan scholar, Mohamed Lahbabi.[13] After praising its author for his pungent criticism of French colonialism and historiography, Ben Barka advances two specific reservations about its methodological approach. The first relates to the negative description of the Moroccan government of the nineteenth century as being neither 'feudal' nor 'theocratic'. He believed that only a thorough sociological and historical study would lead to a positive characterization of its nature and structure. The other concerns the 'excessive importance' that Lahbabi attached to the theory of the Muslim jurist al-Māwardī as regards the delegation of power by the caliph to his vizier. It was a thesis, Ben Barka thought, which unduly idealized a particular state of affairs, and could not therefore be generalized as a timeless exposition. It was a theory that 'never found an echo in the Moroccan tradition' of government.[14]

This was the task that Laroui took upon himself to fulfil. Reading the past and participating in the making of the future became two concomitant activities which are incumbent on the historian of Morocco. In order to do so, one has to discard the partial methodologies of western empiricists and positivists, who perceive reality in its present frozen moment. Such methodologies fail to highlight the inner dynamism of a certain historical period and leave out the future as a positive factor inherent in the structure of the present. Thus the present is not to be understood in itself; it is either the past or the future. The past gave Morocco its specificity, culture, organic cycle of life, and national identity. Its present is an interrupted continuity of its past which has no authenticity or character of its own. The past and the future act as two poles of attraction, obscuring the present and rendering it transient. Hence, there is a rupture between 'social reality and self-consciousness'. Only by postulating the potentiality of the present in its ideological manifestations as an 'objective' development can the present gain its proper significance.[15]

Laroui is therefore interested in the past or the present as either an arrested possibility or a teleological process. It is an endeavour which seeks to identify the progressive elements of an ideology and reveals its anticipated future. The three successive ideologies which he isolates are thus studied as an expression of a promising development and a theoretical consciousness of unrealized potentialities. This study of ideological currents serves as a substitute for the study of economic and social structures which are deemed as mere shadows of a more imposing reality. It is the impact of the west that illuminates more adequately the response of Arab societies. What the west has become, the Arabs are bound to repeat and retrace. They have reached the stage of industrialization under the guidance and direction of the national state. This last stage opens the way for a qualitative leap, and ushers in the birth of a fully fledged ideology which the historian volunteers to deliver. Since all Arab ideologists have internalized the vocabulary of Marxism and use Marxist concepts in the analysis of their history, they consequently practise 'objective Marxism' in a crude and unsophisticated manner. In interpreting certain periods of their past they read into them an image of the west whereby the notions of social classes, the feudal system, and the social contract are introduced as normal features of their historical landscape.[16] Moreover, the Arabs, in appropriating certain elements of Marxism, reclaim their entitlement to a new universal future, the feasibility of which the west persists in denying. Twice before in their history they assimilated the past experiences and intellectual heritage of other peoples and made them their own in a return to 'a common source'. The Qur'ān did not affirm a new message, nor did it simply represent its teachings as 'pure imitation'. Then they had their own Aristotle, quite unlike the one known to the Greeks. In a new phase of their development Marx is reinterpreted to suit their needs. This interpretation is still 'more of a possibility than an effective reality'. Nevertheless, it is an inevitable outcome of the fragmentary models offered by the west to the Arabs in their clerical, liberal, and technocratic phases. Finally they have reached a point whereby a new 'homogeneous and total model' makes its appearance and adoption an imperative necessity.[17]

At this stage Laroui was still not certain of the full nature of his new Marxism. He merely conceived it as an evolutionary concept which 'the national state' was bound to proclaim once its positive implications had been revealed to its leaders. What he had in mind was the adoption of the dialectical method, or what is defined as the Hegelian dimension in Marx's historical materialism. It is a method which the situation of Morocco calls for in order to account for its future development and to bypass the static visions of sociology or positivistic Marxism. In this sense, the historical perspective assumes a far-reaching function which over-rides the mere drudgery of adhering to certain technical and academic principles. One analyses the past in order to lay down guidelines for the future.[18]

A few years later Laroui spelled out what he meant by his dialectical method. In the meantime, the Arab 'national states' were defeated in the 1967 war, and Ben Barka disappeared from the Moroccan scene. The possibility of completing the dialectical progression of Arab ideology from within 'the national state' seemed a far-fetched dream. The regression of one possibility did not, however, deter Laroui from exploring other avenues.

Laroui, in his analysis of the prospects of Arab ideologies, seems to derive his optimism from the sweeping, almost impressionistic, diagnosis which Jacques Berque skilfully adumbrated in his book *Les arabes d'hier à demain.*[19] Both books end on a note of optimistic forecast about the Arab future. They were written at a time when Arabism was enjoying an unprecedented popularity under the leadership of Nasser. All the Arabs appeared to be finally moving in a new direction under the banner of nationalism, socialism, democracy, and industrialization.[20] Berque and Laroui postulated the future of the west as the final horizon of all Arab countries. A scientific age was being inaugurated, leaving behind old values and customs, traditional ways of life, and most important of all, Islam itself as a religion and an exclusive set of ideals. Such a promising outlook is manifested, according to Berque, in the growth of 'historical criticism, which analyses the causes of good or evil conditions, sifts out the useful from the negative in their own behaviour and in that of others'. Hence, Marxism with a humanistic face is gaining new adherents every day as it furnishes the tools to grasp 'totality' and 'restore the wholeness to man'.[21]

Laroui, in his updated version of the dialectical method, and after his failure to indoctrinate Nasser, Ben Bella, the first president of independent Algeria, or Ben Barka with his theories, dwelt at length on his modernizing programme with added vigour and visionary prognostication. In 1973 he revealed to the Arabs that the dialectical method was another name for 'historicist Marxism' or 'Marxist historicism'. Moreover, the identity of his method dawned on him after the French philosopher Louis Althusser had stressed the complete divorce between Marx in his mature works and Hegel, and criticized both Lukács and Gramsci for highlighting the Hegelian strands in Marxism. Laroui suddenly found himself in complete agreement with this particular school which Althusser sought to undermine and refute.[22]

Thus Lukács and Gramsci came to the rescue of Morocco and other Arab countries at an opportune moment. They carried a message of hope and final salvation. 'Cultural retardation' was no longer a chronic ailment or an incurable backwardness:

> The historicism we are leading up to, one that is in many respects instrumental, is not the passive acceptance of any past whatsoever and above all not the acceptance of one's own national past …, rather, it is the voluntary choice of realizing the unity of historical meaning by the reappropriation of a selective past. This choice is motivated by pragmatic considerations, perhaps by modesty, above all by nationalism in the most natural sense of the word: the will to gain the respect of others by the shortest possible route.[23]

In selecting his own past Laroui convinced himself of the historian's ability to bypass the present and look forward to a brighter future. If 'objective Marxism' was temporarily suspended through no fault of his own, another perceptible trend takes its place. Despairing of Arab national leaders and their inadequate response to his 'ideological leap', he now embraced the cause of the intellectuals as the engines of historical change. It is they who are capable of understanding historicism and repeating 'the intellectual movement that developed in Germany at the end of the eighteenth and the beginning of the nineteenth century in opposition to the conception of history defended by the philosophy of the Enlightenment'.[24] Their task is arduous and multifarious. Of the social groups that compose Arab societies they alone are qualified to rationalize their communities and formulate a new programme of modernization. It is a programme which gives 'a rational analysis of the past, the present, and the foreseeable future of the Arabs'. However, they must first achieve 'hegemony' in the cultural field as a *sine qua non* for winning the political struggle.[25] In other words, 'praxis is ... historicism in action', and a rectification of retardation.[26] Praxis is the complete fusion of thought and reality, subject and object. A critical historical theory alters and transforms the reality it studies. Historical consciousness is the ultimate union of correct analysis and revolutionary practice. Since the relationship between object and subject is a dialectical one, the totality of history is perceived and transcended. Facts and values merge in one whole and constitute the realm of the historian-cum-revolutionary. The essence of Arab society expresses itself in its existence as an evolving reality, groping to 'compress historical time' and relive the receding historicism of the west. Moreover, history has its own logic which must be deciphered before a study of the bare facts is undertaken.[27] The Arabs have severed all their connections with the past and their heritage, without realizing this paradoxical situation.[26]

Hence, historicism, which sees society as totality, history as process, and the past and the future as historical entities, is used by Laroui to illuminate the inner logic of Morocco's history and that of the Maghrib as a whole. His main aim is to refute the prejudices and generalizations of western historians and to offer an alternative reading of the same events.

HISTORY AS CULTURE

In his dialogue with the west, Laroui discusses the cultural manifestations of concrete realities. Economic structures, political movements, religious orders, and tribal groups are thus reduced in their various configurations as instances producing cultural symbols and attitudes. It is not the nation that is studied, but rather its concept. The state does not exist as a set of institutions apart from its consciousness in the minds of officials and those subject to its rule. Events are not demarcated in a chronological sequence with a logic of their own: it is what they imply, their future rather than their past, which is of crucial importance. The failure of European orientalists to understand Moroccan history does not primarily lie in their ideological assumptions or the assessment of their evidence. Their methodological shortcomings are directly linked to the absence of a full appreciation of the teleological movement of society, and the discovery of the substance which is concealed by deceptive forms of stasis and stagnation.

Neither western nor Maghribi historians have succeeded in establishing the truth of a past that underwent incalculable distortions. The result is either 'a conspiracy' or a neglect of investigating the general sweep of Moroccan history. But what purpose does this new interpretation of certain facts serve? Laroui has no qualms about stating his intentions:

> Each day we see more clearly the necessity of questioning the past concerning the two phenomena that haunt our political and intellectual life: our historical lag and its conscious compensation, that is, the revolution.[29]

How does one question the past? Simply by denying the 'fragmented and passive character of the Maghribi past'? Or by showing that 'cultural lag can always be compensated, its negative aspects do not necessarily predominate on every level of social life'.[30] The method to be followed is varied and complicated. One variation is to stress the negative character of foreign domination which eliminated the potentially positive aspects of Maghribi history. Seen from this perspective, the Maghribis play no positive role: they are either 'victims or passive onlookers'. This colonial distortion of reality must be rejected, and with it 'the classical conception of a North Africa entering history as a half savage country sparsely populated with shepherds'.[31] In this highly charged atmosphere of polemics, claims, and counter-claims, any plausible hypothesis becomes permissible without being backed up by direct or circumstantial evidence. Instead of the passive and negative Berbers of the French scholars, one may easily postulate the existence of a determined race bent on winning its freedom and positively active in the unification of its society. Laroui manages to use the archaeological summations of Gabriel Camps to prove the existence of a 'sedentary agricultural population' before the coming of the Phoenicians to North Africa. Thus 'the contact between this sedentary society and the Phoenician seafarers at the end of the second century is no longer a meeting between barbarism and civilization, but rather between urban commerce and an agricultural society'. This encounter led to the emergence of Berber kingdoms 'as a reaction to Phoenician pressure'. One of these kingdoms, the Numidian, was on the threshold of accomplishing its goals, when another power intervened. Rome thwarted the patriotic struggle and 'the natural movement for unification'. The first historicist lesson can therefore be solely drawn and applied to subsequent developments:

> Time lost and irretrievable, an ambiguity of attitude imposed by the situation — these are recurrent motifs in the history of the Maghrib.[35]

From that fateful moment onwards, the setbacks and regressions of Maghribi history are largely attributed to foreigners and external pressure. The Romans created 'an inversion of values', and forced the Berbers back to nomadism. History was thus 'arrested'. Its march was thwarted. The reappearance of the tribal system must be considered as a defensive stance, born out of a particular historical situation. 'It was a dialectic response to a blocked historical development'. In this perspective, the Berbers cease to be passive, but they hardly escape the anathema of being victims — a fact which Laroui did his best to refute. Be that as it may, this permanent and transitional aspect causes the historian to admonish his compatriots in these words:

> Herein lies the importance to the modern Maghribi of the period under discussion: it is in this period that a situation which was to be repeated with increasingly grave consequences first appears in the full light of history. In disregarding it, in failing to wrest it from the grasp of colonial ideology, the Maghribi condemns himself willy-nilly to propagating phantasms that prevent us from understanding and from acting.[33]

How to understand and to act is the key question which informs Laroui's history and plagues it with hasty reconstructions of entire periods. He attacks various orientalists and scholars for advancing 'the most adventurous hypothesis', and yet he falls into the same trap and adopts similar methods when the evidence fails him or is not available. Jérôme Carcopino is ridiculed for his theory about the commercial empire of the Phoenicians in the western Mediterranean, and the possibility of a flourishing Carthaginian trade in African gold. Laroui believes that the available archaeological evidence does not warrant such a hypothesis and excludes a Carthaginian traffic in gold, be it maritime or overland. The whole theory seems to him to be 'merely a projection upon the past of another, well-known imperialism, to wit, that of the Portuguese in the fifteenth century'.[34] Laroui was obviously so proud of the way he dismissed Carcopino's theory that he repeated his refutation once more in 1983, and in the context of stressing the importance of basing one's historical judgement on documented evidence and the particularity of each event or society.[35] Unfortunately, our historian resorts to the same techniques he so vehemently rejects, and alerts his fellow Moroccans to their pitfalls and farcical incongruities. As a matter of fact, he reviewed in 1965 a book by an Algerian historian, Mohamed Sahli,[36] who set out to demolish the theories of the French historians on the Maghrib, reveal their ideological deviations and thus decolonize history. While agreeing with the aim and methodology of Sahli, Laroui nevertheless felt the need to remind his colleague that his insistence on established 'positive facts and rational arguments' was widely off the mark, given the paucity of documentation in Maghribi history. If the historian adhered to Sahli's strict demands and refrained from advancing hypothetical theses, he would end up adopting 'l'empirisme total, c'est-à-dire l'incompréhension et le mysticisme'.[37] In order to avoid this misfortune and being accused of empiricism, Laroui follows in the footsteps of his arch-enemies, the colonial historians, and plunges into 'projections' of his own. Hence, in his attempt to show the shallowness of 'Romanization' of Africa, and the inconclusive evidence put forward to support this theory by reference to 'the role played by Africans in the political, administrative and intellectual life of Rome', he uses the analogy of another different empire to support his case:

> If there is such a thing as sociological laws, one might actually draw the contrary conclusions from them. It is not in a very Romanized society that the few Romanized individuals would attain to the highest careers. Compare the Moslem Iran of the second and third centuries H., where the political, administrative and intellectual role of the Arabized Iranians in the Abbāsid Empire was out of all proportion to the degree of Arabization of a country which from the fourth century on recovered its national language.[38]

Laroui believed that there was a dearth of information about the commercial activities in the Maghrib of the ninth century, following the advent of Islam. However, he singles out this period 'as a century of Islamization', which 'went hand in hand with commerce'. Thus Islam spread throughout the Maghrib with the network of 'commercial colonies established by Arabs at the crossroads of an alien world'. How does the historian arrive at this conclusion? Present examples are invoked to confirm the certainty of his deduction: 'We can form an idea of this process by observing the most recent developments in Black Africa.'[39]

Between the fourteenth and the sixteenth centuries the Maghrib witnessed a 'deep-seated regression' in the political and socioeconomic fields. It was a period which followed the failures of what Laroui termed 'the ventures' of the Faṭimids, Zīrīds, Almoravids, and Almohads to unify the Maghrib and bring a reconciliation between state and society. By the time the Zayyānids, Marinids, and Ḥafṣids established their dynasties, and the tribes of Banū Hilāl moved into the Maghrib from Egypt and became a permanent feature of North African life, Western Europe had 'made good its lag' and took the offensive in a new crusade. Thus 'the increasing strength of Western Europe accelerated the internal decay of the Maghrib'.[40] However, it was during this period, from 1358 to 1578, that 'lasting internal frontiers' were established, prefiguring the present political divisions of North Africa. Moreover, the Maghrib missed, at the same time, 'a bourgeois revolution' which could have been brought about by the Andalusian refugees following the fall of Granada in 1492, had they not entered as a new middle class into 'competition with the local merchants and artisans'. The chiefs of Banū Hilāl would have become 'feudal barons', but the conditions of such a development 'were impeded by foreign pressure', and they 'continued to be warlords'. These speculations on missed opportunities are considered by Laroui 'as a working hypothesis'. Nevertheless, the hypothesis is retained for its positive characteristics.[41]

With the coming of the Ottomans, 'the dualism between the state and society' was accentuated, even in Morocco, which escaped direct Turkish domination. Local leaders were detached from the central authority, and the question of legitimacy, a recurring theme in North African history, gained greater importance on 'the eve of foreign intervention' in the nineteenth century. Once again Laroui's account for this state of affairs is almost unambiguous. He asks himself: 'Why did this unstable dual power endure as long as it did?' And he answers: 'The determining reason is probably the permanence of the foreign, chiefly Spanish, threat.'[42] The Spanish, the Portuguese, the Ottomans, and then the French and the British re-enacted the role of the Romans in a new way and under different circumstances. However, the Maghribis did not revert to nomadism, nor did they lose their cultural homogeneity brought about by Islam. 'A return to the coexistence of the primary social cells was impossible.' The military state came to the fore, after the age of principalities, empires, and kingdoms. It depended on an army composed of alien or foreign elements and 'prevented the state from being an organic expression of society'. Traditionalization of society emerged as a defence against the state of outside aggression. The urban élite began to lose its socioeconomic status and privileges in the face of foreign competition. Islam, traditions, and the past, were invoked as symbols of a lost culture and a way of life. Modern Maghribi nationalism, however, was born before the arrival of colonialism proper. The political entities of the Maghrib became distinct, even in their Arabic dialects, and their national consciousness was finally defined:

> Morocco gained self-awareness in its struggles against the Iberians and the Turks, in the strivings of its religious brotherhoods, and through its fidelity to the heritage of Andalusian Islam. Tunisia integrated its foreign rulers and without forgetting the former splendors of Kairouan, opened itself to all the influences of the Mediterranean Orient. And Algeria, despite its Zayyānid and Ḥammādid traditions, achieved individuality through a common awareness of the segregation imposed by the Turkish regime.[43]

It was the resurgence of traditionalism and the response of Moroccans to external pressure that Laroui undertook to analyse in a separate work published in 1977.[44]

A HOBBESIAN SULTAN

The characterization of Moroccan history has acquired a standardized terminology which most western scholars use in their various studies and disciplines. Whether one is writing an anthropological, ethnological, linguistic, literary, or historical study, the famous contrast between 'the land of government' (*bilād al-Makhzan*) and 'the land of dissidence or lawlessness' (*bilād al-sibā*) is bound to crop up as a heuristic device.[45] Hence, the population of the first land gave their consent to the sovereignty of the sultan through a *bay'a*, obeyed his orders, paid their taxes, and answered his call for defending the country against internal or external threat. The other land kept its distance from the central power, paid no taxes, and only acknowledged the spiritual authority of the sultan. Another dichotomy superimposed on the first was that between Arabs and Berbers, plains and mountains, city-dwellers and tribal confederations. The relationship between these was described as that of total antagonism and ceaseless struggle. As no party was able to impose its will on the other, rampant anarchy and social dislocations seized Morocco as a constant iron law. Consequently no centralized state was ever allowed to emerge, and Morocco never managed to become a nation in the European sense of the word.[46] Anarchy, tribal structure, isolation, dispersion, lack of a positive national will, resurgence of nomadism, xenophobia, a primitive and simple central government — these were some of the negative aspects and deficiencies which Laroui sought to explain away or simply inveigh against as empirical platitudes.

Thus Laroui makes a deliberate attempt to describe the problems faced by Morocco in such a way as to show them in conformity with similar problems of a typical European state. In the course of depicting the structures of Moroccan state and society he manages to introduce all the western labels of a bourgeois society such as the social contract, rationalization, civic consciousness and national culture. In order to prove the existence of a Moroccan nation and consequently Moroccan nationalism he divides his thesis into two separate parts. In the first he delineates 'a static image of Moroccan society and culture'. He then offers us a 'dynamic' picture, or the way Morocco responded and reacted to external European pressures.[47] In other words, a sociological and historical enquiry which Ben Barka was thinking of writing himself, although his objective was to cover a more recent period.[48] Laroui, in fact, had initially intended to write a study of Moroccan nationalism as it developed under the French Protectorate. However, owing to the difficulty of extracting useful information from leading personalities who remained active in politics, or because of the lack of authentic documentation, he decided to delve into the nineteenth century. There he sought to locate the origins of his nationalism by studying its ideological manifestations. Thus it turned out to be a philological study but still within a socio-historical framework. The static image depicted by Laroui embraces four main features: the peculiar characteristics and economic foundations of Moroccan society, the organs and structures of the central government, the local forces and organizations, and the culture or ideology which permeates the whole system and animates the national organism. The coalescence of these attributes and elements is pronounced to have constituted the Moroccan nation-state before its subjection to persistent European penetration, which coincided with the French conquest of Algeria in 1830.

The characteristics of Morocco as a national entity are glimpsed through the travel literature of various Europeans who journeyed in one Moroccan area or another in the nineteenth century. Notwithstanding the negative and prejudiced portraits of these Europeans, Laroui manages to extract the nuggets of his national identity in an almost impeccable condition. Thus we learn that the Moroccans wore a peculiar type of shoe, known as the *balgha*, which sets them apart from their neighbours, the Algerians and Tunisians. Moreover, the Moroccans were so attached to their *balghas* that they clung to them wherever they travelled throughout the Maghrib. This national trait manifested itself in a striking manner when the sultan decided to modernize the uniforms of his soldiers: they instantly displayed their utter disgust at the idea, and refused to wear army boots which had been introduced into Algeria.[49] Another nugget or distinctive Moroccan peculiarity is the fact that cigarette smoking was 'practically unknown until 1900'. Then there was that feeling of retardation which gripped Moroccans passing through the green fields of Europe. They immediately sensed their technological inferiority in the cultivation of their land and did not fail to perceive the gap which separated them from France or England. Such a heightened perception of inferiority fostered and sharpened their territorial and communitarian belonging and reinforced 'le sentiment du "nous" contre "eux"'.[50] He even invests the frequent outbreaks of famine with a positive characteristic since they increased the circulation and migration of people and turned in the process into 'an element of homogenization'.[51]

The Moroccan Arabic dialect is brandished once again as a constituent factor in the formation of the national identity, along with the fact that Moroccans had a name for their country, *al-Maghrib*, and possessed a certain knowledge of the geographical configurations and extent of their territory. However, Laroui finds his national traits less malleable when he tackles more tangible socioeconomic factors, such as the existence of a unified economic market, the means of communications, the use of a standard currency and a uniformed system of weights and measures. Nor is he able to explain away the fact that the Moroccan sultan was first and foremost 'the Commander of the Faithful', and the Moroccans primarily recognized and addressed each other as fellow Muslims. He is, moreover, less convincing when we learn that the adage 'love of the fatherland is part of the faith' meant to most Moroccans not their country but the Islamic city of al-Madīna in the Arabian Peninsula.[52] Indeed, all that he succeeds in affirming does not amount to more than a descriptive outline of a community which has its own peculiar customs and way of life. The existence of a true nation is postulated as a potentiality which was cruelly arrested by European pressure, a notion which adds further complications to the theoretical criteria by which the evidence is assessed. In assuming the arrested development of a Moroccan nation owing to external interference, the case for the emergence of a nationalist movement under the same interfering power is rendered all the more puzzling and difficult to sustain.

Laroui's historicism suffers its first setback with his attempt to juxtapose Hobbes's *Leviathan* and the Moroccan *Makhzan* presided over by the sultan. He agrees with E. Gellner that nationalist writers such as Mohamed Lahbabi erred in equating the act of the *bay'a* with the Social Contract of Jean-Jacques Rousseau.[53] He, however, could not resist the temptation of finding another European equivalent. After alluding to the investiture of the sultan, as both caliph and imām, as an act of submission on the part of believers in exchange for security and the maintenance of religious law, he pronounces it to be 'a sociological contract of a Hobbesian nature', and despite the fact that it is modelled on an original Islamic investiture.[54] Thus Laroui's analogy is theoretically and factually untenable. Its weakness is related to a complete reinterpretation of Hobbes's contract, its origin and scope. Whereas the *bay'a* is a contract between a new caliph and a group of persons whereby the latter promise him obedience, that of Hobbes is 'that the power of the person holding authority in the State must be held to rest not indeed ... on a contract which he himself had concluded with the people, but instead on a contract which the people had concluded amongst themselves'.[55] Hobbes's sovereign and people, who together embody the organic unity designated *Leviathan*, are posited as ideal types not to be confused with concrete institutions. In this sense, conducting an analogy with a normative system in a sociohistorical study depreciates the accuracy of the latter and turns it into an opaque depiction.

However, Laroui's insidious insertion of a Hobbesian dimension into his ideological debate allows him to recast his sultan in a variety of shapes and functions. In his real or symbolic authority as *Sharīf* (descendant of the Prophet), *imām*, commander-in-chief of the army, administrator, and finally *mawlā* (religious master, or lord), the sultan condenses and mirrors the unity of the state and society. His multifaceted functions correspond to the structures, social or religious orders and organizations of Morocco at large. The army, the bureaucracy, the religious brotherhoods and orders, the notables and the élite of the élite recognize their true identity and interest in their sultan. They constitute an extension of his largesse, power, and position. Thus, Morocco, bereft of its sultan, ceases to exist as a national entity, be it in a static or dynamic situation. Laroui admits that these different aspects of his polity do not interact, form a hierarchy, or permit individual mobility. Nevertheless, 'the sultanate is at the same time solid and fragile, abstract and yet indispensable'. Is it permissible under these circumstances to speak of a proper state and a proper society? Yes and no. The main object of the exercise is to deny the idea 'd'une "Poussière de tribus autonomes"'.[56]

The authority of the Hobbesian sultan is not confined to 'the land of government'. It spreads its tentacles, spiritually, militarily, or economically, into *bilād al-sibā*, and annihilates its existence as either lawless or independent. A revolt launched by a brotherhood or a tribe does not signify a complete break between its authors and the sultan. It is either a limited act which is not pursued to the bitter end, or an attempt to renegotiate the terms of participation and the conditions of obedience. Thus *al-sibā* is an integral part of the system which renders tribalism, so cherished by western scholars, a redundant possibility.

Had Morocco been left alone and without 'foreign interference', 'the *Makhzan* as an institution' would have lasted a long time. Moreover, culture, in its various religious forms and manifestations, reproduces the social structure at a higher level and acts as a unitary symbol. Its essential role in society made it under European pressure a vehicle of resistance and an embodiment of national identity.[57]

Having thus presented his case for the existence of a Moroccan nation-state with all its specificities and particularities, he now turns to its dynamic response to the outside world. The dynamic nature of this solid yet fragile *Leviathan* is revealed as a long-term process of regression and decline. The different stages of military, administrative, and financial reforms, voluntarily undertaken or forcibly imposed by European powers, are duly noted, and their superficial nature and abysmal failure are highlighted.[58] Poverty and famine became widespread. The central government gradually lost its hold on the economy, and fell victim to European creditors and bankers. The increasing indebtedness of the state and the growing foreign pressure, whether military or commercial, led to a recurring cycle of urban and rural revolts. The sultan and his army proved their impotence in either defending the country against French and Spanish incursions or in curbing various types of rebellions. Consequently, the legitimacy of the Commander of the Faithful was exploded, along with the elaborate system and its 'dialectical synthesis'. The recession of one legitimacy resulted in a counter-movement initiated by a group of religious leaders. The past with its culture and traditions was resurrected as a defensive weapon against external agression. The '*ulamā*' resorted to a direct appeal to the Moroccan individual in order to safeguard his religion and ward off the debilitating effects of falling under European domination. Europe was totally rejected along with its local collaborators, particularly the merchant class. When the last sultan of independent Morocco signed the treaty of a French Protectorate in 1912, the old *Makhzan* had become a totally new institution, hardly recognizable to its former subjects and adherents.[59]

In this perspective, *Salafism* appeared as the only resort of an embattled society. A return to early Islam denoted an endeavour to safeguard the future by means of 'consolidating traditional culture which continued to be the only common language of society as a whole'. Nationalism was born out of 'the specificity', the particular characteristics of Morocco, and expresses the continuity of its past. It confirms 'the predominance of the past over the present', and is bound to reappear under different conditions, and be proclaimed by new social groups in order to serve new purposes. The theory has been vindicated: 'Vue sous cet angle, le nationalisme est essentiellement un aspect de l'historicisme.'[60] Thus historicism reappears in an expected manner, but instead of controlling the future, it now legitimizes the past. Both the historian and the revolutionary have finally been reconciled. One surrenders to the past and the other relieves himself of a retarded present. Nevertheless in 1970 Laroui was still fulminating against the lack of 'cultural unification, politicization of groups, legitimization of the state order', and the negative reactions of his fellow Maghribis. He thought that the fusion of the state and society had long been delayed. In short, he noted the absence 'of a true democracy'.[61]

Shorn of their ideological overtones and historicist assumptions, Laroui's works indicate a marked advance along the long road that modern Arab historiography has traversed since its inception in the 1830s. From being a translating movement or a subservient echo of European scholarship, it now aspired to being treated as an equal partner. Long before Edward Said's *Orientalism*,[62] Laroui was engaged in a critical analysis of the orientalists' methods and the way they viewed Islam, Arab history, and the Maghrib. His devastating criticism of Gustave von Grunebaum's cultural anthropology, first published in French in 1974[63] remains a classic example in its methodological approach and rigorous arguments. His criticism, unlike that of Said, is never confined to a formalistic disclosure of subjectivist judgements and reduction. He always offers an alternative, and often highly illuminating, interpretation of a historical period or an intellectual school. His *L'idéologie arabe contemporaine* contains refreshingly suggestive insights into the nature and scope of Islamic historiography, and which he offers in the course of scrutinizing western works on the same subject.[64] Similarly, Ibn Khaldūn, the great Arab historian, on whose authority French scholars have foisted all their hasty conclusions, is reduced at Laroui's hands to his proper size. Instead of treating his work as an authoritative source on the history of the Maghrib, it is considered as an integral part of the same history, reflecting all its upheavals, pessimistic outlook and deepening crisis. Then he gives his own analysis of certain Khaldūnian concepts which were divested of 'their subtlety' by French historians such as Gautier, Terrasse, and Julien.[65] His book on the origins of Moroccan nationalism includes numerous sections which throw new light on the structure and functions of Moroccan religious orders and social groups such as *al-zāwiya* and the tribe.[66] His cogent observations are only diluted by the artificial bridge which he constructs to link traditional phenomena with modern nationalism.

Laroui reveals in his academic output a potentiality that is blunted by another potentiality — that of a future struggling to control its past. In professing the necessity of seeing historical periods as totalities, and in his adoption of historicism as a dynamic factor underlying the inner development of events, he converted the slogans of nationalist leaders into theoretical constructions. His analytical and interpretative concepts replaced the bare facts of reality and became the living elements of a projected scheme of things. His methodology aspired to telescope two different historical movements and stages — liberalism and socialism — into one single moment of an urgent plan of action. This was postulated under the rubric of a Marxism trimmed and refashioned to suit Arab tastes and Moroccan ambitions. He believed in the ultimate entrenchment of European cultural values in the plains and plateaux of Morocco as the only solution to a historical dilemma. Hence his differentiation between specificity and authenticity in Maghribi history. The first was underlined as the distinctive national identity of his country and the trajectory of its past. The dynamism of his theory turned it into an ever-evolving phenomenon, whereby a regressive movement or an arrested development were held to be momentary pauses and mere phases of recuperation. Authenticity was identified as a fossilized cluster of ideas and attitudes directed towards a dead past.[67] Arab Marxism was, therefore, posited as an organic ideology which lends specificity a more solid character and hastens the decomposition of authenticity in its false survival and nostalgic yearnings. The initial function of the new ideology was to instil and propagate the modern notions of loyalty to the state, and allegiance to the legitimacy of its existence. In order to prove the possibilities of the future, the past was searched for inherent potentialities. Thus, successes in achieving a well-ordered administration and a coherent political organization in Maghribi history were unfailingly ascribed to internal factors and forces, whereas failures in the same fields were almost solely attributed to external pressure or interference.

His narrations, which extend into antiquity, cover the present, and look forward to the future, are overworked reformulations of a certain political programme. Historicism implies constant change at both ends of the spectrum. The dialectical movement of progression opens up infinite prospects and assures the national identity of its inevitable triumph. While the orientalists practise 'de-historization' by casting the Moroccan identity in a rigid mould,[68] his approach unleashes it into the turbulent passage of becoming. Its qualities are constantly changing in the whirlwind of conquests, invasions, and uprisings. State and society are postulated in their capacity to emerge as actual entities; their realization is left to the historian to project and harness. Having rescued the specificity of his nation as a viable polity, he condemns its authenticity as artificial concoctions designed to freeze the present and obliterate the future. The spirit of the age, which was first invoked by Salīm al-Bustānī in the nineteenth century, is reappropriated in the name of an objective alternative — that of democracy merging into a Marxist order. The course of the past is denuded of its viability and considered as an oppressive present. To Laroui, it was no longer a question of endeavouring to dwell among the graves of dead ancestors, or to entice their spirits into a new cycle of life. Ibn Khaldūn's vicious circles, alternating between nomadism and degenerate civilization, had to be broken, and his conceptual frameworks discarded as a sign of unwarranted pessimism. It was now the culture of the future that had to be endowed 'with a national significance'. The task of the historian was to sort out 'the confusion between goals and aspirations', and link the future of Morocco and the Arabs with that of humanity at large.[69]

Whereas the tradition of apologetics in Arabic literature is quite impressive in its quantity, its qualitative value never gained a foothold in the academic world. Ever since Afghānī and 'Abduh voiced their criticism of European views of Islam, the polemic trend began to snowball, producing a mass industry of pamphlets and refutations inspired by the original masters. Their main themes remained almost the same. First, western writers were absolutely right to criticize feudalism, the church, and Catholic Popes for hindering progress, the advancement of reason, or the growth of just laws. Secondly, secularism was a natural outcome which developed out of a specific European context, while, unlike Europe, Islam has always been on the side of justice and science. Finally, the Reformation, inaugurated by Martin Luther, was a latter-day Islamic movement which made both Protestantism and Islam two facets of one single eternal reason.

Laroui was perhaps the first Arab scholar to deprive the Islamic past of its relevance to the present and derive his 'theoretical consciousness and unrealized potentialities' from a different social reality. His stark contrast between a frozen past and a promising future announced the redundancy of the age of apologetics, and heralded the possibility of new perspectives in academic research and political engagement.

NOTES

1. See, for example, Abdallah Laroui, *Les origines sociales et culturelles du nationalisme marocain (1830–1912)* (Paris, 1980), p. 21, where he absolves himself of the requirements of 'perfect detachment'. *Les origines* was originally Laroui's doctorate thesis. It was first published in 1977.
2. *L'idéologie arabe contemporaine* (Paris, 1967). Reprinted 1982.
3. *Ibid.*, p. 3.
4. *Ibid.*, pp. 109, n. 26 and 212.
5. *Ibid.*, pp. 17–28 and 45–9.
6. *Al-Majalla*, no. 255 (London, 29 December–4 January 1984–85).
7. Such as Jacques Berque, Maxime Rodinson, and Charles André Julien.
8. Ben Barka disappeared in 1965 while living in Paris in exile. He was presumed to have been kidnapped and murdered by the Moroccan General Oufkir. The latter was in turn supposed to have committed suicide in 1977. For further details see Wilfred Knapp, *North West Africa*, 3rd edn, (OUP, 1977), pp. 295–8.
9. Laroui, *L'idéologie arabe contemporaine* (Paris, 1967), pp. 47–8.
10. (Beirut, 1970), 4th edn (1981).
11. (Beirut, 1973). The same book appeared in a shorter French version under the title *La crise des intellectuels arabes* (Paris, 1974). It was translated into English as *The Crisis of the Arab Intellectual* (University of California Press, 1976).
12. *Ibid.*, pp. 17–18.
13. Mohamed Lahbabi, *Le gouvernement marocain à l'aube du XXe siècle* (Rabat, 1958).

14. *Ibid.*, pp. 3–6.

15. *L'idéologie arabe*, pp. 65–9 and 124–37.

16. This 'objective Marxism' which Laroui claims to have discovered in contemporary Arab ideology is what Gramsci called in another context 'implicit Marxism'. See Antonio Gramsci, *The Modern Prince and Other Writings*, 4th printing (New York, 1957), p. 83.

17. *Ibid.*, pp. 139–55.

18. *Ibid.*, pp. 157–65.

19. (Paris, 1960). English trans: *The Arabs, their History and Future* (London, 1964).

20. The same optimistic note pervades Albert Hourani's book, *Arabic Thought in the Liberal Age 1798–1938* (London, 1962).

21. Berque, *The Arabs*, pp. 266 and 280. Laroui is awkwardly silent about Berque's work, although it is apparent that he took it as a model.

22. *Al-'Arab wa al-fikr al-tārīkhī*, p. 30.

23. Laroui, *The Crisis of the Arab Intellectual*, p. 100.

24. *Ibid.*, p. 129, n. 1.

25. *Al-'Arab wa al-fikr al-tārīkhī*, p. 35.

26. Laroui, *The Crisis*, pp. 100–6.

27. Cf. Georg Lukács, *History and Class Consciousness* (London, 1971), p. 181: 'The developing tendencies of history constitute a higher reality than the empirical "fact".'

28. *Al-'Arab wa al-fikr al-tārīkhī*, p. 23.

29. Abdallah Laroui, *The History of the Maghrib* (Princeton University Press, 1977), pp. 3–5. First published in French, 1970. Hereafter *HM*.

30. *Ibid.*, pp. 19 and 25.

31. *Ibid.*, pp. 52–9.

32. *Ibid.*, pp. 60–2.

33. *Ibid.*, pp. 65–6. According to Gramsci, *The Modern Prince*, p. 173, historical analysis must not be an end in itself. Its only significance is in serving 'to justify practical activity, an initiative of will'.

34. *Ibid.*, pp. 39–40; Jérôme Carcopino, *Le Maroc antique* (Paris, 1948), pp. 73–163.

35. Abdallah Laroui, *Thaqāfatuna fī ḍaw' al-tārīkh* (Beirut — Casablanca, 1983), pp. 30–4.

36. Mohamed Sahli, *Décoloniser l'histoire. Introduction à l'histoire du Maghreb* (Paris, 1965).

37. *Hespéris–Tamuda*, vol. VI (1965), pp. 239–42. Cf. Germain Ayache, 'Histoire et colonisation, l'exemple du Maroc', *Hespéris–Tamuda*, vol. XVII (1976–77), pp. 47–67.

38. *HM*, p. 45, n. 26.

39. *Ibid.*, p. 107 and n. 4.

40. *Ibid.*, pp. 222–3 and 227–39.

41. 'Its main advantage is that it introduces a social dynamic into the history of the Maghrib.' *Ibid.*, pp. 240–1 and n. 10.

42. *Ibid.*, p. 269.

43. *Ibid.*, pp. 282–7 and 325–6.

44. Laroui, *Les origines sociales et culturelles du nationalisme*

marocain (1830–1912). Hereafter *Les origines*.

45. See, for example, Clifford Geertz, *Islam Observed* (The University of Chicago Press, 1968, 1971), p. 78. This stereotyped image of Morocco was first articulated into a comprehensive theory by French colonial scholars at the turn of the nineteenth century. See Edmund Burke III, 'The image of the Moroccan state in French ethnological literature', in Ernest Gellner and Charles Micaud (eds), *Arabs and Berbers: from Tribe to Nation in North Africa* (London, 1972), pp. 175–99.

46. Or, as Henri Terrasse, *Histoire du Maroc* (Paris, 1952), p. 190, puts it: 'Moins encore qu'un État, le Maroc n'a réussi à devenir une nation.'

47. *Les origines*, pp. 18–19.

48. *The political thought of Ben Barka* (Havana, 1968), pp. 7–8.

49. *Les origines*, pp. 30–2.

50. *Ibid.*, pp. 34–8.

51. *Ibid.*, p. 55.

52. *Ibid.*, pp. 38–65.

53. Ernest Gellner, 'The struggle for Morocco's past', *MEJ*, vol. 15 (1961), pp. 79–90; and *Saints of the Atlas* (London, 1969), pp. 25–7.

54. *Les origines*, pp. 71–80.

55. Friedrich Meinecke, *Machiavellism*, trans. from the German by Douglas Scott (London, 1957), p. 211. Or as Hobbes, *Leviathan* (London and Melbourne, 1973. Reprinted 1983), p. 89, puts it: 'this is more than Consent, or Concord; it is a reall Unitie of them all; in one and the same Person, made by Covenant of every man with every man'. Moreover, Hobbes's sovereign is not necessarily one person, but may be represented by an 'Assembly of men' which is an inconceivable development in a traditional caliphate.

56. *Les origines*, pp. 81–124.

57. *Ibid.*, pp. 126–233.

58. *Ibid.*, pp. 240–62. The reforms alluded to were mainly the brain-child of the British Consul in Morocco, John D. Hay, who was anxious to persuade the sultans to abolish the policy of monopolies, and whose term of service extended from 1845 to 1886. See his work, *A Memoir* (London, 1896).

59. *Ibid.*, pp. 305–36.

60. *Ibid.*, pp. 423–36. For a critical assessment of Laroui's historicism, see Dr Aziz al-Azmeh, 'Bayn al-marksiyya al-mawḍū'iyya wa saqf al-tārīkh', *Dirāsāt 'Arabiyya*, vol. 21, no. 3 (1985), pp. 3–27.

61. *HM*, pp. 386–8.

62. *Orientalism* (London, 1978).

63. *La crise des intellectuels arabes*, ch. 3.

64. See, in particular, pp. 95–106.

65. *HM*, pp. 219–21.

66. *Les origines*, pp. 131–86.

67. *Al-'Arab wa al-fikr al-tārīkhī*, p. 24.

68. *HM*, p. 328.

69. *Al-'Arab wa al-fikr al-tārīkhī*, p. 78; *The Crisis of the Arab Intellectual*, p. 174.

Conclusion

Modern Arab historiography formed an integral part of a wider movement which affected most Arab countries in varying degrees. It accompanied or responded to European influence and expansionism. Its initial manifestations were mere devices used by amateur historians for immediate or hastily constructed purposes. It bore all the marks of a novice intermediary attempting to reconcile a traditional community with an advancing modern world. The novice was consequently caught up in an unfavourable process and suffered the fate of his society. His words became mere apologies, bundled recipes, and a desperate search for a lost dream. Dead heroes of the past were propped up and paraded as living witnesses of a promising future. The present was subsumed under the mantle of a new type of leadership, and the ideals of a putative nation were reduced to a receding echo of a benevolent ruler or sultan. The spirit of the age was invoked as an irrefutable testimony of an assured renewal. Rulers fell, sultans disappeared and the heroes were banished or executed. Europe stepped in to fill the void, and plaster an empty Arab space with its soldiers, commerce, secular and missionary schools. The crumbling walls were verdant again, and blossomed at the hands of skilful masters and adept local pupils. After the death of al-Ṭahṭāwī, the emigration of Zaydān to Egypt and the voluntary confinement of Yannī in his home town, the Arab World veered towards new aspirations and confronted the west with its own weapons. A new generation of Arab historians took up the challenge, and sought to eradicate another vacuum by a leap of imagination.

Ghurbāl, Salibi, and Laroui inherited a new role and a more onerous task. They picked up the torch left smouldering by al-Ṭahṭāwī, al-Bustānīs, Yannī, al-Madanī, and al-Mīlī. They all pointed out the laudable contributions of their amateur colleagues, or announced their intention to ground the same conclusions on a scientific basis.[1] The professional study of the national identity was formally inaugurated. The new historians considered themselves in charge of a message that had to be conveyed to a wider audience. They claimed to possess a practical solution to the backwardness of their societies, and a cultural programme which dwarfed the political tracts and manifestos of various Arab nationalist movements. As they carried out their academic and extra-curricular duties and activities, the historians assumed the air of self-appointed managers of legitimation. Thus the army officer and the scholar in the Arab World share a number of common characteristics: the adoption of certain western ideas, a burning desire to reform society, efficiency, discipline and a perceptible aloofness towards their traditional communities.[2]

Exactly as the military officer wards off or resists foreign invaders, colonial domination, or oppressive rulers, so does the scholar as he engages in demolishing the negative arguments of the orientalists or the distorted views of his countrymen. This confrontation sometimes simulates the tactics of skirmishes without an overall strategy. Ghurbāl's refutation of the way French scholars interpreted the Islamic system of land tenure is such an example. On other occasions, the resistance is fought on a wider scale and a deeper level. The theories and methods of western orientalists are systematically questioned and reduced to mere prejudices and vacuous arguments. Laroui excels himself in pursuing this line of attack.

The military officer attributes the failure of his society to the squabbles of irresponsible politicians and the plurality of political parties and factions. The scholar sees the signs of weakness in the cultural field. His coup d'état is launched to create out of the 'chaos of being' a compact national identity, using the skills and trappings of modern scholarship. The officer paints in his first broadcast to the nation a grim picture of the pre-revolutionary situation. The older order is scathingly dissected as an endless nightmare of confusion, corruption, disorder, social disruption, and economic dislocation. The scholar finds his victim in the numerous, foreign or local, theories and concepts which arrest the natural flow of reality, and fail to depict the true process of events. He therefore weaves the web of historical incidents into a pattern of significance, and captures that 'wonderful moment' in which the nation–state came into existence. The finely divided particles are finally merged into a single substance of an unmistakable identity.

However, when a political upheaval, a military defeat, or an economic crisis grips the nation, and the masses react in the only way they know, the national identity merely goes into hiding. It never vanishes, nor does it become a heap of fine dust; rather, it awaits an opportune moment to manifest itself. The incubation period may sometimes extend for almost a century.[3] Or when it re-emerges its shape and contours are no longer recognizable. Its metamorphosis is only perceptible to the sharp eyes of a Salibi as Lebanism suddenly changed into Arabism. Yet still, it may never desert its adherents, at least in its spiritual incarnation, permeating native dishes, shoes, peculiar dialects, tribal confederations, and religious fraternities. Laroui, once again, freely volunteered to re-enact the whole process.

Be that as it may, these are not fanciful ideas conjured up in the deep recesses of perplexed minds. They point up, reflect, and condense the transitional nature of Arab societies. There is a shift of emphasis accompanying, or coming in the wake of, new shifts in the internal structures and external realignments of the historians' respective countries.[4] This phenomenon is neither the prerogative nor the birthmark of Arab historians. Whether these shifts of emphasis indicate a regressive interpretation or a progressive articulation of the national identity is not an easy question to answer. The temptation at this stage for a new synthesis seems alluring, beckoning with a seductive smile. Perhaps some Arab historians have already succumbed to its synthetic charms. Furthermore, the historians whose works have been studied were not cynics, opportunists, or blindly catering to the whims of presidents and kings. Although they did operate in a constricted environment, their works were not the result of dreading an oppressive authority or an attempt to promote their own careers in a vulgar way. The 'nation–state' in the Arab World was a fact of life, with demarcated international borders, distinctive national symbols, educational systems, administrative structures, armed forces, and full membership of the United Nations. The diversity and unrelated histories of some Arab countries, owing to the fragmentation of the original Islamic caliphate, and the subsequent domination of various European powers, made the writing of an uninterrupted narrative an intellectual impossibility. These are some of the hard facts which may have influenced the general attitude of one historian or another. Nevertheless, they are not meant to appear as direct causes producing equally immediate effects.

The assumptions which underlie this study do not presume a deliberate choice on the part of Arab historians to deceive their readers or choose selective facts out of a surreptitious design and an ulterior motive. At a particular moment, from a certain point of view, according to a political or philosophical theory he entertains, the historian tends to concentrate on certain aspects almost to the exclusion of other minor or major ones. Discussions with academic colleagues, or other intellectuals who may happen to hold contrary views, serve to sharpen the historian's arguments, induce him to review his sources, trigger fresh ideas, and open new horizons. He becomes inclined to embrace an opposite viewpoint when specific events outside his control impinge on his thoughts or life. If the historical past is still a live issue, and a target of controversial debates, brandished by various groups to bolster a contemporary policy or institution, the conversion to a new concept of the same event slowly begins to emerge. Even then, unless the historian believes in his work as a serious undertaking governed by strict rules and principles, the change of emphasis may never take place. It is in this perspective that our historians are judged. Yet, it must be conceded that not all of them had the same degree of integrity or fairness.

Seen from a different perspective, one may say that the unit of study chosen by Arab historians tended to narrow their visions. It made them ask questions already defined by the nature of their subject. As a result, many factors, events, economic developments, social transformations, religious beliefs, and cultural values were either involuted, escaped their attention, or were not fully noted and encompassed within their narratives. What we have is a succession of partial views and glimpses of a richer and more complex reality. The major gap which forces itself on the student of these historical writings is the relative absence of the ordinary Arab man and woman, their needs, fears, and aspirations. One senses his or her presence. They appear as fleeting shadows and elusive ghosts. Yet they are presumed to be part of one national identity, sharing its past, present, and future. Describing the state of Egyptian education at the end of the nineteenth century, Lord Milner states:

> While the Government in 1897 spent more than £E93,000, drawn from the pockets of the general mass of the taxpayers, on educating some 11,000 pupils, mostly of the well-to-do classes, and mainly for the careers of civil employés or lawyers, over 180,000 children found shelter in the village or mosque schools entirely supported by the voluntary efforts of the people. In these indigenous schools … instruction is

> usually confined to learning the Koran by rote. As a result of this neglect of primary education, over 99 per cent of the population are unable to read or write.[5]

One is bound to ask which group of these pupils and their parents represented Egypt, its identity, social structure, and political life. Is this 'the compact nation' which Ghurbāl asserted as a full-blown reality long before British occupation? Why should the sufi orders, the guilds of artisans, the '*ulamā*', and the peasants not be eloquent representatives of Egypt's character and the pulse of its inner depths at the turn of the nineteenth century, rather than 'an adventurer who was already on the scene'? Similarly, Laroui flaunts his abhorrence at the folkloric traditions of Morocco as a token of his modernistic historicism.[6] The longer he studied European brochures and prescriptions for a utopian future, the more Morocco's living culture became a liability to be discarded, an optical illusion or a desert mirage.[7] Salibi described, often brilliantly, the particular traits, customs, and social life of the various Lebanese sects. Yet most of his descriptions convey the impression of being written by an outsider. The beliefs, anxieties, and ambitions of the Sunnis, Druzes, and Shi'ites, are not given a fair representation. He was not appalled by the slums of Beirut until 1976, almost thirty years after they had started to mushroom.

Were these lacunae the result of a specific type of education, the marginality of the historians as intermediaries between two different societies and a certain awareness of not truly belonging to one or the other? Or were they overwhelmed by the rapid changes in the life and fortunes of their countries, and consequently became mere prisoners of their own situation? These are questions implying tentative answers which may shed some light on a complex historical dilemma.

The first generation of modern Arab historians preached the gospel of an absolute ruler with a sense of equity and justice. He was expected to manage and regulate the daily life of a particular nation living within a specific geographical unit. The Egyptian writer al-Ṭahṭāwī placed his hopes of reviving the past glories of his nation in Muḥammad 'Alī and his dynasty.[8] The Syrian intellectuals[9] made no secret of their loyalty to any Ottoman sultan or governor, western protector, or local reformer who would bring about the renaissance of a new Syria. They yearned for a golden age, recently excavated or researched by one western scholar or another, to be re-created and reincarnated in the present. The historical periods of their nations which exhibited a comparatively flourishing culture and an advanced level of material prosperity were considered highly significant and worthy of imitation. Al-Ṭahṭāwī fixed his gaze towards the age of the early Pharaohs, that of Alexander the Great, and the exemplary life of the Prophet Muḥammad. The Syrian historians resurrected Zenobia as a mirror held to posterity. Thus there is no methodical delineation of the various stages of one's national history, and no clear yardstick by which the historian measures the gradual emergence of the nation–state. The available literature on the subject, often secondary or outdated, is used in a selective approach to prop up an argument and highlight a particular point.

These first pioneers were amateur historians. They practised history-writing alongside many other duties, and pursued different careers. Al-Ṭahṭāwī was a technical translator, journalist, editor, school teacher-cum-director, and *'ālim*. Yannī worked as a translator, journalist, vice-consul, and later in his life became publisher and editor. Maṭar specialized as a pharmacist and botanist, then migrated from Beirut to Istanbul where he practised medicine, edited a law journal, worked as a private tutor, school inspector, and translator.

As the rulers of the new nation–states regained full or semi-political independence, such as was the case of Egypt in the 1920s, national universities were established and local scholars were gradually recruited in the various departments, or foreign colleges were transformed by their boards of governors into fully fledged institutions of higher education. A case in point was the Syrian Protestant College which was renamed the American University of Beirut after the declaration of Greater Lebanon in 1920. The second generation of Arab historians made its appearance and contributions within such institutions and as professional scholars trained in European or American universities. This radical change in the professional standard of Arab historians, which crystallized under the direct impact of nationalist movements and ideologies, reflected itself in a new approach towards the past. The narrative of these historians assumed a novel character. It was based on primary sources, and a clear perception of the divergences which separate one historical period from another. Unlike the generation of the nineteenth century, these historians had no golden age to glorify or revive. The rise of nationalism, and consequently the nation-state, is seen as a modern phenomenon. Nationalism develops as a result of a long-term process; it is a historical progression unfolding over time. A set of conditions, a chain of events, a cluster of particular factors lend it a distinct identity. The greater significance of specific incidents lies in their configuration and confluence, leading to the birth of a different current. Thus, the narrative captures a conglomeration of political events and socioeconomic structures and invests them with a decisive role in creating the identity of the nation–state. Disparate elements, formerly considered divisive or incongruous, merge into an organic entity. Inherent contradictions and irreconcilable forces are transformed into a new fabric of harmonious colours. The national identity is thus decreed into existence with the full vigour of a supreme work of art: the art of the historian. If the full flowering of a national identity is still concealed, the events of history persist in prefiguring the inevitable rise of such a phenomenon. This is how the Egyptian historian Shafīq Ghurbāl interpreted the foundation of a central authority in his country at the turn of the nineteenth century.[10] The Lebanese historian Kamal Salibi interpreted the coexistence of various religious sects in his homeland in a similar vein,[11] while the Moroccan historian Abdallah Laroui spoke of the gradual, albeit arrested, growth of a uniform national culture and a potential loyalty to the state.[12]

A reconciliation story of opposed forces is, therefore, embedded in the subject itself. We glimpse a happy romantic play, yet pervaded with a tragic element. A comedy of life implying a sense of tragedy and deep anxiety, bordering on the heroic and eventual triumph of man over nature. The European past and present are projected into Arab history, and made a model for the future. While Ghurbāl considered Muḥammad ʻAlī as a secular western leader bent on building a compact Egyptian nation, Salibi discovered the elusive Lockean social contract in the midst of his Lebanese sects, and Laroui resuscitated Hobbes's *Leviathan* within the labyrinth of the Moroccan sultanate.

A new pattern is clearly discernible. One immediately notices a sharp discontinuity in dealing with the history of the nation-state between the nineteenth and twentieth centuries. Whereas works of al-Ṭahṭāwī, Yannī, Ibn Abī al-Ḍīyāf, Aḥmad al-Nāṣirī, Zaydān, and even Muḥammad Kurd ʻAlī, treated the history of their respective countries in a classificatory and chronological manner, those of the twentieth century were based on a completely different model.

The thought of Arab historians in the nineteenth century was governed by the rules exhibited in the discourse of European thinkers of the classical age which, according to Foucault's analysis, extends from the end of the Renaissance down to the French Revolution. This was the age which listed and described the visible characteristics of natural and historical phenomena. It operated according to four variables of classifying the elements of its discourse. If we apply these variables, as elaborated by Michel Foucault in *The Order of Things*,[13] to nineteenth-century Arabic historiography, the following description emerges: First, the concept of a particular fatherland (*Waṭan*) corresponds to the form of the elements and determines the focus of narration. Second, political events constitute the quantity of these elements. Third, connected linear narrative governs their manner of distribution, space, and relationships. Fourth, the lesson one can derive, or the general principle, such as the necessity of justice, influences the relative magnitude of each element. Thus, the nation-state was 'a fixed space in the foreground'. Its identity became an exercise in tabulating its continuous evolution and nominating its visible structures. This taxonomic enterprise was deployed among other fields, and can be clearly seen in the encyclopedic compilations of Khayr al-Dīn al-Tūnisī and Buṭrus al-Bustānī. Such a concentration on the outer characteristics excluded the possibility of studying the inner workings of a system, or the organic function of events as integral parts of a totality. The organic, or biological model,[14] did not emerge in the Arab World until the 1920s. The nineteenth century can be described as the age of the journalist and the administrator. Or, to be more precise, this classificatory system of knowledge found its fertile soil in newspaper offices, literary clubs, and local councils. In the twentieth century, the sites of the biological discourse were located in political parties, armies, and universities.

These different patterns of discursive formations suggest the emergence of different units of study, a new field of perception, and a new topology. There are definite shifts and transformations which entail a revision of the manner in which modern Arab thought has hitherto been classified and interpreted. These mutations are not simply a qualitative change resulting from quantitative accumulations. Nor are they evolutionary processes, whereby one can detect their origins in a slow maturation of trends and currents. ʻAbduh, for example, did not evolve to become Ṭāhā Ḥusayn, nor did al-Bustānī culminate in al-Ḥuṣrī or ʻAflaq. What made a dialogue impossible between Renan and al-Afghānī is the fact that the first was using biology as a reference point, while the other adhered to the tenets of the Age of Reason. Charles Adams in his *Islam and Modernism in Egypt* could not explain such a discontinuity between Muḥammad ʻAbduh and his two putative disciples, Ṭāha Ḥusayn (1889–1973) and ʻAlī ʻAbd al-Rāziq (1888–1966), and had to reduce it to ʻa spiritual and intellectual succession'.[15]

Unless the Ottoman option is restored to its centrality in the Arab World, a confusion of overlapping phases is bound to arise. This restoration can no longer be the familiar drawn-out decline; but as a response to European penetration and domination. Furthermore, by grasping Ottomanism in its secular dimensions and implications, the dichotomy between Arab Christian and Muslim approaches disintegrates in all its laboured formulations.

The concept of a fatherland, possessing definite boundaries, and endowed with a connected history and a distinct identity, did not emerge in the Arab World until the 1850s. Its emergence can be clearly related to explicit Ottoman endeavours of reform. The theoretical pronouncements and practical measures, generated by the Tanzimat period, made the transition to the adoption of a particular notion of the nation-state possible. Wherever these reforms were introduced or espoused by local élites, such as state officials, army officers, or journalists, a new consciousness of one's national history made its appearance. If other élites or political entities were reluctant to adopt these reforms, no such development took place. Even in Muḥammad ʻAlī's Egypt, national notions were virtually non-existent. Al-Ṭahṭāwī's *Takhlīṣ al-ibrīz*, published at the orders of Muḥammad ʻAlī in 1834, does not call for political allegiance to Egypt as a *Waṭan*, or fatherland. His five-year sojourn and intensive study in Paris do not seem to have engendered in him an alternative awareness of patriotism. In fact, Ṭahṭāwī saw France with the eyes of his patron. Perhaps it is for this reason that Ṭahṭāwī could study under Silvestre de Sacy and praise his eloquence in the Arabic language, while Afghānī could only conduct a vigorous debate with Ernest Renan, the French philologist and historian.[16] Only in the twentieth century was such a dialogue feasible when the biological paradigm became the common language of Arabic thought. Al-Ṭahṭāwī stands on his own as a monumental example of Muḥammad 'Alī's blunted project and its consequences. Unless the whole experiment is seen in its naked brutality, the mediocrity of its intellectual legacy cannot be revealed. Hence Ṭahṭāwī's dull style, austere ideas, and cold pronouncements. It is no accident that he did not leave behind him what is dubbed a school of thought or a group of disciples. One may even go further and consider Ṭahṭāwī's mature ideas, which flourished during the Tanzimat period, as a regression towards a neo-traditional approach. It was in this second phase that he advocated the idea of the king as God's caliph[17] and representative, contradicted Copernicus's theory as regards the rotation of the earth, attacked the ideology of the St Simonians,[18] and advanced his own warped conception of patriotism. While almost all other modern Arab intellectuals recognized the state of decline in their societies, and called for its remedy by imitating the west, al-Ṭahṭāwī masked this growing disparity with Europe. His masters were seen to embody Egypt, civilization, and a recurrent cycle of prosperity. Since Muḥammad 'Alī turned decline into a perpetual struggle with no focus or vision, Ṭahṭāwī followed suit in a submissive and highly unconvincing style of argument. It was al-Jabartī who stood at the threshold which Ṭahṭāwī never managed to cross or identify. The former's warmth is thus instantly felt. His vague awareness of decline and desperate yearning for an age beyond redemption place him in a category on his own. Al-Jabartī anticipates in his peculiar and forceful condemnation of Muḥammad 'Alī's reign the dominant themes of the young Ottomans and other reformists.

Thus regions or systems beyond the direct reach of Ottoman power failed to embrace a modern concept of the nation-state. This was the case in Morocco, the Arabian Peninsula, and even in Mount Lebanon. In fact, it was not until the establishment of the *Mustaṣarrifiyya* that a modern notion of Lebanon began to emerge.[19] Traditional Maronite or Greek Catholic historians of Mount Lebanon do not exhibit such preoccupations in their chronicles.

It was, therefore, as a result of direct involvement in the processes of the Tanzimat, whether as bureaucrats, journalists, or historians, that certain sections of the Arab educated élite began to articulate their ideas in patriotic terms. It can be safely concluded that the appearance of a historical work narrating events unfolding in one particular Arab province, and often written in a modern non-annalistic style, indicates prior introduction of certain Ottoman reforms, and the existence of particular social groups which earnestly believed in their efficacy. The reliance of one intellectual or another on a definite European source is, in this context, of secondary importance. The act of borrowing ideas was a complex and indirect affair. Before taking place, it had to find receptive conditions, and would not have advanced further afield without the availability of local agents and institutions. These channels coloured and reinterpreted the original text and stamped it with a new function.

The Ottoman officials introduced institutional, financial, and social reforms in order to reassert the state sovereignty and halt the decline of the Empire. By contrast, the major European powers intended the reforms to act as a means of facilitating their own economic interests and influence. Thus the reforms were adopted in the face of an advancing capitalist Europe with definite aims and objectives. Europe was bent on asserting its own will, either by opening up the markets of the Ottoman Empire, or through direct colonial occupation. Such an encounter was bound to unfold in an atmosphere of high tension. The reforms only served to defuse a highly charged situation, postpone the inevitable, or arrest the slide towards anarchy. More often than not, they were implemented under duress, ill-conceived, and hastily imposed. Under such circumstances, there is no point in questioning the sincerity of Ottoman governors, or lamenting the haughty attitude of European consuls and officials. Both sides were interlocked in a power struggle in which the weaker party attempted to reverse the inevitability of its downfall.

It is for these reasons that the directives for halting the decline issued from the central authority. The initiative belonged to the sultan or the Sublime Porte. It filtered down into the provinces, and was acclaimed or resisted. When a movement linked itself directly with a European power, no national feeling emerged. Such a connection could only produce a group of individuals either adept at offering their services to a foreign power, or skilled in propagating positive ideas on the progress of the west. A case in point was the Maronite Church in nineteenth-century Lebanon, or the various groups which supported the British occupation of Egypt.

Love of country, as an act of political allegiance, and the necessity of a just ruler, were juxtaposed as two prerequisites of a healthy Ottoman community. The authority of the sultan was perceived to reside in one of his representatives. The nation-state became an axiom in the discourse of all Arab intellectuals, be they liberal or Islamic reformist, Christian, or Muslim. The solution for halting the decline of their societies was postulated as an urgent refurbishment of political institutions. However, social and economic matters were not relegated to the background or ignored. Instead they were considered to be the exclusive prerogative of an enlightened sultan or governor. There was a uniformity of approach which cut across sectarian and religious lines. Contrary to common belief, 'Abd al-Ḥamīd's reign was rarely opposed or attacked by a substantial majority of the Arab élite. This sultan's dilemma expresses the situation of a besieged state, no longer capable of warding off European expansionism. He therefore attempted to carry out his own brand of reforms and keep the Empire intact at the same time. Instead of chronicling the rare manifestations of isolated individuals trying to detach themselves from the Ottoman state, one has to highlight the tenacious manner in which the Arabs struggled to hang on, and renew their attachment to an Ottoman Empire embodied in the authority of the sultan and a network of state institutions. A false impression repeatedly stressed and rehashed is no longer tenable: the Christian Arabs did not initiate secularism or patriotism in the Ottoman Empire. They merely restated, as loyal subjects, the principles and beliefs of Ottoman officials. It is equally misleading to conjure up the spectacle of marginal men, sitting behind their desks and asking themselves puzzled questions about their personal identities. Nor were they insecure members of a minority frightened of their Muslim compatriots, trying to solve their intractable problems by concocting theories of nationalism and liberalism. On the contrary, they spoke in highly confident tones, put across a clear message, and articulated ideas made available and possible by various Ottoman reforms. The characterization of marginal men reflects to a large extent the private experiences of orientalists and their profession.

Al-Afghānī's death in 1897 adumbrates the symbolic conclusion of an era. Thus, it was towards the end of the nineteenth century that a new threshold was reached in modern Arabic thought. Both al-Kawākibī (1849–1902) and Muṣṭafā Kāmil (1874–1908), each in his own way, stand at the dawn of a new configuration of another paradigm, marking the first breach of the classical framework as worked out by al-Afghānī, al-Bustānī, or ʿAbduh. Muṣṭafā Kāmil restored Ottomanism to the centre of Egyptian politics, launched the first modern political party in the Arab World, and made national independence an absolute affirmation of constant struggle.[20] And it was al-Kawākibī who turned the decline of the Ottoman Empire into a pervasive and comprehensive condition. To him, Ibn Khaldūn was no longer valid. Thus oppression was shown to be inscribed in political power, no matter how enlightened or educated its representatives might happen to be. Only the constant pressure and participation of an awakened nation would keep this oppression at bay or succeed in eliminating its institutions. Death and life became two absolute possibilities in the world of human association. Moreover, al-Kawākibī intended to articulate a new science of politics. The opening sentences of his *Characteristics of Oppression (Ṭabā'iʿal-Istibdād)*, published in 1900, illustrate his intention of discarding the tenets of the Tanzimat and their dependence on the goodwill of a just ruler. The age of organic politics was thus inaugurated. The political party thenceforth occupied the centre stage of the Arab struggle for independence. The functions of the different organs of an institution replaced the visible classificatory depiction of an outer structure. Hence, events assume significance in so far as they endow the national identity with a character of its own. The concept of citizenship redistributed the elements of the fatherland in a new totality. Ottomanism slowly disintegrated into localized patriotic movements. Local patriotism, and later on Arab nationalism, situate their discourse at this rupture opened up by the receding role of the Ottomans. Local symbols and native heroes compensate for Ottomanism and its timely absence.

The elements of the national identity, their interaction and function were dealt with as integral parts of an organic structure. Shafiq Ghurbāl detected the unmistakable signs of the Egyptian identity in the emergence of a unified central authority, the birth of a local élite and the implementation of standard laws. This evolutionary process spanned almost a century, during which Napoleon defeated the Mamluks, Muḥammad 'Alī created a modern state, and Egypt was brought under direct British occupation. Salibi perceived his Lebanese national identity as a long-term movement acquiring one further characteristic as its contact with the west accelerated. Political concepts, a liberal culture, an administrative aristocracy, a proper constitution, and, finally, a middle class highly conscientious of civic freedom and democratic values were interwoven into the core of a national identity which slowly emerged between 1800 and 1970. Laroui saw its birth in the repeatedly foiled attempts of the Moroccan *makhzan* (government) to reform itself from within and ward off European domination. Traditionalism, as a cultural defensive weapon, expressed the identity of Morocco and signified its desire to grapple with the future, whilst holding steadfastly on to an ever receding past. He perceived the actualization of independence in an educational effort of instilling loyalty to a state which never managed to establish its own legitimacy, except as a shimmering potentiality.

Furthermore, by the sheer abstractness of this organic model, it becomes feasible to shift emphasis and adopt various characterizations for the same function of the multifarious elements. Egypt could thus acquire successive identities – Pharaonic, Islamic, and Arab – without ceasing to evolve as a modern nation-state. Similarly, the Lebanese identity may easily develop from being an exclusive Maronite invention into a pan-Arab polity, while the interplay of its vitalistic elements keeps striving for kindred principles.[21] Hence, history-writing generated coherence and a sense of direction, both in the individual and the national community. The chaos of reality was transcended in a connected narrative as a symbol of modernity and a worthy imitation of an original inspiring deity. Excluded from participating in direct public life, their writings reveal at once a tense inner dialogue and a vocal protest. Accordingly, the functional properties, brought to the surface by the inner constellations of the identity, obliterate the need for a chronological continuity, and disclose the deeper levels, or significance, of events. The totality of the nation, functioning as a living organism does not, however, unravel its operational being in its full maturation in the absence of its most crucial organ: the state.

Thus the state, born under the watchful eyes of the west, cast its shadow as the embodiment of the nation's development. The direction of events imposed itself as a teleological law depositing in its spiral progression a glowing national identity. The historian, as an employee of the state, or a firm believer in the destiny of his nation, identified himself with one native élite or another. The absence of an independent middle class and the backwardness of the industrial sector did not deter the inception of a secular interpretation. The future was projected into the past, and the two amalgamated to form the structure of the present. The historian interposed his narrative as a transparent link between a class of great families, notables, and politicians and the various groups of artisans, state employees, shopkeepers, and peasants who constituted the majority of the population. An epistemological uniformity regulated the writing of national histories.

It is with contemporary Islamic fundamentalism that the Ottoman Empire, in its Islamic dimensions, is rehabilitated, as an indication of the continuity of history, and a denial of European intervention which led to a rupture of political and religious development. Islamic fundamentalism does not, in this new adventure, stand outside or above history, be it conceptually (in terms of perceiving the process of events) or practically (the role it assigns itself as an integral part of the march of events). Arabism, having established itself after the Second World War, still persists in denying its immediate past. Nevertheless, Arab nationalism was propagated and expounded by Arab intellectuals, formerly associated with the chequered history of Ottomanism. Sāṭi' al-Ḥuṣrī reinterpreted the latest version of Ottomanism and turned it into Arabism. In other words, he continued to survey the scene from a central position, leaving no room for marginality or provinciality. He was so thoroughly Ottoman that he made the transition to Arabism with relative ease. Nasserism and the thinking of al-Ḥuṣrī belong to the mainstream of a movement which settled conclusively the identity of the Arabs as a modern national community.

This study clearly shows that the national identity constitutes a substantial trend in the intellectual discourse of the Arab intelligentsia, and a major preoccupation of a number of prominent Arab historians. It is neither a figment of the fertile imagination of a coterie of intellectuals, nor a passing phenomenon and a passive echoing of European culture. However, it is a problem that historiography itself, no matter how truthful, faithful, or detached, cannot solve on its own. The question itself involves practical solutions carried out by practical persons. It cuts across and touches the material, cultural, and religious life of the Arabs as a whole.

NOTES

1. See M. Ghurbāl, *Muḥammad 'Alī al-kabīr*, pp. 65–7 and 109–10; K. Salibi, *The Modern History of Lebanon*, pp. 144–8; A. Laroui, *The History of the Maghrib*, pp. 4 and 58.
2. Qusṭanṭine Zurayq in his work on the methodology of history, *Naḥnu wa al-tārīkh*, explicitly or implicitly urges the future Arab historian to adopt these characteristics as imperative prerequisites for the writing and making of history.
3. This was the case with Ghurbāl's national identity. It briefly appeared under Muḥammad 'Alī, went out of sight and then reared its head with the arrival of Lord Dufferin in the 1880s, only to disappear once again.
4. Arab countries ruled by military officers have often adopted different ideologies under different circumstances. Nasser's Egypt and General Numayrī's Sudan stand out as apt illustrations.
5. Sir Alfred Milner, *England in Egypt*, 7th edn (London, 1899), pp. 391–2.
6. *L'idéologie arabe*, pp. 87 and 174.
7. *Al-'Arab wa al-fikr al-tārīkhī*, p. 23.
8. See chapter 1 of this study.
9. Particularly Yannī and Maṭar, studied in chapter 2.
10. See chapter 4.
11. Chapter 5.
12. Chapter 6.
13. (London: Tavistock Publications; 1977), p. 134. Originally published in French under the title *Les Mots et les choses* (Editions Gallimard, Paris, 1966).
14. Cf. R.G. Collingwood, *The Idea of Nature* (Oxford University Press, 1945, 1976) pp. 133–6; Foucault, *The Order of Things*, pp. 263–79.
15. *Islam and Modernism in Egypt* (London, 1933), p. 268.
16. The repercussions of this debate have been studied by various scholars. See, for example, Nikki R. Keddie, *An Islamic Response to Imperialism* (University of California Press, 1968, 1983), pp. 84–95.
17. Al-Ṭahṭāwī, *Manāhij al-albāb* (Cairo, 1912), p. 359.
18. Al-Ṭahṭāwī, *Anwār Tawfīq al-jalīl* (Cairo, 1868–69), p. 440.
19. See Y.M. Choueiri, 'Ottoman reform and Lebanese patriotism', paper presented at the Centre for Lebanese Studies Conference, 10–12 September 1987, St Antony's College, Oxford.
20. It was no accident that the most outspoken Christian secularist, Faraḥ Anṭūn (1874–1922), was at the same time the most consistent

believer in Ottomanism, and a supporter of Muṣṭafā Kāmil's party. Donald M. Reid, *The Odyssey of Faraḥ Anṭūn* (Minneapolis and Chicago, 1975), pp. 101–10. In a sense, both al-Kawākibī and Kāmil bequeathed to Faraḥ Anṭūn the formal task of dismantling the intellectual legacy of Muḥammad 'Abduh.

21. An example of a bungled attempt to explain the ideological stance of a certain historian by simply referring to his sectarian affiliation is that of Aḥmad Beydoun, *Identité confessionnelle et temps social chez les historiens Libanais contemporains* (Beirut, 1984). Beydoun takes no account of these shifts of emphasis, and consequently his historians remain static throughout their careers.

Appendix A

HISTORY BOOKS TRANSLATED UNDER THE SUPERVISION OF AL-ṬAHṬĀWĪ:

Note: The Islamic era opens with the migration, Hijra in Arabic, of the Prophet Muḥammad on 16 July AD622 from Mecca to Medina. The Islamic year has twelve lunar months or 334 days. Hence for each Christian century there are about 103 Islamic years.

1 1838: *Bidāyat al-qudamā' wa hidāyat al-ḥukamā'* (Būlāq, 1254/1838). (A history of the ancient world.) No particular author. Translated by Muṣṭafā al-Zarābī, 'Abd Allah Abū al-Su'ūd, and Muḥammad 'Abd al-Rāziq.

2 1841: *Maṭāli' shumūs al-sīyar fī waqā'i' Karlūs al-thānī 'ashar* (Būlāq, 1257/1841). Being the *Histoire de Charles XII* by Voltaire, translated by Muḥammad Muṣṭafā al-Bayyā'.

3 1841: *Nạẓm al-la'āli' fī al-sulūk fī man hakam Faransā min al-mulūk*, (Būlāq, 1257/1841). (History of French monarchs.) Translated by 'Abd Allah Abū al-Su'ūd.

4 1842: *Itḥāf al-mulūk al-alibbā' bi-taqaddum al-jam'īyyāt fī bilād Ūrubbā* (Būlāq, 1258/1842) and *Itḥāf mulūk al-zamān bi-tārīkh al-imbraṭūr Shārlikān*, (Būlāq, 1260/1844 — 1266/1849), 3 vols. Being *The History of the Reign of the Emperor Charles the Fifth*, by William Robertson, translated by Khalīfa Maḥmūd.

5 1844: *Qurrat al-nufūs wa al-'uyūn bi-sīyar ma tawassaṭ min al-qurūn* (Būlāq, 1260/1844), 2 vols, translated by Muṣṭafā Sayyid and Aḥmad al-Zarābī. (A history of the Middle Ages.) Introduced by Rifā'a al-Ṭahṭāwī.

6 1848: *Tārīkh mulūk Faransā* (Būlāq, 1264/1848). (History of the kings of France.) Author unknown, translated by Ḥasan Qāsim and revised by R. Ṭahṭāwī.

7 1850: *Al-Rawḍ al-azhar fī tārīkh Buṭrus al-akbar* (Būlāq, 1266/1850). Voltaire's *Histoire de l'empire de Russie sous Pièrre le Grand.* Translated by Aḥmad 'Ubayd al-Ṭahṭāwī, edited by R.R. al-Ṭahṭāwī and Shaykh Quṭṭa al-'Adawī.

Appendix B

MUḤAMMAD AL-ALFĪ'S VISIT TO LONDON AND THE BRITISH PRESS

This day arrived in London, on a diplomatic mission, Mehmet-Bey-Elfi Murad, one of the Mameluke Chiefs who fought so bravely at Alexandria. He was wounded in the side with a musket-ball, and concealed it for two days, lest, if known, his danger should produce a cabal among the other rival chiefs, and dismay among his troops. His life was saved by the valour of the English. His suite at present consists of 17 persons; but the most valuable part of it, to the number of 13, has not yet arrived. It includes three beautiful females, one a favourite Georgian, to whom he is much attached. The other two are Circassians. One remarkable for dancing, the other for singing. While at dinner, he is waited upon by four pages, and a secretary, who acts always as interpreter. He does not help himself at table; but, when he signifies a liking to any particular dish, one of the pages helps him; he is a great epicure, and drinks two bottles of Champagne or Burgundy after dinner. He is also very fond of spruce-beer, but drinks no malt liquor. He appears to be fascinated with the customs of this country. Of the English ladies he speaks in terms of the most enthusiastic admiration.

Gentleman's Magazine, Fri. 7 Oct. 1803

Our Portsmouth letter states the arrival of a Mameluke Chief, Elfi Bey, who was sent as an envoy from the other Beys of Upper Egypt, to claim the protection of this country, and our interference with the Porte in their favour. That these solicitations will be granted is past all doubt, as a certain degree of popularity in Egypt, joined to the fame of influence already acquired there by our arms, must be of infinite importance in the present, or in any future struggle with the common enemy. Elfi Bey came in the *Experiment* frigate, last from Gibraltar, and was received with due honours on his landing at Portsmouth.

Morning Herald, Sat. 8 Oct. 1803

A Mameluke Chief is come to England in the *Experiment*, of 44 guns. On his landing at Portsmouth he was received by the Admiral and Captains of the fleet.

The Times, Sat. 8 Oct. 1803

In a former letter, I told you that Mahomet Bey Elphi arrived here in the fleet from Egypt. He was not allowed to go in the last fleet to England; because it was necessary to apprize the English Government of his intended visit; the object of which is to claim the fulfilment of promises made to the Mamelukes, when they assisted our army against the French in Egypt. He has not made himself very agreeable to the Government at Malta. He has been tampered with by the French party. He was very much dissatisfied with having been detained so long at Malta; as he was never before subject to any kind of control (controul). He hired a Swedish ship, sent his baggage on board her, and embarked himself, a few days ago. It was then rumoured that he meant to go to Marseilles or some other French port. When this news reached the Governor of the place, sentries were placed on board the vessel to prevent her from sailing; and the Bey was told that he should be furnished with a conveyance, either to Egypt or England; whichever he chose; the latter he has accepted of. I have heard a great deal of the history of this Chief; but as I am very partial to the Mamelukes, I do not wish to say anything of him that might prejudice him in the eyes of the English Nation.

The Times, Mon. 10 Oct. 1803

The Mameluke Chief, Mahomet Bey Elfi Morat, is expected to go to the levee to pay his respects to the King. He is at present attended by a secretary and four pages.

Morning Chronicle, Wed. 12 Oct. 1803

The Mameluke Chief took a ride in coach, accompanied by Lord Blantyre, yesterday morning, through the squares and principal streets at the West end of the town, to view the buildings, and was highly gratified.

Morning Herald, Wed. 12 Oct. 1803

Elfi Bey

This Mameluke Chief is about 44 years of age, five feet and eleven and a half inches high, very stout made, and of a very ruddy complexion. His beard is black, and reaches down to his middle. He wears a very rich inside dress of red and white striped silk, red satin trowsers (*sic*), and red silk stockings, with yellow sandals. Over his inside dress he wears a beautiful shawl, forming a drapery about the body, and over that a rich silk mantle, trimmed with fur. His Excellency dined on Sunday in private, and devoted a considerable time to the pleasures of the table. His deportment is dignified and graceful. A house has been taken for his Excellency in Baker Street. He was visited on Sunday by several persons of distinction. He was wounded on the side by a musket-ball, and concealed it for two days, lest, if known, his danger should produce cabal among other rival chiefs, and dismay among his troops. His life was saved by the valour of the English. He will be introduced at the Levee this day to his Majesty, for whom he has prepared some rich and envious presents, consisting of furs, silks, sabres, etc. His suite at present consists of 17 persons, but the most precious of it, to the number of thirteen, has not yet arrived. It includes three beautiful females, one a favourite Georgian, to whom his Excellency is much attached. The other two are Circassians, one remarkable for dancing, the other for singing. While at dinner he is waited upon by four pages and his secretary, who acts also as interpreter. He does not help himself at table, but when he signifies a liking to any particular dish, one of the pages helps him. He is a great epicure, and drinks two bottles of Champagne or Burgundy after dinner. His Excellency is also very fond of spruce beer, but drinks no malt liquor. He has made many liberal presents to his people since his arrival, and appears to be fascinated with the customs of this country. — Of the English Ladies he speaks in terms of the most enthusiastic admiration. Baker Street was crowded yesterday with dashing Cyprians, in expectation of catching the Bey's eye, but they were disappointed, as he still continues at the St. James's Hotel.

Morning Herald, Wed. 12 Oct. 1803

His Excellency the Mameluke Chief proposed taking a house in Baker Street, but that being found too small, the late residence of Sir Lawrence Parsons, in Berkeley Square, has been engaged for him. It was formerly the scene of Gala Hope's festivities.

The Times, Fri. 14 Oct. 1803

Mohommed Elphy was born in Georgia, and was purchased when a child by Murad Bey for 1000 Sequins. He was uncommonly beautiful, and got the sir name of Elphy, which, in the Turkish language, signifies 1000 Sequins. At the age of fifteen he was made an Aga, for the extraordinary bravery he displayed against some rebel Beys. In consequence of an insult offered him by Murad, he deserted from that Chief, and joined the insurgents. Murad, however, repenting of what he had done, recalled Elphy, and loaded him with fresh favours. Passing over the intermediate rank of Kiaschief, he raised him to a rank equal to his own.

Elphy Bey is remarkable for his courage, agility, and uncommon address and prowess on horseback. He has repeatedly cut off the head of a buffalo, at full gallop, with one stroke of his sabre. He is 43 or 44 years old, about 5 feet 8 inches high, and very corpulent. His countenance is open, and his manners are affable. He is a man of strong natural abilities; which is a very uncommon thing among the Mamelukes. He never was brought to terms by the French, during the whole time of their continuance in Egypt; but constantly remained in the desert (on which account he called himself the *Antelope*), and baffled five divisions of Bonaparte's army who were in constant pursuit of him.

Morning Post, Mon. 17 Oct. 1803

His Excellency the Mameluke Chief took an airing yesterday in Hyde Park.

Morning Herald, Mon. 24 Oct. 1803

The Royal review of soldiers in Hyde Park

Among the persons who attracted most notice in the park, was Elfi Bey, who followed, though from etiquette, he could not join in the Royal Cavalcade. The Bey was in his carriage, accompanied by his Majesty's and his own interpreter, and his Aide-de-Camp. His servants were dressed in scarlet and gold, with green cuffs and collars, gold epaulets, plain cocked hats, with gold loop and button, and high white leather.

Morning Post, Thurs. 27 Oct. 1803

Elphy Bey is already a great favourite with the Ladies. Indeed, bey is such a pretty mincing half-word, so proper for the blushing lips of a young bride!

Morning Post, Thurs. 27 Oct. 1803

The residence of Elfi Bey is almost constantly beset by a number of persons, who are induced to stop from motives of curiosity. A Gentleman, who mixed with the crowd, was asked yesterday, by one of the bye-standers, whether his Excellency was not a *Pacha* with *three tails.* Which an Irish fish-woman happening to over-hear, she instantly turned up her eyes to Heaven, and exclaimed — *O Jasus!* (*sic*).

Morning Post, Sat. 29 Oct. 1803

Patrona Bey has arrived here from Cyprus, and has brought with him those who escaped of the garrison of Damietta; which town, after being a considerable time besieged by Osman Bey and Tamburge (*sic*), was taken by storm. A part of the Turks were massacred, and the unfortunate town was given up to be plundered for 24 hours. The Beys are now sovereign Lords of Egypt.

Morning Herald, 1 Nov. 1803
(Dispatch dated Constantinople, 31 Aug.)

The Mameluks Chief, accompanied by his interpreter, and a numerous retinue, went to the Horse Guards on Thursday, where he remained some hours.

Morning Post, Sat. 5 Nov. 1803

Yesterday morning prince Alexander De Takerhasky arrived in town from Petersburgh. He was the bearer of dispatches to the Russian Ambassador, and report says, that his mission is of considerable importance. Its object is not mentioned; but the general opinion is, that it relates to the present situation in Egypt, in the affairs of which the Court of Russia is understood to take a lively interest. From the Dutch Papers, which, through the favour of a friend, we received on Thursday, we have this day given some further extracts. The article respecting Egypt, copied from a late Paris paper, unfairly charges England with having favoured the rebellion of the Beys, and protected the insurgents. The reasoning of the French writer upon this subject is too contemptible to merit serious attention. As we predicted, the enemy have brought in aid of this unfounded insinuation the recent journey of Elfi Bey to this country; to which, moreover, they affect to attack all the consequence of a regular embassy, though it is notorious that he has never been acknowledged in any public or diplomatic character by His Majesty's Ministers. The illiberal Philippic concludes by observing, that Egypt will ultimately belong to England; and under all the circumstances of the case, the propriety and necessity of the interference, at least, of Great Britain, to remedy the present distracted state of that country, becomes a subject of serious consideration. The importance which it acquired during the last war, from the attempt made by France to obtain permanent possession of it, and the greatness of the effort by which we drove them out, were confined to the consideration of the influence which it was likely to have, as the means of facilitating an attack on the

British dominions in India, or as a barrier for their defence. The resistance which the Beys made in the first instance to the French, and the zeal and gallantry with which they afterwards seconded the British army in reducing the enemy, proved, that notwithstanding their normal subjection to the Porte, they looked upon themselves as the real masters of the country, and that, consequently, they regarded as their friends those who wished to restore the country to its former state, rather than those who wished to make a permanent settlement in it, with a view to the advancement of ulterior projects of ambition, the first step towards which must be the immediate destruction of every power in Egypt that stood in their way. The gross violation committed by the French towards the *Grand* seignior, with whom they boasted the most antient alliance of all those in which the Porte was connected with the European Powers, gave a just and strong impression of what was to be expected from new connections. – The Mamelukes, therefore, however little versed in European politics, could not be at a loss to know which side it was their advantage to take, when they were to chuse between the French and English. The French had invaded them, and compelled them to abandon the best part of the country; the English came to drive out the French, and rescue it from the dreadful gripe of those oppressors. The English were, therefore, from the moment of their landing in Egypt regarded by the Mamelukes as allies and deliverers. Succeeding events proved them worthy of this distinguished consideration. From the moment of the reduction of the French army, the English Commander in Egypt laboured to restore a good understanding between the Beys and the Court of Constantinople.

If they [the Mamelukes] wish for the recognition of their dynasty as an independent power, we see no offence to our ally the Porte in our employing our good offices to that effect, in as much as the Ottoman arms have been expelled from Egypt, and there is little room to hope that they can re-enter it with better success. We see no offence to the existing Powers, in lending our aid towards the establishment of a new and respectable sovereignty, in the room of so many that have disappeared by their own weakness.

Morning Post, Sat. 5 Nov. 1803

Elfi Bey proves himself to be a man of sense, by the eagerness which he manifests in visiting every thing worthy of the attention of a foreigner in this metropolis.

It is said that Elphi Bey, the Mameluke Chief, received by the last Hamburgh mail the pleasing intelligence that the Porte, since the surrender of Alexandria, and the other towns in Lower Egypt, has written to all the Foreign Powers, expressing a desire to come to terms of accommodation with the Beys, and re-establish them in all their antient privileges. If this report be true, it is probable that Elphi Bey will be received at St. James's with all the dignity of his rank.

Morning Post, Mon. 7 Nov. 1803

Last Wednesday evening His Excellency Elfi Bey went to the Royal Circus; and, after the performance, desired his interpreter to assure General Moore of his just sense of the flattering attention paid him by the Surrey Volunteers, and by the whole audience. Indeed every eye was fixed upon him, and every face was strongly expressive of pleasure, as well as respect for this illustrious visitant at our Court. It was the more gratifying to his feelings, as he is known to be a warm admirer of the British Character, and of the devoted attachment of the people to their King, to their country, and glorious constitution.

Morning Post, Tues. 8 Nov. 1803

Curiosity is on tip-toe for the arrival of Elphy Bey's fair *Circassian* Ladies. The attraction of their *naturally-placed, fine, proverbial bloom*, is only wanting, to reduce the *wandering colour* in the 'elbows' and 'ancles' of our *belles*, back to its native *metropolis* and palace, the 'cheek'.

Morning Post, Wed. 9 Nov. 1803

A grand entertainment was given to his Excellency Elfi Bey, and a number of other distinguished visitors, by his Royal Highness the Prince of Wales. The conversation turning upon the very excellent equestrian powers of the Mamelukes and Turks, the prince said, 'I now have in my stud an Egyptian horse, so wild and ungovernable, that he will dismount the best horseman in Elfi Bey's retinue.' The Bey replied, in Italian, to the Prince, 'I shall gratify your Royal Highness's curiosity tomorrow.' An appointment consequently took place next day, at two o'clock, in the Prince of Wales's riding-house, Pall Mall. When the Bey, in company with Colonel Moore, his interpreter, and Mahomet Aga, his principal officer, a young man of apparently great agility, entered the riding house, where the Prince and his royal brothers waited, attended by several noblemen, to witness the management of the horse, which never before could be ridden by anybody. One of the Mameluke's saddles being fixed by the grooms, the animal was led out of the stable into the riding-house, in so rampant and unmanageable a state, that everyone present concluded no one would ever attempt to mount him. There never was a greater model of beauty. He is spotted like a leopard, and his eyes were so fiery and enraged, as to indicate the greatest danger to anyone who dared mount him. Being led around the boundary, Mahomet Aga made a spring, seized him by the reins, and in an instant vaulted on the back of the animal, which finding itself incumbered by a burden, that it had never before felt, and goaded by the tightness of the Egyptian saddle, gave loose to his passion, and, in the height of ferocity, plunged, but in vain, in every direction. The mameluke kept his seat during this proud distraction of the horse, for more than twenty minutes, to the utter astonishment of the prince and every beholder, and the apparently ungovernable animal was, at last, reduced to so tame and accomodating a state, as to yield to the control of the very able rider who had thus subdued him. The Prince expressed himself highly gratified; greatly complimented the officer for his equestrian skill; and after retiring to Carlton House, ordered some refreshment, when Elfi Bey and his retinue departed, not a little proud of the display of their easy victory.

Annual Register, 10 Nov. 1803, pp. 455-6

After the grand entertainment given by his Royal Highness the Prince of Wales to Elfi Bey ... at Carlton House, on Thursday, the conversation turned upon the excellent horsemanship of the Mamelukes.

Morning Chronicle, Mon. 14 Nov. 1803

Elfi Bey is so pleased with the splendour and magnificence displayed in this Metropolis, so far exceeding any idea that he could have formed of it, and so very different from the tawdry, tasteless stile of the East, that it is said he intends to introduce some of our useful and elegant arts into his country, and that in case he obtains permission from our Government, he will invite a numerous train of literati, Astronomers, Geographers, Physicians, Surgeons, Artists, etc. to accompany him to Egypt.

Morning Post, Thurs. 17 Nov. 1803

The Mameluke Chief has paid a visit to Greenwich Hospital, where he was received with every mark of attention and respect. He appeared perfectly sensible of the value of that Institution, and of the beauty of its structure. He was then conducted to the Observatory in Greenwich Park, where he was amused and astonished with the magnificent apparatus it contains. On Thursday he viewed the London Docks, where he was met by several of the Directors, and after taking a complete survey, he proceeded to Blackwall, where he remained for some hours, inspecting the whole of the works, the docks, warehouses etc. After some refreshment given by the Directors, which was prepared on the occasion, he returned to town, and afterwards had the honour of dining with the Prince of Wales.

The Times, Sat. 17 Nov. 1803

Elfi Bey

Yesterday, at twelve o'clock, agreeably to appointment, his Excellency came to the East India House; he was received at the front door by Mr. Roberts, the Deputy Chairman, by whom he was conducted to the Committee of Correspondence Room, where Mr. Bosanquet (the Chairman), and a number of Directors were assembled. His Excellency being properly introduced by the interpreter, was placed on the Chairman's right hand, and partook of an elegant cold collation, which had been provided by the secretary. After the lapse of about half an hour, he returned to his carriage, and inspected the Company's warehouses in New Street, guard-rooms, etc.

On his return to the India House, he was shewn the Court and Sale Rooms, and on re-entering the Correspondence Room, (previous to which he examined, with great attention, the brace of curious brass ordnance taken from Tippuo by Marquis Cornwallis) his Excellency was not a little entertained by a display of the musical Tyger from the Palace at Seringa Patam, which performed several airs, two of them certainly never in the contemplation of its ferocious master, *God save the King*, and *Rule Britannia.* Mr. Wilkins, the Company's Librarian, had also introduced into the Correspondence Room, the famous golden head of a Tyger which formed the foot-stool of the Tyrant's throne. After minutely inspecting the paintings, and more particularly that of the old Nabob of the Carnatic, which adorn this elegant apartment, his Excellency was introduced to the Company's Museum, where he spent a considerable time, expressing, through his interpreter, the pleasure he enjoyed in viewing the various curiosities in that distinguished repository of eastern literature. But what appeared the most to rivet his attention, was the poem of the *Shri Bhagvata*, with the incarnations of *Vishnu*, highly illuminated, and the various pictures illustrative of that popular work, lately presented to the Company by Dr. Fleming.

His Excellency, during the whole of his progress, evidently assumed a solemnity of demeanor suited to the idea he must entertain of the first Corporate Body in the world.

The Times, 9 Dec. 1803

The departure of the Mameluke Bey, is fixed, we understand, for Monday, and we can take upon us with confidence to announce that he leaves the country, confirmed by the attentions and marks of generous consideration, which he has received, in the sentiments of respect and attachment which brought him first among us. While, therefore, Government has properly acquitted itself towards this gallant stranger, it has at the same time, with due address and with the candour of its proceedings, perfectly kept within the rules which etiquette prescribed; and an early and liberal communication of its intentions has counteracted the effects which the jealousy and malignancy of some commentators would have felt a diabolical pleasure in operating, from the circumstance of his arrival here, upon the representative of the Porte, that minister has, however, been perfectly satisfied with the open and confident explanation made to him, and is convinced that the interests of this Government are inseparable from those of his own.

The Times, 17 Dec. 1803

Mahomet Elfi Bey

On Sunday, about twelve o'clock, Elfi Bey, accompanied by Lord Blantyre and Colonel Moore and attended by his interpreter and a suit of Mamelukes, arrived at the Castle Inn, at Windsor, where he was soon after met by General Stuart, when the whole party proceeded to the palace, where they continued for some time to view the apartments. After divine service, the King, Queen, Princesses, and Duke of Cambridge, came also into the Castle, and proceeded to the Armoury, where they met the Bey, who was presented to their Majesties by General Stuart. The Mameluke Chieftain made a bend of low respectful salutation, and was received by their Majesties in a most gracious manner. Both the King and Queen conversed long with him; complimented him upon the gallantry of himself and his party in their frequent discomfitures of the French troops during their late invasion of Egypt; and acknowledged their services to the English armies, in the glorious expulsion of the enemy from that country. His Majesty, we believe, comformably to etiquette, did not enter with him upon any political objects of his mission hither. The Bey said, he was proud of expressing to their Majesties the inviolable attachment of all his party and adherents in Egypt; that he came to bear the homage of their respect to this nation, which, from its conquests as well as its humanity, they considered the greatest in the world; that the happy deliverance of his country, by his Majesty's brave armies, from the cruelty and oppression of the French, whom they still regarded as their common enemy, would ever remain engraved upon the breasts of his people; and that he still hoped that, under his Majesty's auspices, its peace and tranquillity would be finally established, for the honour and glory both of their Emperor, the Sublime Sultan, and themselves, who, like a father and his sons, could have but one common interest. The Bey's speech appeared more the momentary effusion of warm sincerity than a prepared address; and he seemed even affected by the gracious and benignant manner of the British Monarch, whose heart, he said, he read in his deportment. Their Majesties made many enquiries of General Stuart respecting the events of the late campaign, as well as the general affairs of Egypt during his command, and also addressed themselves for some time, with much affability to Lord Blantyre and Col. Moore, who served with much gallantry in that country in the actions in which the French were defeated.

On quitting Windsor, the Bey and the above military officers went to dinner at Lord Hobart's, at Roehampton, at which were present Lord Hawkesbury, Earl St. Vincent, Mr. Sullivan, Sir Even Nepean, and several members of his administration.

Yesterday his Excellency paid his visits of leave to their Royal Highnesses the Prince of Wales and the Commander-in-Chief of the Forces, and the several Officers of State; and this day he sets out for Portsmouth, impressed with every grateful sentiment of attachment to this country, by which he has been so kindly and liberally received. The Argo, which carries him out again to Egypt, waits his arrival at Portsmouth, and is to sail at his conveniency.

The Times, 20 Dec. 1803

Glossary

agha	commander, Ottoman military rank
'ālim (pl. *'ulamā'*)	an expert in religion; an Islamic scholar; canon lawyer
amlāk	property; real estate
'aṣabiyya	tribal or group solidarity
awqāf (s. *waqf*)	religious or charitable endowments; pious foundation
a'yān	notables; leading members of a community
barr	land; territory
bay'a	oath of allegiance
bey	sub-provincial governor; prince
beylerbeyi	Ottoman governor-general of a large province; commander-in-chief of a Janissary (q.v.); military unit
bilād al-shām	geographical Syria
caliph (Ar. *Khalīfa*)	deputy or successor of the Prophet Muḥammad
divan	government department; governing body; Council of State
eyalet	Ottoman province
Fertile Crescent	present-day Iraq, Syria, Jordan, Lebanon and Palestine/Israel
ḥadīth	transmitted saying or deed of the Prophet
Ḥalqa	corps of free-non-Mamlūk cavalry; military unit
iltizām	tax-farming
imam	leader of community prayer in Sunni Islam; divinely inspired successor of the Prophet in Shi'i Islam
iqṭā'	land grant to a government official or military officer
jabal	mountain
Jabal Lubnān	Mount Lebanon

jāhiliyya	the pre-Islamic period of ignorance
Janissaries	the standing infantry of the Ottoman forces: New Force
Khalīfa	successor; deputy
Makhzan	the central administration of Moroccan sultans
mamlaka (pl. *mamālik*)	dominion
mawlā	religious master; lord
millet (Ar. *milla*)	religious community or sect
muqaddams	headmen; paramount chiefs
muqaddima	Prolegomenon: introduction
mulk	freehold property
multazims	tax-farmers or contractors
mutaṣarrif	governor of an Ottoman sub-province; administrator
naqib al-Ashrāf	head of the descendants of the Prophet
Pasha	Ottoman honorific title conferred on a provincial governor
Pashalik	Ottoman province
qā'immaqām	acting viceroy
al-qawm	group of people, dignitaries
Qur'ān	the sacred book of Islam
Ṣāgh	military rank
al-sībā	lawlessness
Salafism (Ar. *Salafiyya*)	Islamic reform; return to the true precepts of Islam
Sharī'a	Islamic law
Sharīf	descendant of the Prophet; noble
Shaykh	religious or lay chief; leader of religious order
Shaykh al-balad	the senior *bey* (q.v.) of Cairo; the paramount bey
Sīra	biography
Tanzimat	reorganization, Ottoman reform
Tārīkh	history; narration
The Porte	the seat of the Ottoman government in Istanbul

vilayets	Ottoman administrative units, replaced *eyalets* (q.v) in 1864
wilāya	period of governorship
Waṭan	fatherland; place of birth
wulāt	governors; dynasties
yaqẓa	awakening
zāwiya	religious fraternity

List of Dynasties

Unless otherwise indicated all dates are AD

‘Abbasids	750–1258
Aghlabids	800–909
Almohads	1147–1269
Almoravids	1053–1149
Ayyūbids	1171–1250
Buḥturids	1147–1516
Faṭimids	969–1131
Ḥafṣids	1236–1574
Ḥammadids	1007–1152
Ḥusaynids	1705–1957
Mamlūks	1254–1517
Ma‘nids	1517–1697
Marinids	1269–1465
Mongols	1206–1502
Muḥammad ‘Ali’s dynasty	1805–1952
Ottomans	1281–1924
Parthians	247BC–AD224
Ptolemies	323BC–31BC
Shihābis	1697–1840
Umayyads	661–750
Umayyads of Spain	756–1031
Vandals	439–533
Zayyanids	1239–1549
Zirids	973–1148

Bibliography

I WORKS STUDIED

'Abd al-Wahhāb, Ḥasan (1953) *Khulāṣat tārīkh Tūnis*, 3rd revised edition, Tūnis.

al-Bustānī, Buṭrus (1859) *Khuṭba fī ādāb al-'Arab*, Beirut.

al-Bustānī, Salīm (1870–74) *al-Jinān*, Beirut.

Ghurbāl, Shafīq (1928) *The Beginnings of the Egyptian Question*, London.

—— (1944) *Muḥammad 'Alī al-Kabīr*, Cairo.

—— (1948) 'Ḥurūb Miṣr fī Filasṭīn', *al-Kitāb*, vol. VI (June), pp. 189–94.

—— (1950–51) 'La contribution de Mohamed Ali à la solution de certains problèmes méditerranéens de son époque', *Annales du Centre Universitaire Méditerranéen*, vol. IV, pp. 9–28, Nice.

—— (1951) 'Markaz Miṣr al-sīyāsī', *al-Kitāb*, vol. X (January), pp. 17–23.

—— (1952) *Tārīkh al-mufāwaḍāt al-miṣriyya-al-briṭāniyya 1882–1936*, vol. I, Cairo.

—— (1953) 'Makān al-thawra al-miṣriyya', *al-Hilāl*, vol. LXII (July), pp. 32–5.

—— (1955) 'Aḥkām al-mū'arrikhīn 'alā al-rijāl', *al-Hilāl*, vol. LXIII (April), pp. 40–3.

—— (1957) *Takwīn Miṣr*, Cairo.

—— (1961) *Minhāj mufaṣṣal lidars al-'awāmil al-asāsiyya fī binā' al-umma al-'arabiyya*, Cairo.

al-Jabartī, 'Abd al-Raḥmān (n.d.) *'Ajā'ib al-āthār fī al-tarājim wa al-akhbār*, 3 vols, Beirut, Dār al-Fāris.

Laroui, Abdallah (1967) *L'idéologie arabe contemporaine*, Paris. Reprinted 1982.

—— (1970) *L'histoire du Maghreb, un essai de synthèse*, Paris. Reprinted 1982. English translation, *The History of the Maghrib* (Princeton University Press, 1977).

—— (1974) *La crise des intellectuels arabes*, Paris. Reprinted 1978. Published in Arabic as *al-'Arab wa al-fikr al-tārīkhī*, Beirut, 1973. English translation *The Crisis of the Arab Intellectual*. California, 1976.

—— (1977) *Les origines sociales et culturelles du nationalisme Marocain (1830–1912)*, Paris. Reprinted 1980.

—— (1983) *Thaqāfatuna fī ḍaw' al-tārīkh*, Beirut and Casablanca.

al-Madanī, Aḥmad (1927) *Qarṭajanna fī arba'at 'uṣur*, Tunis.

Maṭar, Ilyās (1874) *Al-'Uqūd al-durriyya fī tārīkh al-mamlaka al-Sūriyya*, Beirut.

al-Mīlī, Mubārak (1963) *Tārīkh al-Jazā'ir fī al-qadīm wa al-ḥadīth*, 2 vols, Algiers.

Salibi, Kamal (1957) 'The Maronites of Lebanon under Frankish and

Mamluk rule (1099–1516)', *Arabica*, vol. IV, pp. 288–303.
—— (1959a) 'Lebanon in historical perspective', *Middle East Forum* (March), pp. 16–21.
—— (1959b) *Maronite Historians of Mediaeval Lebanon*, Beirut.
—— (1960) 'Six aspects of Lebanon', *Middle East Forum* (March), pp. 30–3.
—— (1961a) 'Lebanon since the crisis of 1958', *The World Today*, vol. 17, no. 1 (January), pp. 32–42.
—— (1961b) 'The Buhṭurids of the Ġarb. Mediaeval Lords of Beirut and of Southern Lebanon', *Arabica*, vol. VIII, pp. 74–97.
—— (1962a) 'Ta'rīf tārīkhī bi-Lubnān', *al-Abḥāth*, vol. XV, no. 3, pp. 364–84.
—— (1962b) 'The traditional historiography of the Maronites', in Bernard Lewis and P.M. Holt (eds) *Historians of the Middle East*, Oxford, pp. 212–25.
—— (1965a) 'L'historiographie libanaise: histoire de vanité', *L'Orient*, 23 May, pp. 12–13.
—— (1965b) *The Modern History of Lebanon*, London.
—— (1966a) 'Lebanon under Fuad Chehab 1958–1964', *Middle Eastern Studies*, vol. II, pp. 211–26.
—— (1966b) 'The personality of Lebanon in relation to the modern world', in Leonard Binder (ed) *Politics in Lebanon*, New York, pp. 263–70.
—— (1967) 'The Lebanese Emirate 1667–1841', *al-Abḥāth*, vol. XX, no. 3, pp. 1–16.
—— (1970) 'Fakhr al-Dīn wa al-fikra al-lubnāniyya', in Antoine Qāzān (ed.), *Ab'ād al-qawmiyya al-lubnāniyya*, Juniah, pp. 85–111.
—— (1971) 'The Lebanese identity', *Journal of Contemporary History*, vol. 6, pp. 76–86.
—— (1973a) 'The Sayfās and the Eyalet of Tripoli, 1579–1640', *Arabica*, vol. XX, pp. 25–52.
—— (1973b) 'The secret of the house of Ma'n', *IJMES*, vol. IV, pp. 272–87.
—— (1976) *Crossroads to Civil War — Lebanon 1958–1976*, New York.
—— (1979) *Munṭalaq tārīkh Lubnān*, Beirut.
—— 'Fakhr al-Dīn', *The Encyclopaedia of Islam*, new ed., E.J. Brill, Leiden, 1979, pp. 749–51.
al-Ṭahṭāwī, Rifā'a Rāfi' (1250/1834) *Takhlīṣ al-ibrīz ilā talkhīṣ Bārīz*, Būlāq.
—— (ed.) (1254/1838) *Bidāyat al-qudamā wa hidāyat al-ḥukamā*, Būlāq.
—— (1285/1868–69) *Anwār Tawfīq al-jalīl fī akhbār Miṣr wa tawthīq Banī Ismā'īl*, Cairo.
—— (1291/1874–75) *Nihāyat al-ījāz fī sīrat sākin al-Ḥijāz*, Cairo.
—— (1912) *Manāhij al-albāb al-miṣriyya fī mabāhij al-ādāb al-'aṣriyya*, Cairo.
Yannī, Jurjī (1881) *Tārīkh Sūriyya*, Beirut.
Zaydān, Jurjī (1889) *Tārīkh Miṣr al-ḥadīth*, Cairo.

II WORKS IN ARABIC

'Abd al-Karīm, Aḥmad 'Izzat (1972) 'Nadwat Muḥammad Shafīq Ghurbāl', *al-Majalla al-Tārīkhiyya al-Miṣriyya*, vol. 19, pp. 25–31.

Anīs, Muḥammad (1961) 'Shafīq Ghurbāl', *al-Majalla*, no. 58 (Nov.), pp. 12–17.

'Awaḍ, Lūwīs (1969) *Tārīkh al-fikr al-miṣrī al-ḥadīth*, vol. II, Cairo.

al-Ayyūbī, Ilyās (1923) *Tarīkh Misr fī 'ahd Ismā'il*, vol. I, Cairo.

al-Bustānī, Buṭrus (ed.) (1852) *'Amāl al-Jam'iyya al-Sūriyya*, Beirut.

al-Bustānī. Buṭrus and Salīm al-Bustānī (eds) (1876, 1883) *Dā'irat al-Ma'ārif*, vols I and VII, Beirut.

Buṭṭī, Rafā'īl (1947) 'Anastase Marie al-Karmalī 1866–1947', *Majallat al-Kitāb*, vol. III, pp. 747–57.

Choueiri, Youssef (1988) *Bayn al-naṣṣ wa al-hāmish. Dirāsa fi al-tārikh wa al-dīn*, London.

Dāghir, Yūsuf (1973) *Maṣādir al-dirāsa al-adabiyya*, vol. III, Beirut.

Ḍaw, Buṭrus (1976) *Tārīkh al-mawārina*, vol. III, Lebanon.

al-Dūwayhī, Isṭifān (1951) *Tārīkh al-azmina*, Beirut.

Farrūkh, 'Umar (1980) *Tajdīd al-tārīkh*, Beirut.

Farrūkh, 'Umar and Zakī al-Naqqāsh (1935) *Tārīkh Sūriyya wa Lubnān*, Beirut.

Gharāyiba, 'Abd al-Karīm (1961–62) *Sūriyya fī al-qarn al-tāsi' 'ashar*, Cairo.

Ibn Abī al-Ḍīyāf, Aḥmad (1963, 1964) *Itḥāf ahl al-zamān bi-akhbār mūlūk Tūnis wa 'ahd al-amān*, vols IV and V, Tunis.

Ibn Yaḥyā, Ṣāliḥ (1969) *Tārīkh Bayrūt*, edited by Kamal Salibi and Francis Hours, Beirut.

al-Jabartī, 'Abd al-Raḥmān (1975) *Tārīkh muddat al-Faransīs bi-Miṣr*, edited and trans. by S. Moreh, Leiden.

Kāmil, Muṣṭafā (1898) *al-Mas'ala al-sharqiyya*, Cairo.

al-Karmalī, Anastase Marie (1919) *Khulāṣat tārīkh al-'Irāq mundhu nushū'ih ilā yawminā hādhā*. Basra.

al-Khālidī, Aḥmad b. Muḥammad (1969) *Lubnān fī 'ahd al-amīr Fakhr al-Dīn al-ma'nī al-thānī*, edited by F.I. al-Bustānī and Asad Rustum.

Khayr al-Dīn (al-Tūnisī) (1978) *Aqwam al-masālik fī ma'rifat aḥwāl al-mamālik*, Beirut. first published 1867.

Kurd 'Alī, Muḥammad (1925–28) *Khiṭaṭ al-Shām*, 6 vols, Damascus.

al-Ma'lūf, 'Isā Iskandar (1934) *Tārīkh al-amīr Fakhr al-Dīn al-thānī*, Jūniah.

Mubārak, 'Alī (1305/1887) *al-Khiṭaṭ al-tawfīqiyya al-jadīda*, vol. XIII, Būlāq.

al-Najjār, Ḥusayn Fawzī (1962) *Rifā'a al-Ṭahṭāwī*, Cairo.

al-Nāṣirī, Aḥmad (1954) *Kitāb al-istiqṣā' li-akhbār dūwal al-Maghrib al-aqṣā*, Casablanca.

Riḍā, Rashīd (1931) *Tārīkh al-ustādh al-Imām Muḥammad 'Abduh*, vol. I, Cairo.

Rustum, Asad and Fū'ād Ifrām al-Bustānī (1937) *Tārīkh Lubnān al-mūjaz*, Beirut.

Rustum, Asad (1939) *Muṣṭalaḥ al-tārīkh*, Beirut, 1939; Sidon, 1957.
Sarkīs, Yūsuf (1928) *Mu'jam al-maṭbū'āt al-'arabiyya*, Cairo.
al-Shayyāl, Jamāl al-Dīn (1953) *al-Tārīkh wa al-mū'arrikhūn fī Miṣr fī al-qarn al-tāsi' 'ashar*, Cairo.
al-Shidyāq, Ṭannūs (1855–59) *Akhbār al-a'yān fī Jabal Lubnān*, Beirut.
al-Ṣulḥ, 'Ādil (1966) *Suṭūr min al-risāla*, Beirut.
Ṭarabīn, Aḥmad (1970) *al-Tārīkh wa al-mū'arrikhūn al-'Arab fī al-'aṣr al-ḥadīth*, Damascus.
Ṭarāzī, Philippe de (1913–33) *Tārīkh al-ṣaḥāfa al-'arabiyya*, 4 vols, Beirut.
Zurayq, Qusṭanṭīn (1959) *Naḥnu wa al-tārīkh*, Beirut.

III WORKS IN OTHER LANGUAGES

Abdul Rahman, A.R, and Yuzo, N. (1977) 'The *iltizām* system in Egypt and Turkey', *Journal of Asian and African Studies*, no. 14, pp. 169–94, Tokyo.
Abu-Lughod, I. (1963) *Arab Rediscovery of Europe*, Princeton.
Abu-Manneh, B. (1980) 'The Christians between Ottomanism and Syrian nationalism', *IJMES*, vol. XI, pp. 287–304.
Abun-Nasr, J.M. (1975) *A History of the Maghrib*, Cambridge.
Adams, Charles (1933) *Islam and Modernism in Egypt*, London.
Amin, Samir (1970) *The Maghreb in the Modern World*, Harmondsworth.
Anderson, M.S. (1966) *The Eastern Question, 1774–1923*, London.
Antonius, G. (1938) *The Arab Awakening*, London.
Ayache, Germain (1976–77) 'Histoire et colonisation, l'exemple du Maroc', *Hespéris–Tamuda*, vol. XVII, pp. 47–67.
Ayalon, D. (1953) 'Studies on the structure of the Mamluk army', *BSOAS*, vol. XV, nos. 2 and 3, pp. 203–28 and 448–76.
—— (1960) 'The historian al-Jabartī and his background', *BSOAS*, vol. XXIII, pp. 217–49.
Barka, Ben (1968) *The Political Thought of Ben Barka*, Havana.
Berque, J. (1960) *Les Arabes d'hier à demain*, Paris.
—— (1964) *The Arabs, their History and Future* (English trans.) London.
Bey, Ali (1816) *Travels of Ali Bey*, vol. II, London.
Beydoun, Ahmad (1984) *Identité confessionnelle et temps social chez les historiens Libanais contemporains*, Beirut.
Binder, L. (ed.) (1966) *Politics in Lebanon*, New York.
Bodin, J. (1945) *Method for the Easy Comprehension of History*, translated by Beatrice Reynolds, Columbia University Press, New York.
Bosworth, C.E. (1977) 'al-Jabartī and the Frankish archaeologists', *IJMES*, vol. 8, pp. 229–36.
Bowman, H. (1942) *Middle East Window*, London.
Bowring, J. (1840) *Report on Syria. Parliamentary Papers*, London.
Brown, L.C. (1974) *The Tunisia of Ahmad Bey, 1837–1855*, Princeton.
Browne, W.L. (ed.) (1976) *The Political History of Lebanon, 1920–*

1950. Documents on politics and political parties under French Mandate, 1920–1936, vol. I, North Carolina.
Burke III, Edmund (1972) 'The image of the Moroccan state in French ethnological literature: a new look at the origin of Lyautey's Berber policy', in Ernest Gellner and Charles Micaud (eds), *Arabs and Berbers, from tribe to nation in North Africa*, London, pp. 175–99.
Bury, J.B. (1909) *The Ancient Greek Historians*, London.
Butterfield, H. (1949) *The Origins of Modern Science*, London.
Cahen, C. (1960) 'Féodalité', *JESHO*, vol. III, pp. 1–20.
Chebli, M. (1946) *Fakhreddine II Maan, Prince du Liban*, Beirut.
Chejne, A.G. (1967) 'The concept of history in the modern Arab world', *Studies in Islam*, vol. IV, pp. 1–31.
Choueiri, Y.M. (1987a) 'Neo-Orientalism and Islamic Fundamentalism', *Review of Middle East Studies*, vol. 4, pp. 52–68.
—— (1987b) 'Ottoman Reform and Lebanese Patriotism'. Paper presented at the Centre for Lebanese Studies Conference, 10–12 September 1987, St Antony's College, Oxford.
—— (1987c) 'Two Histories of Syria and the Demise of Syrian Patriotism', *Middle Eastern Studies*, vol. 23, October, pp. 496–511.
Churchill, C.H. (1862) *The Druzes and the Maronites under Turkish Rule from 1840 to 1860*, London.
Collingwood, R.G. (1976) *The Idea of Nature*, Oxford University Press.
Crabbs, J. Jr (1975) 'Politics, history, and culture in Nasser's Egypt', *IJMES*, vol. 6, pp. 386–420.
David, J., and Yanosky, J. (1848) *Syrie, ancienne et moderne*, Paris.
Declair, S. (ed.) (1946) *Napoleon's Memoirs*, London.
Douin, G. (1925) 'L'ambassade d'Elfi Bey à Londres', *Bulletin de l'Institut d'Egypte*, vol. VII, pp. 95–120.
—— (1926) *Mohamed Aly, Pacha du Caire 1805–1807*, Cairo.
—— (1927) *La mission du Baron de Boislecomte*, Cairo.
—— (1930) *L'Angleterre et l'Egypte*, vol. II, Cairo.
Douin, G. and Fawtier-Jones, E.C. (eds) (1929) *L'Angleterre et l'Egypte: la politique Mameluke*, vol. I, Paris.
Fahmy, M. (1913) *La vérité sur la question d'Egypte*, Saint-Imier.
Farag, N. (1972) 'The Lewis affair and the fortunes of al-Muqtataf', *MES*, vol. VIII, pp. 72–83.
Farrington, B. (1963) *Greek Science*, Harmondsworth, Middlesex.
Fawaz, L.T. (1983) *Merchants and Migrants in Nineteenth Century Beirut*, Harvard.
Foucault, Michel (1966) *Les mots et les choses*, Paris; English translation *The Order of Things*, London, 1977.
Ganiage, J. (1959) *Les origines du protectorat français au Tunisie 1861–1881*, Paris.
Geertz, Clifford (1968) *Islam Observed*, Chicago, 1968, 1971.
Gellner, Ernest (1961) 'The struggle for Morocco's past', *MEJ*, vol. 15, pp. 79–90.
Gibb, Hamilton (1947), *Modern Trends in Islam*, Chicago.
—— (1962) *Studies on the Civilization of Islam*, Princeton, 1962 and 1982.

Gibbon, E. (1898) in J.B. Bury (ed.) *Decline and Fall of the Roman Empire*, vol. V, London.

Graf, G. (1944–53) *Geschichte der christlichen arabischen literatur*, vol. III, Vatican.

Gramsci, Antonio (1957) *The Modern Prince and Other Writings*, New York, fourth printing, 1970.

Green, Arnold H. (1978) *The Tunisian Ulama, 1873–1915*, Leiden.

Grunebaum, G.E. von (1962) *Modern Islam: The Search for Cultural Identity*, Berkeley and Los Angeles.

Hamilton, W. (1809) *Aegyptiaca*, London.

Hershlag, Z.Y. (1980) *Introduction to the Modern Economic History of the Middle East*, 2nd revised ed, Leiden, E.J. Brill.

Heyworth-Dunne, J. (1938) *Introduction to the History of Education in Modern Egypt*, London.

—— (1950) *Religious and Political Trends in Modern Egypt*, Washington.

Hill, R. (1967) *A Biographical Dictionary of the Sudan*, London.

Hitti, P.K. (1957) *Lebanon in History*, London.

—— (1977) *History of the Arabs*, 10th edn, London.

Hobbes (1973) *Leviathan*, London and Melbourne. Reprinted 1983.

Holt, P.M. (1966) *Egypt and the Fertile Crescent 1516–1922*, London.

—— (1973) *Studies in the History of the Near East*, London.

Hourani, A. (1962) 'Historians of Lebanon', in B. Lewis and P.M. Holt (eds), *Historians of the Middle East*, Oxford.

—— (1968) 'Ottoman reform and the politics of Notables', in W. Polk and R. Chambers (eds), *Beginnings of Modernization in the Middle East*, Chicago, pp. 351–81.

—— (1970) *Arabic Thought in the Liberal Age 1798–1939*, Oxford.

al-Husry, K.S. (1966) *Three Reformers, Beirut.*

Irwin, R. (1977) 'Iqṭā' and the end of the Crusader states', in P.M. Holt (ed.), *The Eastern Mediterranean Lands in the Period of the Crusades.* Warminster, England.

Ismail, A. (1955) *Histoire du Liban du XVIIe siècle à nos jours, Tome V: Le Liban au temps de Fakhr-ed-Din II, 1590–1633*, Paris.

Jorga, N. (1894) 'Un projet relatif à la conquête de Jérusalem, 1609', *Revue de l'Orient Latin*, vol. II, pp. 183–9.

Keddie, Nikki (1983) *An Islamic Response to Imperialism*, California.

Lahbabi, Mohamed (1958) *Le gouvernement Marocain à l'aube du XXe siècle.* Rabat.

Langlois, Ch. V., and Charles Seignobos (1898) *Introduction aux études historiques*, Paris.

Lewis, Bernard (1964, 1968) *The Middle East and the West*, London.

—— (1968) *The Emergence of Modern Turkey*, London.

Lukács, Georg (1971) *History and Class Consciousness*, London.

Mannheim, K. (1976) *Ideology and Utopia*, London.

Marsot, A. (1975) 'Political and economic functions of the 'Ulamā' in the 18th Century'. *JESHO*, vol. 16, pp. 130–54.

Maundrell, H. (1810) *Journey from Aleppo to Jerusalem in 1697*, London.

Meinecke, Friedrich (1957) *Machiavellism*, trans. from the German by

Douglas Scott, London.
Milner, Sir Alfred (1899) *England in Egypt*, 7th edn, London.
Mosca, G. (1939) *The Ruling Class*, New York and London.
Owen, R. (1976) 'The political economy of Grand Liban, 1920–1970', in R. Owen (ed.) *Essays on the Crisis in Lebanon*, London.
—— (1981) *The Middle East in the World Economy 1800–1914*. London.
Plato (1974) *The Republic*, trans, and intro. by D. Lee, 2nd edn Harmondsworth, Middlesex.
Poliak (1937) 'Some notes on the feudal system of the Mamluks', *Journal of the Royal Asiatic Society of Great Britain and Ireland*, January 1937, pp. 97–107.
Polk, W. (1963) *The Opening of South Lebanon, 1788–1840*, Cambridge, Mass.
Polk, W.R., and Chambers, R.L. (eds) (1968) *Beginnings of Modernization in the Middle East*, Chicago.
Porath, Y. (1986) *In Search of Arab Unity 1936–1945*, London.
X Poujoulat, B. (1841) *Voyage à Constantinople, dans l'Asie Mineure, en Mésopotamie, à Palmyre, en Palestine et en Egypte*, vol. II, Paris.
Rabbath, E. (1973) *La formation historique du Liban politique et constitutionnel*, Beirut.
Raymond, A. (1973) *Artisans et commerçants au Caire au XVIIIeme siècle*, vol. I, Damascus.
Reid, Donald M. (1975) *The Odyssey of Faraḥ Anṭūn*, Minneapolis and Chicago.
Richmond, J.C.B. (1977) *Egypt 1798–1952*, London.
Ristlehueber, R. (1918) *Les traditions françaises au Liban*, Paris.
Rosenthal, F. (1952) *A History of Muslim Historiography*, Leiden, E.J. Brill.
Runciman, S. (1958) *The Sicilian Vespers*, Cambridge.
Rustum, A.J. (1924) 'Syria under Mehemet Ali', *The American Journal of Semitic Languages and Literatures*, vol. XLI (Oct), no. 4, pp. 34–57.
Sabry, M. (1919–21) *La révolution égyptienne 1919–1921*, 2 vols, Paris.
—— (1920) *La question d'Egypte*, Paris.
Safran, N. (1961) *Egypt in Search of Political Community*, Cambridge, Mass.
Sahli, Mohamed (1965) *Décoloniser l'histoire. Introduction à l'histoire du Maghreb*, Paris.
Saliba, N.E. (1978) 'The achievements of Midḥat Pasha as Governor of the Province of Syria, 1878–1880', *IJMES*, vol. 9, pp. 303–73.
Saunders, J.J. (1961) 'Islam and the Mongols: The battle of Goliath's spring', *History Today*, vol. XI no 12 (Dec.) pp. 843–51.
Sédillot, L.A. (1877) *Histoire générale des Arabes*, 2nd edn, vol. II, Paris.
Shamir, S. (1974) 'Midhat Pasha and the anti-Turkish agitation in Syria', *MES*, vol. X, pp. 115–41.
X Smith, C.D. (1973) 'The "crisis of Orientation". The shift of Egyptian intellectuals to Islamic subjects in the 1930s', *IJMES*, vol. 4,

pp. 382–410.
Terrasse, Henri (1952) *Histoire du Maroc* (Édition abrégée), Paris.
Tibawi, A. (1966) *American Interests in Syria*, Oxford.
Tibawi, A.L. (1967) 'History of the Syrian Protestant College', *MEJ*, vol. XXI, pp. 1–15 and 199–212.
Tlili, B. (1970) 'Note sur la notion d'état dans la pensée de Ah'mad ibn Abî Ad'-d'Iyâf', *Revue de l'Occident Musulman et de la Méditerranée*, vol. VIII, pp. 141–70.
Toynbee, A. (1962) *A Study of History*, vol. III, Oxford.
Williams, A. (1968) *Britain and France in the Middle East and North Africa*, London.
Yamak, L.Z. (1966) *The Syrian Social Nationalist Party*, Cambridge, Mass.
Zeine, Z.N. (1958) *Arab–Turkish Relations and the Emergence of Arab Nationalism*, Beirut.
—— (1960) *The Struggle for Arab Independence*, Beirut.

Index

Bayhum, Ḥusayn 41
Beirut 38–9
Ben Barka, Mehdi 166–8, 170, 178
Ben Bella, Ahmad 170
Berbers 58–60, 173–4, 178
Berque, Jacques xi, 170
biography 4–7
Blantyre, Lord 94, 208, 218-19
Bliss, Daniel 118
Boughton, Sir G.C. Braithwaite 92
Bourgeois, Emile 66
Bowen, Harold 129
Bowman, Humphrey 56
Buḥturids 127–9, 132
bureaucracy *see* administration
al-Bustānī, Buṭrus xiv-xv, 25–8, 32–4, 138, 189, 196
al-Bustānī, Fū'ād Ifrām 117
al-Bustānī, Salīm xiii, 26–32, 35, 185, 189
Byzantines 11, 44, 58–60

Camps, Gabriel 173
Canaanites 123
Carcopino, Jérôme 174–5
Carthaginians 58–60, 174
Catholic Patriarchal School 34
Caussin de Perceval, A.P. 5
Chebli, Michel 131
Chiha, Michel 122–3
Churchill, Charles Henry 153
Clemenceau, Georges 116
colonialism xv-xvi, 58, 117
Conférence de la Paix (1919) 66, 116, 125
Copernicus 16, 198
corruption 19, 47, 105
Cromer, Lord 105
Crusades 12, 45, 118, 176

Daḥdāḥ (family) 152
al-Damanhūrī, Muḥammad 9
David, Jules 43, 45–6
Dāwūd Yuḥannā, Maronite Patriarch 142
Depping, Georges-Bernard 5
Drovetti, Bernardino 98
Druzes 127–8, 130, 150–4, 158; *see also* religion
Dufferin Report 81
al-Dūwayhī, Isṭifān 136–8, 140–2

Eddé, Emile 117
education; in Egypt 103, 105; Iraq 56; Lebanon 27, 34–5, 38, 41–2, 55, 117–18, 194; Syria xvi, 25, 27, 34–5, 38, 41-2, 47, 55, 117–18, 194
Egypt xv, xvii–xviii, 193; as geopolitical unit xv, 11, 71; education 103, 105; feudalism 77, 81; history 65–108; to 640 8-12, 104-5, 641–1797 12–15, 21, 71–3, 101, 142, 1798–1801 18, 73–83, 1802 84–90, 1803 91–6, 207–19, 1804–1807 96–9, 1808–1848 4–7, 11–13, 17, 21, 100, 102–4, 1849–1951 65–70, 105–7, 1952- 104, 106–8; intellectuals in 102; invades Syria 4, 25, 103, 153; newspapers in 42; '*ulamā*' in 9, 18–19, 75, 85, 95–6, 98–100, 102
Elgin, Lord 80, 82
élites 18, 104–5, 151, 177, 200–1; *see also* social classes
epic poetry 140–1
equality 27–8
Europe xiv, xvii, 3–4, 20, 30, 47, 179

Fakhr al-Dīn II, Ma'nid amir 130–5
Fāris, Nabīh Amīn 119
Farrūkh, 'Umar 118
Fārūq, King of Egypt 67, 69–70, 102
al-Fāsī, 'Allāl 166
Faṭimids xvii, 176
Fayṣal, King of Syria and Iraq 116–17
feudalism 77, 81, 127–30, 132, 143, 185
Foucault, Michel xii, 196
France 3–5; and Egypt 1798–